THE PSYCHOLOGY
OF EXECUTIVE
COACHING

THE PSYCHOLOGY OF EXECUTIVE COACHING

Theory and Application

Bruce Peltier, Ph.D., M.B.A.

Published in 2001 by
Routledge
Taylor & Francis Group
270 Madison Avenue
New York, NY 10016

Published in Great Britain by
Routledge
Taylor & Francis Group
2 Park Square
Milton Park, Abingdon
Oxon OX14 4RN

© 2001 by Taylor & Francis Group, LLC
Routledge is an imprint of Taylor & Francis Group

Printed in the United States of America on acid-free paper
15 14 13 12 11 10 9 8 7 6

International Standard Book Number-10: 1-58391-072-7 (Softcover)
International Standard Book Number-13: 978-1-58391-072-7 (Softcover)
Library of Congress catalog number: 2002037555

Library of Congress Cataloging-in-Publication Data

Catalog record is available from the Library of Congress

Taylor & Francis Group
is the Academic Division of Informa plc.

Visit the Taylor & Francis Web site at
http://www.taylorandfrancis.com

and the Routledge Web site at
http://www.routledge-ny.com

CONTENTS

ACKNOWLEDGMENTS

There are many people to thank.

First, to my family—Tracey, Drew, and Carly—for their support and flexibility and love. What a great family.

Thanks to Dave Chambers for taking an interest in this project and reading early chapters; to Dave Nielsen for crucial, quiet support, and to many others at the University of the Pacific School of Dentistry, including Bob Christoffersen and Art Dugoni, the Dean of a very special place. Thanks also to Morley Segal for graciously contributing to the idea; to Robert H. Fisher, M.D., for teaching me and giving me the chance to practice; and to Al Hedman for always being in my corner.

Much appreciation goes to Tim Julet for nurturing the project and to Kimberly Shigo for extremely competent editorial work.

And thanks, once again, to John Vriend, the writer.

ABOUT THE AUTHOR
AND CONTRIBUTORS

Bruce Peltier is Professor of Psychology at the University of the Pacific School of Dentistry, a licensed psychologist, and an executive coach in San Francisco, California. He is a 1970 graduate of West Point. His M.Ed. and Ph.D. are from Wayne State University and his M.D.A. is from the Eberhardt School at the University of the Pacific. His post-doctoral internship was at the University of Southern California, and he has taken additional training at Stanford University, Georgetown, and Loyola of Chicago.

The author can be contacted at bruce.peltier@mindspring.com.

Alan Hedman is a psychotherapist and management consultant in Pasadena, California. His undergraduate degree is from Pacific Lutheran University in Tacoma, Washington, where he was inducted into the University's Sports Hall of Fame. His Ph.D. is from the University of Maryland, and he served for five years as the Associate Director of the Student Counseling Center at the University of Southern California.

Ana Maria Irueste-Montes, Ph.D., is a psychologist and coach, specializing in gender issues in the corporate world. She is a faculty member at the College of Executive Coaching and an adjunct staff member at the Center for Creative Leadership, where she is regularly involved in the assessment and coaching of senior executives. She has a deep commitment to helping those in leadership positions treat their members and themselves with dignity and respect.

Show up and choose to be present.
Pay attention.
Tell the truth.
Be open to outcome, not attached to results.

Adapted from Angeles Arrien's
Four-Fold Way Principles
(HarperCollins, 1993)

PREFACE

The purpose of this book is to translate psychotherapy theory for executive coaches. Its goal is to make the principles, research, and wisdom of psychology accessible to the practice of executive coaching. This psychological information can and should form the basis for effective coaching in the business consulting environment.

Executive coaching has become a popular way for companies to assist and develop talent, and there is a growing body of literature on how to do this kind of coaching. But most coaching books do not effectively establish a direct relationship between psychological methods and coaching practice. Many are written in the popular style of business self-help books, and they occasionally exhort more than they enlighten. This book begins with psychological theory and provides a conceptual foundation for the business coach.

The author is a counseling psychologist with two decades of clinical experience, as well as an M.B.A. and entrepreneurial, small business experience gained over a ten year period.

There is a primary and a secondary target reader for this book. It is first written for psychotherapists, including psychiatrists, psychologists, Master's-level therapists, marriage and family therapists, and social workers who would like to expand their practice into the corporate or small business environment. Opportunity clearly exists there, and psychology has plenty to offer the business world. But psychological concepts and methods must be translated for the corporate world first, before it is applied there. The business point of view and its vocabulary must be accommodated if coaches are to be successful.

The second audience includes business people, managers, leaders, and human resources directors who want to enhance their own coaching skills. Coaching is an important part of their present job, and it is likely they lack an adequate understanding of the psychological basis for effective coaching. This book takes readily applicable lessons from psychology and makes them available to the management coach. These ideas and principles, when properly applied, can help grow a promising employee, remediate one who has run into difficulties or limitations, and can enhance the entire organization and company culture.

The book is organized in the following way. Good coaching usually begins with an assessment, and Chapter 1 describes the application of psychological testing principles and methods. Chapters 2 through 9 each describe an important psychotherapy theory, beginning with a brief history and a description of its essential components. Examples are provided to explain how each model can be optimally applied to executive coaching. Strengths and weaknesses are discussed in terms of the theory's applicability to the business world. Chapter 10 summarizes lessons from athletic coaching books, as there is much to be gleaned from this intriguing body of literature, a literature widely read by business executives. Chapter 11, on the coaching of women in business, points out that, in the male world of corporate life, there is a need to understand gender politics and differential gender communication patterns. Chapter 12, Ethics in Business Coaching, translates well-established codes and principles from psychotherapy into the executive coaching setting, were no formal ethics codes currently exist. The two final chapters provide important business information for psychotherapists who are unfamiliar with the business culture and point of view. Chapter 13 describes the important, but poorly understood, differences between management and leadership, while Chapter 14 describes how to make the transition from therapist to coach. Most chapters end with a list of summary points for those readers in a hurry to translate their skills and get going. There is a comprehensive, annotated list of the important points at the end of the book, so that readers can quickly access answers to important questions. Extensive references and additional recommended readings are listed at the end of each chapter for the reader who wishes to study in greater depth.

If you are a psychotherapist with established counseling skills, you may want to skip selected parts of the text and go directly to your areas of relative weakness. These might include theories you learned years ago, but have forgotten. Many of the chapters will provide a useful "brush-up." You certainly will want to study the chapters that focus on the business world and how it works.

If you are a manager or executive yourself, you will certainly want to study the theory chapters to gain essential background on their development, evolution, and core ideas and skills. You may even want to seek additional training or find a mentor from the psychotherapy field.

These are exciting times in psychotherapy and in business. Each of these two worlds has much to offer the other. This book strives to help you make the most of the available opportunities and to make a positive impact on workers and on the business environment, as well.

INTRODUCTION

Take a course in psychology, rather than technology.
                                              —Tom Peters (Weinstein, 1999)

This book is for two audiences. It is written primarily for psychologists, counselors, social workers, and other trained psychotherapists who seek to apply their clinical experience to the corporate workplace. The second reader is the executive coach or management coach who would like more background on the psychological theory underlying the practices of executive coaching. The goal is to translate psychological theory into practical executive coaching skills.

Two Forms of Coaching

Coaching has become a popular, mainstream way to improve executives and organizations. Although little has been written on the subject, two basic forms of coaching have evolved. "Executive coaching" provides one-on-one services to top level leaders in an organization, on the principle that positive changes can be leveraged to filter down and enhance the entire organization. (The alternative view is that a toxic executive can pollute an organization and cause widespread damage.) In the present economy, many are promoted into leadership positions based on previous diligence and technical excellence. They never intended to have a leadership position and didn't prepare for it, but they couldn't resist the money and prestige that came with the promotion. Others simply had a great idea and boundless creative energy, so they started a company. Now they have to figure out how to lead. At the same time, companies are well aware of the importance and cost-effectiveness of retaining their best people, even when it means spending money to develop them.

A second approach called "management coaching" views coaching as a set of day-to-day skills exercised by managers at all levels of the organization. Some even view coaching as a primary way for managers to conduct their work. It replaces standard ways to manage people. Managers coach rather than control. In this view, workers are all seen as team members and assets to be continuously developed for promotion. This version makes coaching an integral part of succession planning, for employees must be coached to move up into more demanding positions as the organization and its human capital evolves.

While this book accommodates both views of coaching, and the principles and techniques described here can be used throughout the organization, the primary focus is on coaching the executive. Basic psychological theories are described, reviewed, and focused specifically on coaching the corporate executive.

Much executive coaching is presently atheoretical, from the point of view of mainstream psychology. This book is for those who desire a framework for what they do. The Center for Creative Leadership in Greensboro, North Carolina, recently published an annotated bibliography of executive coaching (Douglas & Morley, 2000, p. 39). They define the executive coach as "a consultant who uses a wide variety of behavioral techniques and methods. . . ." This text describes many of the available methods for coaching along with their theoretical background.

Psychologists and other mental health counselors are facing significant changes in work patterns, and many psychotherapists are seeking alternative ways to apply their hard-earned skills. Much of the change is driven by the powerful influence of managed care health plans, which have driven payment for and access to psychotherapy downward. Some of the change reflects current social and cultural values which de-emphasize personal therapy and, perhaps, introspection as well. Biological psychiatry has demonstrated an increased power with new medications, and managed care organizations are quite happy to take advantage of the associated cost savings. The "talking cure" has lost its place in mainstream American culture. It's too slow, too personal, it provides no guarantees, and it lacks the punch and focus demanded by those in the fast lane.

What Business Do Therapists Have Doing Executive Coaching?

Why should psychotherapists consider coaching? Is it within their training and scope of practice? Is it appropriate? Who should consider the practice of coaching? Is it for everyone? The business strategy literature is helpful in addressing these questions. Two strategy questions are useful.

Strategy Question One:
What Business Are You In?

This is a question that strategists insist must be answered with care, because it aligns all future efforts of an organization. The answer can open doors or it can close them.

> You can miss the strength of competitors by looking only at their end products, in the same way that you miss the strength of a tree if you look only at its leaves. (Prahalad & Hamel, 1990)

By way of example, if a railroad views its business as *running trains*, it runs into severe constraints as airlines grow, penetrate new locations, and drive down the time and cost of transporting goods and people. A railroad may benefit by thinking of itself as being in the business of *transportation*. Such a shift in viewpoint opens doors and potential new markets and services. A business is best viewed as a "customer-satisfying endeavor" rather than a specific product or service (Kerin & Peterson, 1998). Products and services are transient. They must change as customers and environments change. This begs the second strategy question.

Strategy Question Two:
What Are Your Core Competencies?

No company can do everything, and it is unwise to stretch oneself too thin. Railroads don't own or fly airplanes, and they don't employ pilots. They are in a poor position to compete directly with airlines, if they interpret that to mean buying and flying planes. A core competency is that set of skills that you know best, and it represents your collective learning. When companies are clear about their core competencies, they can function in a variety of lucrative markets, as long as their products and services derive from those competencies.

The reader may want to read Prahalad and Hamel's 1990 essay in the *Harvard Business Review* titled "The Core Competence of the Corporation." In it they list three defining attributes:

1. A core competence provides potential access to a wide variety of markets.
2. A core competence should make a significant contribution to customers.
3. A core competence should be difficult for competitors to imitate.

The Core Competencies
of Psychotherapists

Core competencies are the wellspring of new business development. (Prahalad & Hamel, 1990)

Although the definition of core competence varies somewhat between psychologists, family therapists, social workers, and psychiatrists, it varies more between individuals in those fields. Someone who identifies as a psychotherapist is likely to view her basic competencies more narrowly than, say, a psychologist, who may engage in a wide variety of assessment and consultative activities.

Nonetheless, here is a definition of the business of the psychotherapist that opens the door to executive coaching.

> The psychotherapist facilitates the growth and development of individuals in intrapersonal and interpersonal functioning, as well as the remediation of problems in those areas.

Core competencies may include one-on-one interpersonal instruction, behavior analysis, psychological assessment, counseling, or psychotherapy.

You may not agree with the above definition, and you may choose to tweak it to suit you, but you need a clear idea of your core competencies along with a definition of your "business" in order to focus your transition from therapy to coaching. You may even decide, as a result of this value clarifying exercise, that executive coaching is not for you.

The Potential

Executive and management coaching are ideal ways to bring the positive potential of psychology into the workplace. Psychologists have always recognized that the workplace has a powerful influence on a person's mental health, and efforts to make the work environment more humane can have a healthy impact on large numbers of people, as well as on the bottom line. There is a growing interest in coaching (on the part of psychotherapists), as evidenced by recent publications such as Iris Martin's book *From Couch to Corporation*, Len Sperry's *Corporate Therapy and Consulting*, and an entire issue of the *Consulting Psychology Journal* devoted to executive coaching. It is no wonder that providers of psychological counseling, accustomed to focusing their skills on individuals in private sessions, now look to corporations and small businesses for a new market.

Counseling and clinical psychologists, as well as marriage and family therapists, social workers, and even psychiatrists possess powerful interpersonal change skills. This book puts old wine into new bottles, so that more can appreciate the vintage. It is written to help psychotherapists adapt their valuable skills to the corporate culture and its needs.

Coaching: What Is It?

It is no accident that management consultants often start by declaring what coaching is not. "Coaching is specifically not therapy," they typically state. Although some business practitioners include "counseling" in the repertoire of skills used by managers on a day-to-day basis, counseling is reserved for troubled employees with "psychological problems." Counseling is personal and it is aimed at personal problems. Coaching carries a much more positive implication in the corporate world. High performance athletes are coached; sick, weak, or crazy people get therapy. Such thinking goes like this: "Anyone with a lick of sense seeks coaching, but competent people don't need therapy. They can handle things on their own." Competent people, however, want coaching. High-performers seek it out. Tiger Woods apparently works with his coach on a daily basis, even after a stellar performance.

Carol Macmillan (1999) performed an extensive literature review as part of her dissertation on role definitions of management consultants. She concluded (p. 75):

> As more mental health clinicians move into organizational consulting positions, it becomes more important to establish what the role of the organizational consultant is, particularly when the consultant is trained and experienced in clinical work. The consulting literature in general is poorly defined, poorly documented, and poorly integrated, particularly as it relates to clinical theories, which may be relevant and useful for consulting work.

Despite the unsavory implications of psychotherapy in the corporate culture, there is no denying that the literature of psychotherapy is important and highly relevant to coaching in the work world. The baby can't be thrown out with the bath water. Here is an example of the relevance of psychological theory in executive coaching:

> Within this systems orientation, we draw from the frameworks of humanistic, existential, behavioral, and psychodynamic psychology and choose our techniques eclectically to fit the client, the situation, and the need.

This quote is from the article "Coaching at the Top," by Kiel, Rimmer, Williams, and Doyle (1996, p. 68) of KRW International, a firm that specializes in the coaching of CEOs at Fortune 500 companies.

Lester Tobias (1990, p.1) made the following observation in his book, *Psychological Consulting to Management:*

> Consulting psychology, management psychology, or corporate psychology, as it is variously called, is the application of the principles of psychology to help people in organizations become more effective.

The Center for Creative Leadership (Douglas & Morley, 2000, p. 40) provides the following descriptions of coaching:

> Reduced to its essence, executive coaching is the process of equipping people with the tools, knowledge, and opportunities they need to develop themselves and become more effective (Peterson, 1996). Executive coaching involves the teaching of skills in the context of a personal relationship with the learner, and providing feedback on the executive's interpersonal relations and skills (Sperry, 1993). An ongoing series of activities tailored to the individual's current issues or relevant problem is designed by the coach to assist the executive in maintaining a consistent, confident focus as he or she tunes strengths and manages shortcomings. (Tobias, 1996)

W. T. Anderson of the Meridian International Institute weighs in with a similar opinion in a 1998 essay in *The Family Therapy Networker:*

> Although management thinkers are notoriously eclectic in their plundering of intellectual resources . . . there's really no way the modern discipline of management would have evolved as it has without theories and practices borrowed from psychology. (p. 36)

Coaching Defined

Coaching, as described in this book, is defined in the following way:

> *Someone from outside an organization uses psychological skills to help a person develop into a more effective leader. These skills are applied to specific present-moment work problems in a way that enables this person to incorporate them into his or her permanent management or leadership repertoire.*

Examples of skills derived from psychotherapy literature include active listening and empathy, self awareness, process observation, giving and getting feedback, assertive communication, conflict resolution, cognitive restructuring and learned optimism, effective use of reinforcement, hypnotic language, resistance management, detriangulation, reframing, even paradoxical intent. These skills are described in the chapters that follow, and examples demonstrate their application to the workplace. Other essential skills which can be coached include more basic elements of leadership and management, such as delegation, public speaking, presentation of self, time management, strategic planning, goal setting, use of information technology, and project management. Consulting which focuses directly on a business's content skills or technical skills is not included in the scope of this book, nor is it seen as a typical coaching focus, although there is a small, but growing demand for coaches who can provide specific business or project-related expertise, as well. Examples include dentistry, law, sales, and technology industries.

The skills that psychotherapists possess are of enormous potential to business executives and corporate leaders. They ought not go to waste.

> The most important workplace skill was, is, and always will be the ability to get along with people. If you don't have that skill, any success you will have will only be temporary. (Dave Murphy, 2000)

Coaching Executives

Organizations are often willing to spend time and money on the ongoing development of top executives. They assume that such a commitment will, down the line, pay compounded dividends. The organization will perform more effectively, profits will increase, and life will be more comfortable for everyone in the organization. The company's reputation will be enhanced, and key people will be retained. Intervention is especially important when a top executive has a blind spot or some poor quality or tendency that drives others "up the wall." Organizations suffer when exceptional technical workers are promoted into leadership positions when they don't have leadership skills. It is common for companies to promote people with an excellent technical record into leadership positions on the assumption that they will be able to learn how to lead on the job. Some of these newly minted "leaders" don't even possess much interest in leadership, but they take the "promotion" because it is a step up and it means that they will be paid more money. Some young executives actually find interpersonal interaction to be distressing. Many aren't even aware that a distinctive set of essential leadership skills exists!

Organizations are often willing to give coaching a try at top levels because it is at top levels that important strategic decisions are made.

One or two critical strategic decisions can literally make or break a company. Good strategic thinking is rare and difficult. Sometimes the decision-making process is risky and lonely, and an executive can often use a trusted advisor, someone who is not inside the organization. This is where therapeutic methods, translated to fit the corporate culture, can be enormously valuable. There is great potential for the win–win result. Therapists use existing skills to make a good living, and executives benefit from a source not previously available in the corporate setting.

Where Coaching Can Help

There are at least four general situations that call for executive or management coaching. Coaching works best when it is seen as a *benefit* for high achievers, key people, and those with great potential. When it is seen only as remedial, executives are likely to run from it, and a coach becomes the "angel of death," the last step before you're shown the door. No one in an organization wants to be stigmatized or marked for elimination, so they avoid or resist. If coaching is going to work it must be framed as a benefit—an *opportunity* for the most promising or valuable executives and managers.

Here are four general ways that executive coaches can help:

1. **When big things in the organization change.** Coaching is extremely useful when an organization realizes that it must change. This decision might be an adaptation to changes in the market or the environment or it could be a decision to respond to a perceived opportunity. Such changes usually require new executive approaches, and a coach can help leaders adapt. Coaching is of special importance during mergers and acquisitions. Organizational sea change can become a disaster without outside help.
2. **Skill development for individual transitions.** Coaches can help high performers acquire the necessary new skills as they move to positions of greater authority and responsibility. When someone is rewarded for technical excellence and given a promotion into a leadership position, he or she typically needs to learn new leadership skills. He or she may even need to learn a whole series of new and sophisticated social skills (e.g., delegating, public speaking, or entertaining clients at dinner). This is likely to require a solid assessment or self-evaluation. A coach can facilitate and accelerate this process. The essential leadership skills do not come "naturally" and must not be taken for granted. They must be identified, evaluated, taught, and discussed.

3. **Specific skill development.** Sometimes an executive realizes that he or she has never learned one specific critical skill, such as how to work with an advisory board or board of directors. A coach can be extremely cost effective in such a case, especially if the coach has expertise in that specific area.

    Sometimes executives realize that they lack one important leadership or social skill such as public speaking in front of large audiences or working a cocktail party. Sometimes they must improve the way they present themselves in public settings.

    Frequently executives have been able to hide a shortcoming for years, but are now faced with awareness of the limitation. The time has come to deal that shortcoming and fix it. Sometimes they are only dimly aware that they have a skill deficit, but know that something is getting in the way.

4. **Resolving specific problems.** Frequently a powerful and successful person possesses one or two sets of dysfunctional behavior that cause repetitive difficulties. He or she may have an annoying habit or gap in self-esteem or self-confidence that didn't show before. Perhaps the increased responsibility is a heavy burden, and the person lacks adequate stress management skills, so he or she takes it out on others. Perhaps the person finds it difficult to trust.

    In this situation, the coach is called on for specific remedial help. When done well, this kind of help can save a career and a lot of corporate expense. It can also eliminate considerable human friction and misery.

Steps in the Process

Effective coaching involves a four-step process:

Step One: Get Things Started

Either the company must find a coach or a coach must find the company. Regardless of how this happens, the coach must, in some way, sell the service. This means that he or she must call attention to a deficit, make a case for skill enhancement, or offer a solution to a problem. Coaches must be able to define their work in terms of outcomes and solutions. What will be better as a result of coaching? How will we know, and what difference will it make? Ground rules and parameters such as confidentiality, reporting relationships, and dimensions of the project (targeted people, time, and money) must be established.

A contract must be negotiated and signed. Much of this is discussed in detail in Chapter 12 (Ethics in Business Coaching) and Chapter 14 (Making the Transition) of this book.

Step Two: Gather Information and Make a Plan

This phase typically includes an assessment of the executive to be coached—the client. The assessment process is described in Chapter 1. Supervisors, colleagues, direct-reports, and customers are often called upon to provide input to the coaching process. Extensive data are carefully fed back to the client. A clear plan is developed, and the plan includes measurable outcomes. This plan is locked in and written down. The coach and client agree on what will change.

Step Three: Implement

The coach has an extended period (typically three months to two years), to produce tangible results. This process includes regular meetings (in person, through e-mail, and over the telephone) between the executive and the coach. The focus of meetings may be to solve problems, to develop new skills, or to work on objectives described in the plan for change. Good coaching often includes shadowing, where the coach goes to the executive's workplace and observes the action in person.

Step Four: Lock in the Changes, Arrange for Ongoing, Continuous Improvement and Support

Improvements that do not last are of little value. Absent effective arrangements for permanent long-term change, coaching will take its place on bookshelves full of other trendy, passing management fads. Activities of value to organizations are those that have a lasting influence, long after the consultant has left town. Steps must be taken to cement short-term gains.

Coaching as a Mainstream Leadership Skill

Coaching can have an egalitarian influence on organizations. When its premise is that each employee is valued, time and money are justified, as they will benefit the entire organization in the end. When people are viewed as assets worthy of development, coaches can be employed to stimulate growth in areas of organizational importance or weakness. Such areas might include regular, on-the-job coaching in areas like these:

- interpersonal communication
  listening skills
  assertiveness skills
  ways to read other people
  effective use of language
  giving positive and negative feedback
- delegation skills
- team building skills
- diversity in the workplace
- running an effective meeting
- writing skills for business and management
- planning skills
- decision-making
- project management
- conflict management
- organizational culture
- dealing with difficult or problem employees or colleagues

Referring Pathology Appropriately

Executive coaches can certainly identify and even remediate occasional personality pathologies, however the corporate coach typically refers such cases to professionals outside of the organization. This is where psychotherapy is appropriate. Coaches must possess skills that allow them to make such referrals in an effective way. They need to understand how to refer and must have some familiarity with local referral sources. There are good reasons, discussed later, to keep these activities (coaching and therapy) separated.

Don't Throw Out the Therapy Baby with the Bathwater: Coaching and Psychotherapy

Some business consultants and some executive coaches go out of their way to distance themselves from the models and language of psychotherapy. This is easy to understand, as therapy brings with it all kinds of negative images and implications in the corporate world. If you need a psychotherapist, according to this way of thinking, you are sick or crazy or weak; strong people can solve their own problems, and effective executives don't have those kinds of problems, anyway. "We hire stars, not mental cases," some might say. But to run from the therapy model, to abandon it completely would be a mistake. The core ideas from accepted therapy theories have significant value for executive or management coaches.

Numerous unfortunate impressions of therapy linger in the management world, and many still attach a stigma to therapy. Therapy is seen as appropriate for Woody Allen types who would rather sit around and whine than go out and make things change. This is hardly an attractive image for the corporate executive, charged with the task of moving market mountains. Therapy is viewed as slow, expensive, tedious, often ineffective, and for people with "real" problems. It can drag on for years, with no attempt at evaluation or accountability. In my experience, therapists are seen by some executives as complex, wimpy, gloomy types who don't live in the real world—they won't give you a straight answer, they've never accomplished anything significant, and they are probably a little goofy themselves. In therapy, they believe that you talk a lot about your feelings and you complain. You go over and over things. Many business people have no real experience with psychotherapy, and some are uncomfortable with the idea that they might have to confront themselves, their feelings, and their behavior. Others dread the negative feedback they might get from a coach or from co-workers.

If executive coaches allow themselves and their work to be seen this way, they are dead before they get through the door.

Differentiating Coaching from Therapy

A coach must be able to provide a good working definition of coaching and articulate the difference between coaching and psychotherapy. The table below summarizes the major differences.

As can be seen in Table I-1, coaching is action oriented, data driven, present-moment focused, and designed for a high-functioning client. Confidentiality is complex and much less secure than it is in therapy. Even the definition of the concept of "client" is complicated, as the organization (which pays the bill) has a stake in the outcome. Boundaries are much less rigid, as the work usually takes place outside of the coach's office, and it often includes social events, large business meetings, and company outings.

TABLE I-1. Differentiating coaching from therapy

Therapy	Coaching
Focus on the past	Present and future focus
Passive orientation (listening), reflective	Action orientation
Data from client	Data is information from key others, as well as from the client
Pathology orientation	Growth or skill development orientation
Problem is intrapsychic (found in the person)	Problem is found in person–environment mix
Information not shared with others	Information sometimes fed back to key members of organization (with great care)
Client is clearly the person you work with	Definition of "client" unclear (may be the organization that is paying coach's fees)
Client (person) must feel enriched	Organization must feel enhanced by the coaching
Confidentiality is clear and absolute	Confidentiality is complex
50-minute sessions	Meetings of variable length
Work in therapist's office	Meet in executive's workplace or a "neutral" site
Rigid boundaries	Flexible boundaries, including social settings
Work through (resolve) personality issues	Work around personality issues
Client or HMO chooses therapist	Organization may choose coach

See also Sperry's chart in *Corporate Therapy and Consulting*, 1996, p. 184.

Certainly there are aspects of therapy that are inappropriate and counterproductive when dragged into the corporate environment. If a therapist attempts to provide coaching without significant knowledge of the business world or the corporate environment, including its vocabulary, its motivations, its assumptions, and its bottom-line orientation, he or she is destined to fail. A psychotherapist who has spent all of his or her time in the therapy world, isolated from the corporate environment, is likely to face significant difficulties in coaching. If you have spent your entire professional life at universities, in counseling centers, in a private therapy office, and at professional meetings with psychologist colleagues, you are going to have to make a significant transition.

Values

As a starting point, mental health professionals must often overcome their own serious value biases about the business world. Psychologists sometimes don't respect a "bottom-line" profit orientation. *Money* is a primary method for evaluation in the business culture, and many therapists do not think in those terms.

Competition

Business executives *compete* and expect others to compete with them, moment-to-moment, day-to-day, all the time. Competition is a way of life; it is accepted and expected—even welcomed by effective executives. Counselors aren't used to this focus. Counselors generally think cooperatively.

Appearance

Corporate executives are used to dressing for success, on the assumption that *the way you look* carries real weight. If you appear successful and powerful, they believe, others will give you respect and you will be taken seriously. Mental health workers often ignore this part of life, dressing for comfort on the assumption that appearance is superficial and insignificant.

Pace

Things move *fast* in the corporate world, and decisions must be made now, without enough information. Therapists are trained to reflect, to work through, and to give things time to settle out.

What Therapists Can Offer the Business World

Therapy, nevertheless, has much to offer the corporate world. Here are some of the most important general things that therapists can bring to business:

1. **Insight.** At its best, therapy produces hard-earned wisdom about how life really works. The executive who knows how to study the undertow of psychological currents and patterns in a work environment will have a significant advantage. This includes insight into self and insight into the dynamics and motivations of others. An executive who cannot read and understand other people does not stand much of a chance in the long run. And one who is ignorant of self is at a real disadvantage. Some people develop these skills on their own; others must work at them in a structured way . . . with help. Everyone can use another set of eyes and ears and another point of view.

2. **Adult development.** Each of us goes through a series of expectable changes in life. To behave like a thirty-year-old when you are fifty is to ask for trouble. It just doesn't work, and an understanding of development brings an important expertise to the mix. Developmental changes and urges are important motivators, and they must be considered when making significant corporate decisions. Executives must develop, as well. Many exceptional young executives are promoted ahead of their contemporaries, only to find themselves in a new cultural milieu with new rules and priorities. Their previous scorn for (or comfort with) conformity or self-promotion or social schmoozing puts them at odds with their new colleagues. Such leaders may need help to move through this developmental phase within their career.

3. **Modeling effective listening skills.** Most psychotherapists are far better listeners than most business executives are. Therapists have taken courses in graduate school on how to listen effectively. Many have read research on listening and how it functions, and most have experienced internships or traineeships where they received feedback on their listening skills. At the very least, excounselors can serve as a useful model of these skills for executive clients. Simple listening techniques such as restatement, summarizing, and physical listening are new to executives, and highly valued, once they are seen and understood.

4. **Resistance.** People don't change when they say they will. People don't grow when they decide they need to. Therapists are used to resistance, and they come to expect it. It doesn't throw them; they don't find it discouraging or annoying. It simply comes with the territory. It is actually useful in some ways.

5. **Cooperation.** The therapist–coach is not competitive in any way with the executive client. When the executive succeeds, the coach succeeds. Therapists bring this rather unique slant to the business world, and it is rare and valuable in that context.

Sometimes executives compete compulsively, when they would be better off to cooperate. There is evidence that cooperative models of leadership are advantageous with modern workers in the present economy.

Other, more specific themes must be considered in the coaching-therapy mix. The table below summarizes some important themes to keep in mind.

Positive and Negative Themes from Therapy (What to Keep; What to Throw Out)

As shown in Table I.2, there are aspects of psychotherapy that must be left behind if the coach is to be perceived as useful and relevant in the corporate world. This is most often true at the beginning of a coaching relationship. Once trust and effectiveness have been demonstrated, a coach can be less wary about being confused with a psychotherapist, although this issue never completely goes away.

TABLE I-2. Positive and negative themes from psychotherapy in regard to coaching

Positive themes (useful in coaching)	Negative themes (leave these behind)
Insight	Passive approach
Awareness as a goal	Data from client only
Self-examination	Slow movement
Intrapersonal understanding	Focus on feelings or intrapersonal information
Talking about things is superior to: • not talking about them • ignoring them • pretending things are OK • hoping things will get better	Meeting only in office (of clinician) at a regular time, for a standard period of time (50 minutes)
Rapport building/special relationship	Reliance on the coach
Feedback from impartial party	
Confidential relationship	

The Overall Purpose of This Book

Simply stated, the goal of this book is to help the reader synthesize the best lessons from psychological theory in a way that they can be quickly understood and effectively applied to executive and management coaching. There are two target audiences: the psychotherapist who wants to enter the world of executive coaching and the manager seeking to enhance everyday coaching skills. Each chapter begins with a history of the theory and its basic concepts, followed by examples of the way that the theory can be applied to coaching in the workplace. Strengths and weakness of each theory are discussed, along with situations that are well suited or poorly suited for each approach. There is a chapter specifically aimed at coaching female executives, and it explores the unique problems that women face when they enter the corporate arena and move from survival to thriving in the executive suite. One chapter describes the important differences between "workers," managers, and leaders. Another summarizes the lessons an executive coach can learn from successful athletic coaches. A final chapter provides tips for the psychotherapist who is just getting started. References and additional readings follow each chapter.

References

Kerin, R., & Peterson, R. (1998). *Strategic marketing problems: Cases and comments.* Upper Saddle River, NJ: Prentice-Hall.

Kiel, F., Rimmer, E., Williams, K., & Doyle, M. (1996). Coaching at the top. *Coaching Psychology Journal: Practice and Research, 48* (2), 67–77.

Macmillan, C. (1999). *The role of the organizational consultant: A model for clinicians.* Unpublished doctoral dissertation, Massachusetts School of Professional Psychology.

Murphy, D. (2000, June 25). On the fringe: Survival lessons. *San Francisco Sunday Examiner and Chronicle,* J-1-2.

Tobias, L. (1990). *Psychological consulting to management, a clinician's perspective.* New York: Brunner/Mazel.

Weinstein, B. (1999, November 21). Career search: Peters sees black hole for white collars. *San Francisco Sunday Examiner and Chronicle,* J-2.

Recommended Readings

Anderson, W. (1998, January/February). New kid in the boardroom. *The Family Therapy Networker,* 35–40.

Benton, D. (1999). *Secrets of a CEO coach.* New York: McGraw-Hill.

Block, P. (2000). *Flawless Consulting: A guide to getting your expertise used* (2nd ed.). San Francisco: Jossey-Bass (Pfeiffer).

Christmas, B. (1994, April). Coaching vs. managing. *Apparel Industry Magazine, 55*(4), 70.

deLisser, P. (1999). *Be your own executive coach*. Worchester, MA: Chandler House Press.

Douglas, C., & Morley, W. (2000). *Executive coaching, an annotated bibliography*. Greensboro, NC: Center for Creative Leadership.

Doyle, J. (1999). *The business coach: A game plan for the new work environment*. New York: Wiley.

Gilley, J., & Boughton, N. (1996). *Stop managing, start coaching!* Chicago: Irwin Professional Publishing.

Hall, D., Otazo, K., & Hollenbeck, G. (1999). Behind closed doors: What really happens in executive coaching. *Organizational Dynamics, 39–52*.

Hargrove, R. (1995). *Masterful coaching*. San Francisco: Jossey-Bass (Pfeiffer).

Kilburg, R. (1986). *Professionals in distress: Issues, syndromes, and solutions in psychology*. Washington, DC: American Psychological Association.

Kilburg, R. (2000). *Executive coaching: Developing managerial wisdom in a world of chaos*. Washington, DC: American Psychological Association.

Kilburg, R. (Ed.). (1996, Spring). Executive coaching (Special Issue). *Consulting Psychology Journal: Practice and Research, 48*(2).

Kochalka, J. (1995, February). Shrink office problems down to size. *Real Estate Today, 37–39*.

Koonce, R. (1994). One on one. *Training & development, 34–40*.

Martin, I. (1996). *From couch to corporation: Becoming a successful corporate therapist*. New York: Wiley.

Miller, J., & Brown, P. (1993). *The corporate coach*. New York: St. Martin's Press.

Olesen, M. (1996). Coaching today's executives. *Training & Development, 22–27*.

Peterson, D. (1996). Executive coaching at work: The art of one-on-one change. *Consulting Psychology Journal: Practice and Research, 48*(2), 78–86.

Prahalad, C. K., & Hamel, G. (1990, May–June). The core competence of the corporation. *Harvard Business Review, 79–91*.

Richard, J. (1999). Multimodal Therapy: A useful model for the executive coach. *Consulting Psychology Journal: Practice and Research, 51*(1), 24–30.

Segal, M. (1997). *Points of influence: A guide to using personality theory at work*. San Francisco: Jossey-Bass.

Singer, E. (1974). *Effective management coaching*. London: Institute of Personnel Management.

Snyder, A. (1995, March). Executive coaching: The new solution. *Management Review, 29–32*.

Spector, E., & Toder, F. (2000, March). Coaching 101: A primer for psychologists. *The California Psychologist, 33*(3), 18.

Sperry, L. (1993, June). Working with executives: Consulting, counseling and coaching. *Individual Psychology, 49*(2), 257–266.

Sperry, L (1996). *Corporate therapy and consulting*. New York: Brunner/Mazel.

Thach, L., & Heinselman, T. (1999, March). Executive coaching defined. *Training & Development, 35–39*.

Tobias, L. (1996). Coaching executives. *Consulting Psychology Journal: Practice and Research, 48*(2), 87–95.

Vriend, J. (1985). *Counseling powers and passions*. Alexandria, VA: American Association for Counseling and Development.

Wallace, W., & Hall, D. (1996). *Psychological consultation: Perspectives and applications*. Pacific Grove, CA: Brooks/Cole.

White, R., & Hodgson, P. (2001). *Relax, it's only uncertainty: Lead the way when the way is changing*. Upper Saddle River, NJ: Prentice Hall.

Witherspoon, R., & White, R. (1997). *Four ways that coaching can help executives*. Greensboro, NC: Center for Creative Leadership.

1
CHAPTER

Assessment

Whatever exists at all exists in some amount.

— Thorndike, 1918

Anything that exists in amount can be measured.

—Thorndike, 1939

There is one essential area where psychologists have a clear edge over all other kinds of consultants: psychological testing and assessment.

Testing is central to the professional identity of psychologists, and to some extent, it represents psychology's historic core competency. Psychologists in the 1950s and 1960s often defined themselves as psychometricians, and psychological testing was, for many, their single important professional activity. Only psychologists are formally trained to conduct psychological assessments. Psychologists study testing in school, receive supervision in residencies, and are licensed to conduct formal evaluations and submit them as evidence in court. Psychologists are identified with psychological testing in the eye of the consuming public. Most psychologists possess a basic understanding of the important elements of assessment, including knowledge of the important tests, the clinical interview, concepts of validity and reliability, and how to tell people about the results of testing in ethically effective ways. Other psychotherapists are familiar with assessment methods, and all assess their clients in some fashion as a regular aspect of individual treatment.

1

The Role of Assessment in Coaching

Assessment is an essential element of executive coaching. It is important because people in the workplace tend to avoid frankness when they deal with each other, especially when they interact with people to whom they report—those who formally evaluate them. The higher leaders get in an organization, the less frank feedback they get. Leaders at the top of organizations rarely get any "negative" feedback at all, and sometimes, because of flattery, they have a distorted sense of their strengths, weaknesses, and abilities.

Assessment is also important because people are generally not accurate self-reporters, in spite of how certain they may be (Erdberg, 2000). We cannot rely on what people tell us about themselves.

Most executive coaches fly by the seat of their pants when it comes to assessment, and many use an informal 360° process. This chapter outlines the important components of an effective executive assessment process along with ways to incorporate them in coaching.

A Brief History of Psychological Assessment

Attempts at objective assessment have been around for centuries, and there is evidence that formal mental testing has roots in the sixteenth century, if not before (Drummond, 2000). Psychologists have always used the clinical interview to assess patients and clients, but modern clinical practice has moved toward structured interviews, which have the potential to be more reliable and more consistently comprehensive than unstructured ones. Objective psychometric instruments were originally conceived out of the need to standardize the way that psychologists collect and interpret client information, particularly during wars and times of rapid educational or economic expansion in the United States.

Alfred Binet was studying the relationship between palmistry, phrenology, and intelligence when the Ministry of Public Education in Paris commissioned him to develop procedures to distinguish between students who could be educated and those who could not (Drummond, 2000). This work led to the development of the first standardized IQ tests. Testing was originally conceived as an objective and fair way to allocate precious educational resources (even though it has not generally accomplished that purpose. If anything, widespread IQ testing in education seems to have served to maintain the status quo).

World Wars I and II led to accelerated activity in test development, as the American military establishment sought to quickly and efficiently screen out "dull" young men using the Army Alpha test. They added the Army Beta when it became clear that many immigrant recruits could not be adequately tested using a written English format. Intelligence testing seemed successful, and the Army eventually moved toward personality testing to screen out problem recruits.

Hathaway and McKinley (1943) pioneered the Minnesota Multiphasic Personality Inventory (MMPI) at the University of Minnesota as a way to differentiate between normal, neurotic, and psychotic people. They combined questions from the best personality inventories that existed in the 1940s and developed comprehensive norms that were widely accepted in the psychological community as the "gold standard" for personality testing.

Hermann Rorschach developed a projective method to assess personality in 1921 using inkblots. Several scoring systems evolved until John Exner consolidated the best features of those systems and subjected them to rigorous systematic, data-based evaluation in the 1970s. His system can be used to enter data into a computer that produces information on a wide range of cognitive-personality factors. Exner moved the inkblot test forward in terms of validity and reliability, although skeptics remain. The Rorschach is an excellent comprehensive instrument that produces a large amount of important personality information, but it is difficult and time consuming to use, and it lacks a certain face validity in the corporate world.

Recently, the convergence of extensive historical norms, developed over the past century with the data reduction power of the personal computer, has produced some extraordinarily convenient and useful tools. Testing via the Internet appears to have great potential value to psychologists and executive coaches. Data can be entered on an office PC, uploaded to a testing service, and the results can be downloaded back to the end user in moments. Numerous testing companies are standing by to sell you their assessment products.

Assessment Methods for Coaches

Assessment is one of the early steps in any successful coaching effort. There are four different ways to get the assessment information needed for good coaching. An optimal evaluation of your client would include all four, although all four are not always feasible.

Method 1. Multipoint or 360-Degree Feedback

This is an area of accepted organizational development (OD) practice that is different from the normal practice of psychotherapy, and is likely to seem strange and even a little uncomfortable to a coach first trained in psychotherapy. It is not new, as it apparently has roots in assessment centers developed by the German military in World War II (Fleenor & Prince, 1997). The method solicits feedback from people all around your client. Since there is some controversy over whether or not the term "360°" is proprietary, many use the terms "multipoint" or "multi-rater" feedback or full-circle evaluation, or even multi-source assessment. It represents a diminished approach to confidentiality and an expanded view of client data collection, in that significant others are brought into the mix right at the beginning of the coaching process. Many business organizations are used to the 360-degree process and are likely to already be comfortable with it (at least in the United States). Some businesses use this process routinely in organizational development and personnel evaluation, and they use it as an organizational change method. Everyone in the organization contributes feedback to everyone else, and the information is fed back to organizational consultants and members.

Coaches tend to use multi-rater feedback to get information for their single client, one client at a time. In this method, all the important people in a client's world are solicited for input. This includes people your client reports to, people who report to your client, and peers. It should also include internal customers (people within the organization to whom your client provides a service) and, when feasible, outside customers. It may also include family members, if there is a chance that they can provide useful information, and it should include self-assessment input from your client. The receptionist and the custodial staff can be included if their point of view has a chance to be useful.

Figure 1.1, the Johari window, created by Joseph Luft and Harry Ingham (Luft, 1970; Jones & Pfeiffer, 1973) is a helpful model here. It can be used to orient the executive and coach and it can be used to organize 360° information.

In coaching, the general goal is to move knowledge from cells II, III, and IV toward cell I. The Johari Model teaches us the following (Luft, 1970):

- A change in one quadrant causes a change in other quadrants.
- It takes psychic energy to keep information in quadrants II, III, and IV.
- Threat tends to decrease awareness while mutual trust tends to increase movement to quadrant I.
- Forced awareness (exposure) is usually counterproductive.
- The unknown, hidden, and blind quadrants are maintained by social training, custom, and fear.

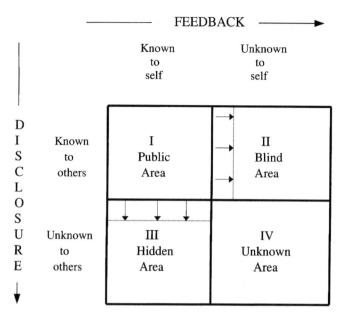

FIGURE 1.1. The Johari window.

Executives sometimes confuse good intentions with good leadership. Obviously, intentions do not equal action, and people do not react to a leader's intentions. They react to his or her behavior, particularly in terms of what it means to them, not to the leader. So, leaders must actively solicit feedback from direct reports. They simply cannot assume that their intentions "work" or that their good intentions accurately or adequately speak for them.

Confidentiality in Assessment

The issue of confidentiality must, of course, be dealt with early on, and executives might not seem concerned about this at first. (Executives in other countries may tend to be more cautious about personal information.) The key is a clear understanding of what's at stake, along with an agreement about where the information goes or does not go. Coaching is different from therapy in that it often has more than one purpose; that is, the organization which pays for the coaching has a legitimate stake in the outcome. This implies that the organization, in the form of a boss or supervisor or human relations professional, has a claim on the information that would otherwise be confidential if the client were seeking counseling privately (and paying for it). This does not mean that some level of discretion isn't possible or important. It is, and many coaching clients are actually quite interested in how and where information will be shared. Some coaches insist on a confidential relationship with their clients, while others do not offer such an arrangement, as it is not always feasible or realistic to do so. A discussion about this must take place at the beginning of the relationship, and the coach must not overestimate his or her ability to manage information flow. If a coach is uncomfortable with the situation, he or she should reconsider the appropriateness of the assignment and perhaps decline to proceed.

There are several important steps to managing confidentiality. Check out your client's assumptions. Temper expectations at the onset, and assert that a coaching client cannot count on absolute confidentiality as would a psychotherapy client. The coach can follow that statement with a commitment to discretion, making it clear that the coach has the client's best interests in mind. The question of whose interests prevail (the organization's or the person's), must still be discussed and determined honestly and openly. In most cases it will be possible to provide great discretion to the individual client, and in some cases very little. The key is to figure this out at the onset, reach an understanding, and stick with it. Don't promise something that can't be delivered, and don't reveal anything unnecessarily. If your client wishes assessment information to go forward to support his or her career, think carefully about the request. If it will change the balance of feedback and make accurate or hard-hitting information impossible to get, rule it out. But if you and your client decide to forward some of the information to others, consider a written agreement that specifies the details.

Objections to Multipoint or 360-Degree Feedback

There is a good case to be made for avoiding the use of multipoint feedback for personnel purposes (e.g., selection and promotion), as you cannot count on its validity. There are many sources of potential bias in multi-rater information. Occasionally, someone will use "feedback" as an opportunity to take a cheap shot at your client or to get revenge. Happily, this is a rare event. The greater threat to validity comes from various halo effects. When your client is an upbeat and kind person, these global positive attributes spill over and influence other, unrelated bits of feedback. If your client is grumpy or moody, these qualities also affect ratings in other specific areas. There is simply no way to know exactly how valid 360-degree ratings are, and it can be extremely unfair (and perhaps illegal) to use the information for personnel decisions. Most 360-degree evaluations are not vali-dated against specific job content. It is the job of the coach to filter the inherent bias and help clients make accurate sense out of the data, so that they can apply it to the process of self-improvement.

The level of feasible confidentiality will vary from organization to organization, but all managers (of the clients being coached) will ex-pect some information about the progress of the coaching. Are goals being met? Is the coaching productive? What can the boss do to help? What can the organization learn about itself from this client's assess-ment? Take care to provide appropriate ongoing information to those who pay the bills.

Next, discern the organization's familiarity with the 360-degree process. If those who hired you are comfortable with the idea, get started. If not, discuss and sell the idea to the coaching client. Assessment re-quires coaching clients to agree to receive feedback that may be un-comfortable and negative. Do not underestimate how difficult and threatening this can be. It is easy for a coach to become inured to the painfulness of unflattering feedback that clients may get from col-leagues. Remember: when they first hear it, it can break their heart.

Create a set of questions that will be posed to all participants. You can get these questions from various sources, and you can suggest several of your own. First, consult the coaching goals and see which questions naturally derive from them. Then ask supervisors, bosses, or mentors what the best questions would be. Then ask your clients what they think they would like to learn. Then offer some question of your own. These questions are not difficult to create. Most multipoint evaluations include questions like the following:

1. What are this person's strengths? What does he or she do well?
2. What are this person's weaknesses or skill deficits?
3. What is it like to work with this person?
4. What would you like this person to know about working with you?
5. Give an example that would be instructive to the client (about coaching and the client's development).
6. What does this person need to learn in order to be successful at the next level?

Homemade Instruments

Although there are commercially available instruments, you can cer-tainly develop your own. For example, you could create Likert-type scales based on interviews with your client and important others, us-ing the format in Figure 1.2.

Example Question 1:

"How much does Joe Executive allow you to operate autonomously?

0	1	2	3	4	5
None	Some	Moderate amount	Quite a bit		Lots

Example Question 2:

"How well does Joe delegate?

0	1	2	3	4	5
Poorly	Needs to improve	Adequately moderate	Quite well		Terifically

FIGURE 1.2. Likert-type scale.

The question of confidentiality must also be addressed with those who provide the feedback. They have a stake in it. While it is usually possible to tabulate and synthesize the information into a "group" consensus so that your client cannot tell who-said-what-about-whom, this is sometimes tricky. A coach cannot assume that people won't be able to correctly connect comments to specific people—or worse, to erroneously do so. People who report to your client, whose job may depend upon the good will of your client, may understandably be nervous or reticent about providing precise negative information, even though that information might be extremely useful to the coach and the executive. It is wise to have a conversation about this with each person who provides information. Warn them that even though you intend to completely disguise what they say, there is a possibility that you might not be able to do just that. Ask them for direct, useful input, but recommend that they take care of their own position and comfort level. Certain parties will not be able to provide information in a disguised or confidential way, of course, when there is only one person with certain information. When a supervisor tells the coach that a client doesn't meet deadlines, for example, that client will know exactly where that piece of feedback came from. It is the coach's job to effectively combine and synthesize the information so that a few important points are made without indicting those who contributed.

Discussing the Results

When it comes time to provide feedback to the client, think carefully about how to do it. Clients and circumstances vary, and some would be well served to get information in a direct and hard-hitting way. Others need it to be softened, and the feedback must be framed in gentle, positive terms, so that it can be "heard." Take care to avoid overwhelming your client with negative information. Titrate it if necessary. Mix positives in with the negatives. Like a good piano teacher, don't overload your client with too much information at one sitting. Watch for signs of feedback fatigue. Often, executives will not show their feelings of hurt or disappointment, because they have learned to hide those feelings at work. You must be aware of the impact that negative feedback can have.

The 360-degree evaluation can be repeated at set intervals or at the beginning or ending of coaching phases. For example, you can set goals to be accomplished in three months, and then conduct a mini-360-degree evaluation (a useful variation by Robert Fisher, M.D.) to check progress. You can even begin each coaching meeting with a review of the most important or relevant 360-degree finding.

Method 2. The Interview

Psychotherapists have a special skill and advantage in this area, as they have relied on assessment interviews throughout their career. They know how to create rapport quickly in a one-on-one interaction, they know how to ask difficult personal questions, they are used to carrying a checklist in their head, they know how to focus a rambling person in a brief period of time, and they know how to "bring out" a shy client.

The one-on-one interview is a powerful and important coaching skill, because it sets the scene for most of the coaching that will follow. Rapport must be established, goals must be set, guidelines laid down, and, while all of this is happening, coaches can assess their client. Check out their interpersonal skills such as the ability to listen, ability to speak clearly and concisely, ability to focus, their openness and defensiveness, sense of humor, and the general interpersonal impression that they make, along with the reactions they invoke in the interview.

The First Meeting

The first interview in coaching is different from the counseling interview. Many psychotherapists focus much of their attention on history and intrapersonal development. This is unnecessary and probably counterproductive in coaching. Certainly, the coach is interested in how a client developed, especially as it pertains to the matters at hand. "I am interested in how you came to be this way" is a fair question that most clients will welcome. But an extended interest in psychosocial history is liable to detract from the action focus that coaching requires.

There are essential aspects of the first interview with a coaching client, and clients are assessing coaches during that meeting, as well. This interview can last anywhere from 45 minutes to several hours, depending on the circumstances. Often, executive clients want to move quickly, so a longer first meeting can be a good way to cover a lot of ground at the outset.

Here are some important components of the first coach–client contact.

1. Get off on the right foot. Present yourself confidently and calmly. Assure yourself that you can make an important contribution, because you can. Discern how to dress for the situation. Some companies are formal, some are casual. Some expect consultants to dress the same way that they do, others expect a more professional, dressed-up look. Feel free to ask about how people dress at the company if you do not know. Determine quickly the meaning of coaching to your client, especially whether he or she considers it to be a growth opportunity for those on the fast track, a remediation effort, or a way for the company to shed executives who aren't working out. Make sure that you reach an understanding about reasonable expectations. Deliver a clear working definition of what you have to offer. It is imperative that you get clear about this and rehearse it ahead of time, if necessary, for if you cannot do this, you are in trouble. Your client probably has some ideas about who you are and what you intend to do, but these may not be accurate.

2. You may have to "sell" the assessment to your client. Executives are sometimes skeptical of consultants, as most have had poor or mediocre experiences with them in the past. This is especially important when coaching has been suggested or mandated by the boss. Find out what your client thinks of coaching before you start. Check out his or her previous experiences with consultants, and see if mistakes were made that could now be avoided. Find out if your client is interested in the coaching process. Find out if he or she trusts, values, or believes in the information you could provide through an assessment. See if the client welcomes feedback.

3. Discuss and agree upon the level of confidentiality that is optimal

and possible. Do not promise more than you can give in this area. Get an expressed, written agreement about how information will be shared, how much, with whom, and when.

4. Set reasonable, important goals and agree to help your client meet them. Conceptualize these goals in a way that can be measured, so that you both will know, at a specific point in the future, whether or not they have been met. This may require creativity. While everything can be measured, the metrics are not always obvious. For example, if you are working with someone's feelings of inadequacy, your client can count the number of times that he or she thinks a specific thought or feels a specific feeling. If you are working with listening skills, you can evaluate his or her empathy behavior using a Likert-type scale (e.g., from "none" to "perfectly empathic"). You can count almost anything. You can express most questions using a "scale-from-one-to-ten" format.

5. Establish ground rules and a structure for the coaching. This includes scheduling, cancellation policies, and the amount of time you will spend together to accomplish goals, as well as the efforts expected of both of you outside of your meetings together. This requires that you describe a clear and useful definition of coaching to your client. Discuss your views of what coaching is and is not, what it can and cannot accomplish, as well as a preview of its methods, as you see them.

6. Continuously assess your clients. How do they treat you? Rate their interaction skills, listening skills, and speaking skills. Do they interrupt, do they talk on and on long after their point should have been made? Do they have annoying behaviors? Do they ask questions about you? Are they able to focus in a calm manner, or are they jumpy and all over the place? Do they think positively or negatively? Is their thinking expansive or constricted? Check out their vocabulary. Is it appropriate? Do you like being with them and look forward to meetings, or do you feel uncomfortable or dread them? These observations will be useful later. Make notes and remember them.

7. Prepare a written memo or letter to the client after the first meeting. Doing so documents agreements and goals and provides a starting point for later benchmarking.

Method 3. Direct Behavioral Observation

Most psychotherapists will find this area new. Executive coaches get important information about their clients by observing them directly, and in context. This happens in several settings, including the one-on-one contact that coaches have with them. Begin your evaluation from the very first contact you have, including the voice-mail message that initiated your relationship. Notice your reaction to this person's message. It is likely to be instructive. Write it down, so that you can compare it to your impressions later in the relationship.

Seek opportunities to observe your clients as they work. Listen to them on the phone, read their e-mail messages if you can (with their permission, of course. You may even need to get permission from the larger organization to do this, as well). The best way to get a comprehensive and accurate sense of your clients is to "shadow" them. Accompany them at work, sit in meetings with them, watch them as they interact with people in the hallways, and sit in as they give instructions to people who report to them. This is an aspect of coaching that is very different from psychotherapy, and it offers a tremendous advantage. The information that counselors get from their therapy patients is useful, but flawed, in that it is virtually all self-report. It is filtered through the needs and biases of that person. Direct observation is so important and powerful that coaches must forcefully advocate for its use. This usually means that they must push through their own natural inclination to be shy about shadowing. It is a powerful assessment technique, and clients accommodate to it more readily than most coaches imagine, especially when having a coach is seen as a benefit for high-potential executives rather than as a remediation. It makes sense to paint the coach as a status symbol for those with a future rather than as the "angel of death." You and your client can decide how you should be introduced to others in the workplace. For example, "This is my coach. She will be joining us this morning to observe how I operate at team meetings. We're working on ways to make the team meetings more effective." You will be surprised at how quickly a coach can fade into the background.

It is important to create key questions for shadowing. Some examples are:

- How do others behave around this client? How do they react?
- Do you see deficits or signs of target behaviors (those to be changed)?
- Does your client's behavior match his or her self-perception?
- Does your client do what the client says he or she is doing?
- How does this person reinforce others, consciously and unconsciously?
- What unintended messages does your executive send to others?
- Is this someone you would want to be around? Why or why not?

Method 4. Objective Assessment Instruments

A wide variety of standardized, pre-packaged instruments are available to the coach. They can be of extraordinary value, but they can also be a significant waste of time and energy. In fact, they can serve to "turn off" a client and damage rapport. Before purchasing and using instruments off the shelf, evaluate them carefully.

Testing Tools: The Basics

There are two important ways that formal instruments can add value to the coaching process:

1. **Accuracy.** Interpersonal interviews and even behavioral observations are subject to several sources of distortion, including bias and missed data. Formal, structured instruments can minimize these problems.
2. **Efficiency.** Large amounts of information can be quickly obtained and tabulated. Data can be mechanically "crunched" in a way that is virtually impossible to accomplish otherwise. Clients can be compared to extensive norms that answer the question "compared to what?"

In order for testing to make a legitimate contribution to the coaching process, the following components must be in place.

Selection.   The coach must be familiar with the available tools and instruments and must be able to match them with their client and with the task at hand. This is no easy task, as there are thousands of tests and inventories out there (with new ones on the market each month), and coaches have to experiment with tests to determine which instruments are legitimate and which is optimal for their purpose. New instruments appear on the Internet and in the literature on a regular basis, some of which are excellent and many which are weak. Most are expensive, at least at start up. Most become relatively inexpensive once initial costs (for booklets, manuals, and software) have been met.

Evaluation.   Most testing tools are proprietary, and the "seller" of the instrument cannot be counted on as a valid source of information. There are hundreds of inventories that are, at best, a worthless and whimsical distraction, and at worst, a source of distorted information accompanied by the patina of technical truth.

The Construct.   The first, and perhaps most important task, is to decipher the basic concept that the instrument tests ("personality" is an example of a construct). Clients rely on coaches to do a good job with this. They count on us. They naively assume that we have done this adequately, yet it is a daunting task. Tests don't always test what they sound like they are testing, so you have to do a little checking to get a good feel for what the results really mean. For example, there are several available scales and measures of depression, but they don't all test the same thing. Each test starts with a different conception or definition of depression (the construct). You have to understand the test maker's definition of depression to be able to understand the results. Clients don't know this, and they are liable to swallow results without scrutiny. It is easy to confuse matters when you get test results that don't make sense, if it is because the test isn't measuring what it purports to measure. Test developers use a particular theory or viewpoint from which to develop their instrument, and it is important to explore the conceptual underpinnings. For example, many consultants use the Meyers-Briggs without a clear understanding or explanation of the theoretical basis for the instrument, or even a clear sense of what the essential concepts mean. This leads to confusion and misinformation, especially when the test is a relatively simple one.

Validity.   Aside from the question of construct validity (above), there are a couple of other questions that must be answered before an instrument is used. Validity asks the question: "Is this test measuring what it says it measures?" Is it accurate? Do the questions address content that is relevant to the results that it produces? Is there evidence that the results tend to accurately predict things in real life? Will the results work in the specific environment at hand? Do the results work better than a cheaper or easier method of getting the same information? Was this instrument developed for people similar to your client? Does the test appear (to your client) to be asking important and relevant questions, or do the questions seem mysterious or incomprehensible (face validity)?

Reliability.   Another set of evaluative questions has to do with the stability of the instrument. Can you use it and get the same results that the designers get? Can you use it in your coaching setting and get accurate results, or is it only useful in narrow settings and circumstances? Do you get consistent results when you use the instrument with different kinds of clients? (Was it designed for nurses, for example?) Is it a "sturdy" instrument; can your client take the test at home or on an airplane, or in a hotel room? Can your client take the test again a year from now and get relevant and valid results for comparison purposes? Can you ask a member of your staff to administer the test and expect valid results?

Standardization.   This is the norms question. How does the test determine and represent results? To whom or to what is your client compared? It makes little sense to use an MMPI for business coaching, because the purpose of the test is to assess psychopathology, and because norms were developed in clinical and hospital settings. The best tests for coaching use business and executive norms, meaning that your client's responses are compared to similar people in the same kind of circumstances. If you get a result that puts your client at the 95th percentile, you must be able to answer the question: the 95th percentile of what or whom? Were all members of the norm group from the Midwest? Were they about the same age as your client, the same gender, and (the most vexing problem) similar in race, culture, and ethnicity? If the answer to these questions is "yes," then your results will be more accurate, more relevant, and more cogent. A second question, in addition to the similarity question (Is the client similar to the norm group?) is the question of norm-group size. How many people were used to establish the test's norms? Is the size adequate? Larger is generally better, to a point.

Practical Issues.   Is the test written in a way that sounds smart and competent? Many are not, and they sound silly, or trivial. This can be a turn-off to a client. (Although it must be said that business people are generally unfamiliar with personality tests and inventories.) Are the questions clear and coherent? Are the questions written in a way that is difficult for your client to understand? Is the inventory too long to hold your client's attention, or so long that your client won't make time to get it done? If you are going to ask an executive to spend a couple of hours filling out questionnaires, the results had better be worth it. Also, evaluate whether or not the administrator of the inventory will need to be trained, especially if the task of administration or scoring will be delegated to a member of your staff or theirs.

   It is a bad sign when the information needed to evaluate an instrument is not available or if the testing vendor is unwilling to help. Think about rejecting this test and seeking other instruments. There are alternatives for every inventory or test that is currently available. Testing companies should be able to provide you with a sample packet so that you can adequately evaluate their instrument. Care is necessary because many vendors are not eager for you to know these essential qualities of their instruments. They just want you to buy them.

Specific Instruments

There is a wide range of prefabricated, proprietary, self-report instruments available. Most suffer from the problems associated with self-report data, although some incorporate a mechanism for input from those who work with your client. It is important to seek tests which provide results in the form of relative "strengths and weaknesses" rather than psychopathology.

There are a few well-known and well-respected companies that have produced and sold instruments for years. Listed in Table 1.1 are the names and contact information for five of the oldest and most widely-used companies. Each of these companies has created products that can be extremely useful in assessing executives and managers. You can generally rely on their instruments for validity and reliability.

Each of the companies listed in the above table produce a wide range of instruments designed to assess the "normal" population. Results are presented in several formats that can be used to help executive clients understand their personality strengths and weaknesses relative to their current job or career aspirations. While executives typically find lengthy questionnaires to be annoying, they are persuaded by data. The combination of standardized test data, input from 360 degrees, and their coach's professional opinion can be particularly persuasive.

Administration

Remember that assessment, especially by a psychologist, is threatening. Most people have unrealistic views of what psychologists can "tell"

TABLE 1.1. Key sources for assessment instruments and products

Company	Products	Internet address	Telephone
NCS Pearson	Various personality inventories (MMPI)	www.ncs.com	(800) 627-7271
Institute for Personality & Ability Testing (IPAT)	Various personality inventories (16PF)	www.ipat.com	(800) 225-IPAT
Consulting Psychologists Press	California Psychological Inventory (CPI)	www.cpp-db.com	(800) 624-1765
Center for Creative Leadership	360° instruments and assessment tools	www.ccl.org	(336) 545-2810
The Psychological Corporation	Various personality inventories	www.psychcorp.com	(800) 211-8378

about them, and they may be wary that a coach may pathologize or diagnose. Don't oversell testing if you decide to use it.

Presentation of the assessment is critical. Engineering and management vocabulary is optimal when discussing the evaluation process. For example, the term "instrument" is likely to fare better than "psychological test." Corporations are used to thinking in terms of "metrics" (data from the measurement of outcomes), and "benchmarks" (goals considered to be excellent and achievable). "Data" is preferable to "information." This is obviously not true across the board or for every client, so consider the circumstances and mirror the organization's vocabulary.

Make sure that the purpose of assessment is clear to all parties, and that there is agreement about what will happen to the data. If the information is to be used for "developmental" purposes (to develop the executive-client), make certain that this is clear and adhered to. Your client must know that data will not be used for selection, promotion, or retention purposes (assuming that this is, in fact, the case). Such a use of data is certainly not part of a *coaching* process.

Set the scene for realistic, truthful data collection that is aimed at discerning goals that you and your client can use. Emphasize strengths and weaknesses (or areas for future growth or development). Find one or two things to work on, rather than a whole bunch at once, even if your client seems to be interested in changing many things. Prioritize, if necessary. One thing at a time.

What to Evaluate

The circumstances, client, and goals determine the variables of interest. There is an extremely wide range of dimensions along which a client can be studied, and it is smart to give these some thought before you begin. Targets are determined by the circumstances that led to the coaching. If coaching is necessitated by a client's deficit, the evaluation must begin by focusing on what is lacking, what is "wrong." When coaching is offered as a developmental benefit to an executive with great potential, choice of evaluation variables is open for discussion and careful selection, and might start with a discussion of the particular strengths and assets that have served that executive so well, thus far.

The following section describe examples of the kinds of variables typically assessed by coaches and executive clients. In some cases, these are skills or qualities that are essential to high performance in business.

Interpersonal Skills

This may be the single area in which the coach possesses the most valuable expertise. It is common in business for a valuable executive to lack certain areas of interpersonal development. Most of us have interpersonal blind spots and relative weaknesses. A person who feels that he or she could not use input or improvement in some area of interpersonal interaction is a fool. Many successful executives have been promoted because of their drive, their content skills, or their technical track record. Some never intended to be managers or leaders, but they have taken a promotion into such a position because of the money attached. They now need additional skills to continue to succeed. The skills they developed in technical excellence are inadequate for the manager. The skills required to propel a person to middle management or to a VP position are different from the skills needed to lead a company. Some of the important interpersonal skills required of effective executives are shown in Table 1.2.

Daniel Goleman's view of Emotional Intelligence (1995, 1998) is very helpful here, and executives can be assessed using his five categories (self awareness, self regulation, motivation, empathy, and social skill). According to Goleman, effective leaders possess high emotional intelligence or EQ. There are numerous websites providing instruments and ideas about how to use EQ for executive coaching (www.eqi.org and www.eqi.mhs.com are current examples).

Content Skills

A successful executive who can contribute to organizational effectiveness possesses a high degree of *content skill*; he or she understands the core competency of the organization in a deep way and knows how to enhance it. It is helpful if key executives understand the history of the organization and of the product. For example, if you are an executive in the coal industry, do you understand and appreciate the history of coal and mining operations in this country and in the world? Does it excite you? Do you understand how historical factors influence the present culture and environment?

Political Skills

Success requires the ability to understand the organizational culture and a willingness to honor the rules of the culture. There are "political"

TABLE 1.2. Assessment variables

Skill	What to look for—sample components
Listening	Does client value listening? (Or is it lip service?) Amount of listening Active or passive listener? (Does client participate, ask questions, rephrase?) Physical listening/attending skills? (client appears to be listening)
Speaking	In front of large audiences? In small groups or meetings? One-on-one? On the telephone?
Empathy	Notices other people? Grasps the concept? Cares about others and their point of view? Is capable of putting self in others' shoes?
Management	Is well organized? Can control things? Delegates appropriately? Has clear communications? Is loyal?
Leadership	Is passionate about the work and organization? Presents a confident image? Has a positive attitude, point of view? Knows how to motivate others; is persuasive? Understands leadership role. Has strategic vision. (See Table 12.1.)
Self awareness	Has an accurate sense of self. Values self-understanding. Is open to input from others.
Self presentation	Overall appearance is appropriate for the situation? General impression they give? Optimistic? Energetic?
Sense of humor	Is this person too serious? Can the person make light of himself or herself? Can they see the funny side of things? Is their humor out of control or over the top? Do they tell racial or sexual jokes?

dynamics that are common to most organizations and there are dynamics that are unique to each. An effective executive is adept at both kinds. This requires an attitude of acceptance of a modicum of political game playing (with integrity). Some executives never accept the necessity to play the requisite organizational games, and skillful executive coaching can be extremely useful in helping clients reexamine and decide how to reframe such a posture. Technical workers who possess contempt for the organizational politics have little chance for success as managers or leaders. They may be able to thrive for a while in some organizations as a "rebel," but their demise is pretty much inevitable, especially if they are promoted.

Personal and Industry Vision

It is useful to have a view of where one is going, what is possible, and how to get there. For some, this comes naturally. Others need coaching. Vision becomes incrementally more important the higher one goes in an organization. At the top, it is essential.

Feedback and Goal Setting

When you have tabulated all of the assessment information (from initial interviews, from the 360-degree evaluation, from written instruments, and from your own reactions and observations) sit down with your client and go over it all at length. Focus on a discrete number of factors rather than every single data point. Compare your client's perceptions with the information. Does your client accurately understand his or her strengths and weaknesses? (Remember to emphasize strengths!) How accurate is your client's self-perception? Is any of the assessment information surprising to you or to your client? Use this information to help your client set a small number of achievable and measurable goals.

Summary

An accurate assessment is essential for good coaching. You have to know much about a client in order to provide excellent help. Interview checklists, behavioral observation (including shadowing at the work site), a 360-degree evaluation, and prefabricated pencil-and-paper instruments can all ensure that assessment meets three important criteria: accuracy, efficiency, and comprehensiveness. Psychologists are in an excellent position, by training, background, and point of view, to provide such an assessment, but they have to work with a diminished level of client confidentiality where third parties are involved in data collection and when the organization has a share in the outcome. Social workers and other psychotherapists may need to enhance their formal assessment skills as they learn executive coaching.

References

Fleenor, J. & Prince, J. (1997). *Using 360-degree feedback in organizations: An annotated bibliography.* Greensboro, NC: Center for Creative Leadership.

Goleman, D. (1995). *Emotional intelligence.* New York: Bantam.

Goleman, D. (1998). *Working with emotional intelligence.* New York: Bantam.

Jones, J., & Pfeiffer, J.W. (Eds.). (1973). The Johari Window: A model for soliciting and giving feedback. *The 1973 Annual Handbook for Facilitators.* San Diego: Pfeiffer & Company.

Recommended Readings

Business & Professional Publishing. (1999). *360° Feedback manual.* Warriewood NSW: Woodslane Pty Limited.

Cattell, R., Eber, H., & Tatsuoka, M. (1970). *Handbook for the sixteen personality factor questionnaire (16PF).* Champaign, IL: Institute for Personality and Ability Testing.

Drummond, R. J. (2000). *Appraisal procedures for counselors and helping professionals.* Upper Saddle River, NJ: Prentice Hall.

Erdberg, P. (2000). Assessing personality: Psychology's unique contribution. *The California Psychologist.* March.

Groth-Marnat, G. (1997). *Handbook of psychological assessment* (3rd ed.). New York: Wiley.

Hathaway, S. R., & McKinley, J. C. (1943). *The Minnesota Multiphasic Pesonality Schedule.* Minneapolis, MN: University of Minnesota Press.

Jude-York, D., & Wise, S. (1997). *Multipoint feedback: A 360° catalyst for change.* Menlo Park, CA: Crisp Publications.

Kaplan, R., & Palus, C. (1994). *Enhancing 360-degree feedback for senior executives: How to maximize the benefits and minimize the risks.* Greensboro, NC: Center for Creative Leadership.

Lepsinger, R., & Lucia, A. (1997). *The art and science of 360° feedback.* San Francisco: Jossey-Bass.

Luft, J. (1970). *Group processes: An introduction to group dynamics* (2nd ed). Palo Alto, CA: National Press Books.

Maddox, T. (Ed.). (1997). *Tests: A Comprehensive Reference for Assessments in Psychology, Education, and Business.* Pro-Ed.

McAllister, L. (1988). *A practical guide to CPI interpretation.* (2nd ed). Palo Alto: Consulting Psychologists Press.

Ward, P. (2000). *360° Feedback.* Woodstock, New York: Beekman Publishers.

The Psychodynamic View

Psychoanalytic consulting maintains the position that the presenting problem may at best be a symptom and often is an issue that serves to protect the real problem.

— Czander (1993, p. 183)

No text on the application of psychological theory would be complete without a chapter on psychodynamic theory. It is the oldest of the psychotherapies, and there are several modern variations, including object-relations theory and self psychology. Virtually all psychotherapists trained in the twentieth century have been exposed to psychodynamic ideas, and for many, it was the foundation of their training. This can be an asset and a liability, and this chapter discusses both. While many variations of Freud's thinking can be extremely useful to the executive coach, the psychoanalytic psychotherapist is the butt of "Woody Allen" jokes, and the source of stereotypes that can seriously damage a coach's attractiveness and credibility. Indeed, some coaches go out of their way to distance themselves from Freud and from psychotherapy, especially when it is stereotyped as endless probing in search of childhood memories. Some psychotherapists have more to *unlearn* than to learn when it comes to the application of psychodynamic principles to executive coaching. Prior to about 1990, even clinical training that was not analytic contained artifacts of psychoanalysis. The fifty-minute hour, the transparent therapist, strict adherence to boundaries, and the therapist's inclination to interpret everything, are examples of methods likely to be more useful for the couch than the coach. One classic and unexamined example is the assumption that "depth" equals "strength" (Harrison, 1970/1994). Many clinicians operate on the unchallenged assumption that deeper interventions or interpretations are, de facto, better. This assumption can ruin a coaching relationship, where analysis is often less trusted than action. Deep interpretations may actually be too threatening for the coaching relationship.

Many of the essential rules and conventions of psychodynamic therapy are violated in executive coaching. For example,

- coaching is goal- and action-oriented rather than reflective or introspective. Business executives move at a pace not generally comfortable for psychotherapists.
- coaching usually takes place on the client's turf, not the therapist's office.
- time frames are flexible, and the 50-minute hour is irrelevant or counterproductive.
- client-coach contact includes a mixture of professional and social interactions in various settings.
- confidentiality is almost assuredly weakened or threatened.

There is danger when a coach becomes associated with Freud, because coaching can then be viewed in the organization as corrective action mandated for losers, a remedial effort for damaged executives just before they are moved out. Coaching works best when it is seen as an activity for executives who are looking for an edge, some way to push their limits and expand their effectiveness.

The trick is to integrate "analytic" or "dynamic" thinking into coaching without pathologizing the client or relationship. The task is to think analytically and behave proactively. That said, the action-oriented and psychodynamically informed coach can be very effective.

Usefulness

Psychodynamic ideas can be extremely useful in coaching. Here are some examples:

1. When an executive wants to develop political or interpersonal skills.
   - to understand the behavior of board members
   - to deal with people above in the power structure
   - to sell work
   - to develop effective relationships

- to lead and manage team members
- to choose key personnel for important tasks

2. When an executive desires enhanced self-understanding.
   - of his or her own behavior
   - of strengths and weaknesses
   - of future development
   - of optimal career choices

3. When an executive behaves in ways that are self-defeating.
   - over controlling or under empowering
   - abrasive
   - self-centered
   - disorganized
   - angry or hostile
   - poor listener
   - perfectionistic or rigid
   - authoritarian
   - too timid in certain situations
   - distrustful
   - easily threatened
   - procrastinates

4. When an executive needs to deal with difficult colleagues or employees.
   - working with talented or key people who are difficult
   - dealing with people who are self-centered or narcissistic

Theoretical History and Basics

Sigmund Freud was a pioneer—even a revolutionary—in his time and place. He broke ranks with philosophers and physicians in his day by insisting that reason could be used to fearlessly explore deterministic forces motivating human behavior. He believed that behavior could be understood, if only we looked closely enough. He pinpointed strange and even ugly impulses, and exposed us to the fact that we do not run our lives on a rational basis. We are all irrational, in spite of our rational pretenses. And we are irrational in predictable patterns and configurations. Central to this viewpoint is the idea that we rarely deal directly with external reality. Instead, we interact with the world based on internal representations. We "see the outside world in terms of internal concerns" (Czander, 1993, p. 45).

What follows is a basic summary of Freudian ideas from the point of view of their utility in executive coaching. Many of Freud's ideas will be discarded, as they seem more useful to therapists than to coaches. (Mainstream psychotherapists have already rejected some of Freud's ideas, as well.) These will not be presented. The views of Freud and related theories, such as object relations theory and self psychology, will be presented here in ways they can be useful to the executive coach.

What Motivates People?

Business thinking is essentially economic; that is, it sees enlightened self-interest as the primary motivational force. We work hard (and smart) because we want to thrive. In this view, when we work hard and smart, we will get what we want. We get houses, cars, and financial security. Others admire us for our success. There is a linear relationship between thoughtful, goal-seeking behavior and success. Psychoanalytic thinking rejects this view (Czander, 1993), replacing it with an irrational set of motives and causes for human behavior.

In the psychodynamic view, behavior is the result of the interplay of conflicting internal forces. The view is *dynamic* in the sense that when two forces come into conflict a third, and different, force is produced. (Freud was influenced by the dramatic advances that were taking place in the physical sciences of his day, such as thermodynamics.) Human psychic energy is expressed through one of three channels: the id, the ego, and the superego. The *id* is the original way that children control energy, and it is motivated by the desire for pleasure as well as the avoidance of pain. It is primitive, simple, and instinctual, and is called the "Pleasure Principle" (Czander, 1993). The *ego* is reality oriented and pragmatic, and its main job is to control the id and still satisfy needs. The ego is sensible, and it rules with the "Reality Principle." The *superego* is the moral channel, and is often thought of as the seat of the conscience. Its goal is the ideal, rather than the real, and it strives for perfection. It subdues the impulses of the id and attempts to substitute moralistic goals for realistic ones. It rewards a person with feelings of pride. It punishes with feelings of guilt or inferiority (Corey, 1982).

The Role of Fantasy

Fantasy is important to psychodynamic theory. In the workplace context, we strive to gratify fantasies about our career aspirations (Czander,

1993). We have an idealized notion of who and what we are in the world of work (called the "ego ideal"), and often it is pretty fantastic. In most cases, of course, the workplace cannot fully service our fantasies, especially when we work in a hierarchical organization. By definition, only a few make it to the top. Few are able to sustain status as a "rising star." The rest are disappointed, and they experience psychic conflict and even hostile or aggressive impulses. Such conflict is rarely discussed openly or directly. It manifests itself in frustrated, disguised, and camouflaged forms. Psychodynamic thinking can help sort it all out.

The Unconscious at Work

Freud contributed the idea of the *unconscious* to modern behavioral science, the idea that we do not know much of our own mental activity. Recent research by cognitive scientists has essentially confirmed the existence of unconscious psychological processes, so we now know that the unconscious is real (Cramer, 2000). A central goal of psychoanalysis is to make the unconscious conscious; that is, to become more self-aware, to understand more about how we think, feel, and react. In that way, we can exercise conscious choice and make decisions in line with our espoused values and the interests of the organizations we lead.

Defense Mechanisms

One of the most durable legacy ideas in Freud's work proposes that we have many ways to protect our ego or sense of self. We use defense mechanisms to distort or deny reality so that we aren't too hurt or too threatened. The id, ego, and superego compete to control available psychic energy, and the urges of the id often feel dangerous. Anxiety is a signal that we are struggling to control these desires. When we can't rationally control these primitive urges (to attack or to flee), we use defense mechanisms to keep threatening feelings out of consciousness and painful thoughts out of awareness. Defenses protect us from painful emotions or realizations. They are ways to distort reality by behaving irrationally in order to protect one's ego ideal or sense of self. These are typically useful in the short-run and self-defeating in the end. We use defense mechanisms like we use aspirin: to temporarily blunt pain until we get a better handle on things. Defenses smooth out the emotional bumps in the road and are useful unless they become extreme or habitual. Like aspirin, they work well in small amounts, but become toxic if we consume the whole bottle or become too reliant on them. When a person clings to defenses, when they are too quick to defend, or when defenses interfere with accurate perceptions of reality, they become troublesome. There are many such mechanisms in the psychodynamic literature, and a knowledge of them can be extremely useful in the organizational setting. People aren't usually aware when they are using them, but the alert coach or executive can spot the use of defense mechanisms in the business setting. Some defenses are healthier than others. Detailed descriptions of all the defenses can be found in the back of the Diagnostic and Statistical Manual of Mental Disorders, 4th edition (DSM-IV; American Psychiatric Association, 1994, pp. 751–757). What follows is a description of defenses most likely to be employed by healthy executives in the workplace. Coaches must be able to spot them and incorporate them into their understanding of their clients.

Adaptive Defense Mechanisms

Altruism.   Rather than experience feelings that are threatening, you dedicate yourself to actions that benefit others. You use this difficult psychic energy to help. This helps you avoid your own uncomfortable feelings. Instead of taking care of the business that is right in front of you (because you are intimidated by it, or because you are scared that you don't know quite how to do it) you spend time mentoring a younger executive or you help someone with a project of his own. No one could criticize you for this, including yourself. But the primary motivation is to avoid something that must be faced.

Sublimation.   In this case, you channel uncomfortable emotional energy into something socially acceptable. Rather than feeling hurt or angry, you "get busy." You redirect energy toward a positive goal. When you are anxious or upset, you focus on a big project that needs to be done, and seem to have boundless energy for it, even though the true source of energy is avoidance. Channeling aggressive impulses into athletics is a common example. Sometimes executives inexplicably head for the golf course when the pressure gets extreme. This mechanism is less of a problem when you are taking on a challenge that is worth doing, even if it means that you are not "facing" a different primary task.

Humor.   When faced with painful or threatening feelings, you emphasize the funny aspects of the situation. This defense works very well unless it gets out of control and becomes an irritant to others. It can also be a problem when humor is sarcastic or, alternatively, too self-deprecating. We laugh and joke about things rather than face them. Gallows humor is an example; the person who makes jokes in the emergency room is another. It is occasionally misunderstood to mean that a person is not taking a difficult problem seriously or that he or she doesn't care about it. Constant or inappropriate humor is a tip-off: maybe this person is actually anxious about something she doesn't care to face. Consider that possibility. The overall level of humor in an important meeting can indicate that a problem is overwhelming. Some organizational cultures allow for more humor than others. If a client's main defense is humor, but he finds himself in an uptight organization, he will certainly be uncomfortable, and perhaps misunderstood. Laughter when someone else is panicking is rarely appreciated.

Substitution.   We substitute one (comfortable) behavior for a threatening one. This happens when, instead of sitting down and writing a difficult memo, we clean our desk, refile things, or make telephone calls. In this way, we can tell ourselves that we are accomplishing something with our time. Such behavior can be productive, but it can also mean that we are winning a small battle while losing the war. It can be very helpful for a coach to find a way to point this out to a client who is stalled or inadequately productive.

Compensation.   We over-strive in certain areas as a way to handle a perceived weakness. For example, when a business client is weak in the accounting area, he overcompensates by spending excessive time on the shop floor, where he is comfortable. Sometimes people with extraordinary skills in one narrow area have done this. As executives move up in a hierarchical organization, they need to expand their repertoire or change the few things that they are very good at. For example, the transition to "partner" often requires a person to learn how to find new clients and to sell work. If psychic compensation throws energy in those directions, all the better, but this defense usually invests effort in the same old direction, causing a person to get better and better at something he or she is already good at.

Rituals.   Although this can sometimes be negative, the repetition of behaviors can effectively cover or manage anxiety (Bounce the ball three times before you shoot a free throw. Use a pre-shot routine in golf. Always sit in the same seat in important meetings. Park in the same spot each day. Take the same route to work. Use a certain pen to sign documents or write important notes.) Many companies could not survive without their organizational rituals. A coach must quickly learn the rituals and decide how to accommodate to them. They are an integral part of the organizational culture, and executives are often quite reactive to the rituals of the CEO. Occasionally, a leader's rituals are damaging to others, and it may be a coach's job to find a way to point this out.

Identification.   One way to avoid feelings of inferiority is to take on the identity of the organization or the leader. We become "company men" (women do this, too) and we give up our own values or independent judgment. In this way, we don't have to face negative things we think about ourselves. People take on aspects of important cultural or sports figures, allowing them to feel good without actually accomplishing much. This, of course, can be good or bad, depending on how one identifies. Sometimes a coach can actively help a client consciously choose good models.

Affiliation.   Rather than suffer threatening or negative feelings, you turn to others for support and comfort and you share your perceptions. You don't expect them to solve your problems, just to be a comforting "ear." Organizations need people who will serve as such an "ear," and coaches can provide some of this service. Clients will expect much more than just listening and affiliation from their coaches, however.

Defense Mechanisms that Deny

Denial.   This is a simple defense, and it amounts to an unconscious ignoring of the facts. Things happen and we just pretend they aren't there. They can be obvious to everyone else, but we still exclude harsh truth from our reality. We behave as if something does not exist, even though it is directly in front of us. Entire organizations can indulge in group denial, especially if things are going poorly or if there is a huge looming crisis and no one has an answer. Coaches can often spot the denial before others in the organization, and sometimes they are in a good position to point it out. Sometimes, however, a coach would be a fool to "make the unconscious conscious" even when the temptation is great. Here's an example of how one coach handles psychoanalytic insights in executive coaching (Macmillan, 1999, p. 142):

> So I feel that I have a sophisticated understanding of analytic thinking and I know that I bring it into the world of work. But it is never directly spoken about. . . . I see a lot of connections to what goes on in corporate consulting . . . as long as it stays in the mind of the consultant.

Repression.   This is an extreme version of denial, in that we "banish" a particular thought or line of thinking from our reality. This can happen at an organizational level, when certain topics are known to be "off-limits for discussion." Once again, it may well be the coach's job to point out areas of organizational or personal distortion. Such a mandate requires exceptional interpersonal tact and courage, and when things go well, a coach can make an extraordinary contribution in this way.

Isolation.   This mechanism can be helpful or harmful, but it is an essential one when we have to perform a distasteful task, such as firing someone we care for. We simply detach the feelings from a behavior. A good surgeon probably uses this defense. Isolated leaders are usually not healthy, however, and it is rare that someone inside of the organization can effectively intervene.

Defense Mechanisms that Twist Reality

Rationalization.   This may be the most common of all the defenses. We simply change the explanation to make it more acceptable, make excuses, or explain things away. We come up with excellent reasons for the things already done. "I really didn't want that promotion anyway. I would have had to move to Los Angeles, and my family would have hated that." "It's just as well," we say. "We didn't need that account, anyway. It would have been an enormous headache."

Intellectualization.   We use this defense when we ignore feelings and are able to discuss pressing matters only as intellectual arguments. Even the most obvious emotional or difficult aspects of a situation are swept under the rug of complex arguments. A coach is likely to be called upon when a bright executive is promoted to a position requiring excellent communication. It is then that the coach must discern whether complex jargon is motivated defensively or is just a matter of a learned communication style. Style can be attacked directly, while defenses must be explored and understood if they are to be acknowledged at all.

Projection.   Sometimes, when we experience a desire that is unacceptable we put it out of mind by attributing it to others. It is present, but in someone else. Instead of saying "I hate him" we say "He hates me" (Hall, 1954). There is ample room for projection in the daily life of an organization. The trick is to understand the difference between projection and reality. This is no mean feat.

Defense Mechanisms that Cause People to Behave Strangely

Reaction Formation.   In order to tolerate a threatening impulse, we express its opposite. That way we don't have to notice it, and we have terrific deniability. We express great affection for someone we really despise. Conversely, when we have a crush on someone at work, we behave inexplicably rudely toward him or her. (This, of course, mystifies others.)

Help-Rejecting Complaining.   People use this defense when they complain or make repetitious requests for help that aren't sincere. No actual help could suffice, and offers are rejected without consideration. These behaviors actually cover feelings of hostility that cannot be expressed directly. This one is very common, and it drives others crazy. Some people seem always to complain. This is not so much that they object to things, but that they are covering up their own unacceptable feelings of inadequacy or even rage.

Displacement.   We express hostile urges toward safer targets. Instead of yelling at a boss, we yell at our kids. Hardly anyone takes on the CEO. We snap at each other, or worse, at the consultants.

Regression.   When anxiety becomes unmanageable we revert back to earlier, less mature behavior. For example, an executive stops delegating under pressure and regresses to a time when she took care of all the details herself. One's worst developmental habits sometimes come back under pressure (Kernberg, 1979).

Conversion.   Instead of dealing with anxiety through appropriate action, we express it through a physical response. Examples include coughing when you have to speak at a meeting, getting a rash, getting the flu, or even cold sores. Many people become sick when difficult or threatening tasks loom. Remember: This is an unconscious mechanism; they are not simply weaseling out or malingering.

Passive Aggression.   When we feel hostility, anger, or other negative emotions toward someone dangerous, or when it would be difficult or inappropriate to express those feelings directly (as it usually is in business), we behave in passive ways that have the effect of being aggressive or negative. We can then remain blameless, because we didn't actually do anything aggressive. An example: You are upset at your boss. Rather than saying something, you forget to set up a hotel room for her when she is on the road. She gets stuck with the problem and you can simply say "I'm sorry." You didn't actually do anything aggressive, you just forgot. And she had to scramble around for a hotel room in Cleveland in the winter at midnight.

Provocative Behavior.   This one is associated with adolescents, but sometimes seen in grown-ups, as well. It is a way to express hostility without feeling guilty about it. You simply behave in a way that provokes the other person to behave poorly so that you can (justifiably) retaliate. Coaches may find clients who have inexplicably goofed up, blown an assignment, or created a rift in the team or department.

Usefulness

There are two ways that an understanding of defense mechanisms can be useful in coaching. In the first place, a coach must be able to recognize the use of defenses in his or her executive client. The coach must then decide whether to call attention to those defenses or to simply integrate them into an overall understanding of the client. Some executives may resent the mention of defenses. The tricky part of this process is that it can raise defenses itself. People use defenses precisely because they feel threatened, so sophisticated communications skills are essential here. Coaches can add important value by making executives aware of their characteristic defenses. Normalize these mechanisms. *Everyone* uses them from time to time. Give examples of how you, the coach, have used a defense recently and how things worked out (positively or negatively). Make it easy to discuss defenses by normalizing such a discussion. Use humor, if appropriate. Many of our standard defenses are pretty silly when we isolate and discuss them, even though they serve important functions.

Nonetheless, some coaching assignments preclude the overt discussion of defenses. A clearly understood set of coaching goals can determine how defenses are handled or discussed. Some goals might preclude analysis of defenses, as might some client personalities. If a client is averse to introspection, discussion of defenses might even be counterproductive.

The second important use of defense mechanisms in coaching is to teach clients how to observe them in other people. That way, your client doesn't need to react stupidly; that is, to go for the bait. When an employee complains and complains, even after the executive makes serious efforts to solve the problem, it is useful to consider "help-rejecting complaining" as a cause. Maybe they really feel hostile or afraid, but cannot express the feeling. It often helps to simply label someone else's defenses in your own head and to avoid taking things personally. An understanding of the use of defenses can help in a greater understanding of organizational politics, and it can prevent you from "spinning" or acting foolishly. This process might also result in development of specific strategies for specific workplace defenses.

It is important to note that in Freud's model, one cannot simply "look in the mirror" to discover these things. A second, impartial party is required, and that is where the coach comes in. A coach has a special mirror for the executive, and the clinically trained coach is armed with theoretical assets not generally available to clients. A coach also has a vested interest in the development of the executive, and is willing to inform him or her about these tricky psychological games.

Social Defenses

Defense mechanisms are not exclusively intrapersonal. Organizations use them, as well, and they use them to the same ends: to manage threat and anxiety. They use them to reduce uncertainty and to handle uncomfortable feelings of inadequacy, intimacy, and dependency. Sometimes a corporate culture is organized to protect against the uncomfortable feelings its members resist. Bureaucratic structures are used to stabilize the difficult inner world of leaders and managers. Rules for interaction serve to buffer people from each other. The physical layout of offices even reflects these defensive rules. In many organizations, top leaders have their own floor.

Older organizational cultures are more able to "get away" with such social defenses, and modern companies are less likely to offer the safety of a lumbering bureaucracy. The post-modern company has a flat (rather than hierarchical) structure, and technical workers can (and do) readily interact with chief executives. The days are gone when the boss could hide behind closed mahogany doors or extensive layers of memoranda. Roles are much less rigid now, and they don't protect people from contact with each other. Modern companies are discarding the old routines. Communication rituals (which are used to protect and stabilize our inner world) are changing, and the absence of social defenses makes interpersonal skills all the more important. Companies depend on the sophisticated interpersonal ability of its leaders and managers, and it is unreasonable to expect most members of modern organizations to possess them. Coaches are of great importance in the modern, fast-moving organization, because we can help people develop adaptive social skills.

Core and Related Concepts

Object Relations Theory

This point of view emphasizes the ways that people use each other to stabilize their own inner world. In this theory, humans develop internal representations of people and of things with which they can "connect." These connections help us to manage our inner lives and are called "objects." People are seen as "object seeking," and these objects are both real and fantasized. The object can be a person or an organization or even an idea that we hold dear. For example, many men (and a few women) use football teams for this purpose. When their favorite team does well, they identify with the team's success and feel competent and comfortable, even though they might otherwise feel inadequate or insecure. We use these objects to feel safe and to manage internal conflicts that derive from the complexities of real life. One way to do this is to "split" objects into good or bad. This is an infantile tactic that allows us to manage difficult feelings. It is difficult to think of a person as having a combination of good qualities and bad qualities all at the same time, and the ambivalence can be intolerable. So we idealize them or we disparage them, depending upon whether they conform to our wishful expectations or meet our own internal needs. We also do this to ourselves, in the way that we represent ourselves internally. It is difficult to think of one's self as an integration of good aspects and bad aspects all at once, so we tend to move back and forth between them, depending upon how things are going (and according to deeply entrenched cognitive habit patterns). When something negative happens at work, we are threatened with the possibility of a "narcissistic injury," an injury to our sense of self or our self-esteem. We then have to figure out how to integrate this information into our perception of self. If we are "good," how could this new (negative) information be true? There are many ways to respond, some healthy and some unhealthy. One common way is to project the negativity to the outside, onto someone else. Another is to take it in, and collapse, on the presumption that we are totally bad. It is just easier and simpler (and more childlike) to do this all or nothing thinking.

It is important for a coach to observe the way that clients handle negative events as well as the ways that they idealize themselves and others. Sometimes coaches are called in to help out with negative situations. Observe how key players respond to negativity, loss, and disappointment.

A Developmental Point of View

Psychodynamic thinking is developmental, and it can help set goals for growth. This means that we all go through rather predictable stages of development, both personally and in our career. In this view, there are several qualities associated with healthy development. They provide us with a framework for sizing executives up.

Trust

The healthy person is able to trust others, the world, and himself. Every executive must be evaluated along this dimension, for a deficit in this area manifests itself in ways that handcuff a leader. The ability to trust is a relatively rare quality, and it implies a solid self-esteem. It is virtually impossible to succeed without enormous trust in others, in the market, and in one's own abilities to get things done. At the same time, effective executives must discern those who cannot be trusted, and there are plenty of them in typical business environments. Most clinicians-turned-coaches are able to evaluate the level of trust their client feels for them and then to extrapolate that trust level to others in the corporate arena. In other words, coaches must evaluate their client's characteristic ways of trusting or not trusting based upon how they treat the coach.

Accurate Perceptions

The fully functioning person is able to accurately assess surroundings, including threats, opportunities, and the strengths and weaknesses of others, including their motivations. Effective people don't distort things much. They are clear-eyed observers. They don't exaggerate the faults of people they don't like; they don't idealize those in the inner circle.

Accurate perception of others implies accurate empathy, beginning with a natural interest in others, followed by the ability to correctly guess what others might be thinking and feeling.

Psychodynamic theory points out that humans perceive the world, particularly other people in the world, based upon their own internal needs, wishes, and development. This produces a distorted view of things. It is the wise executive who can cut through his or her own internal filters in order to understand things in a relatively objective way. This is a valuable skill, and coaches can help clients develop it, for they come to the organization as an outsider, and they aren't constrained by the normal pressures of the organizational culture. Most coaching will not include a detailed examination of the development of distortions, but it may be useful to point out distinctive patterns to clients, normalizing them along the way.

Independence and Autonomy

Executives and leaders must be able to operate independently. This important dimension must be evaluated and strengthened. The independence–isolation balance has to be just right. It is important to be able to "team-up" and function cooperatively, and it is essential to be able to think for one's self. This balance is difficult for most people. Our temperament typically dictates that we lean one way or the other.

Some jobs or tasks require more autonomy than others, and a good match between personality and position makes a big difference. Sometimes coaches are called in to help an executive who is not comfortable with the level of autonomy required by her position. The CEO's position can be lonely. Some jobs require interdependence and great cooperation. Still others demand that many are kept "in the loop," and a lone wolf will not fare well in such a job. The management literature is increasingly turning away from models that stress an isolated, hierarchical leader-at-the-top organization. Some industries seem to require an *interdependent* style of leadership at the top (and throughout the organization).

Self-Awareness and Self-Management

An effective executive cannot function without these skills, and they are often hard earned. As Clint Eastwood (as Dirty Harry) observed, "A man's got to know his limitations." An executive has also got to know his or her strengths and inclinations, as well. Executives must be able to discover their own areas for growth. They must be willing and able to take advantage of strengths. And they must be able to find ways to minimize the impact of personal weaknesses. A coach can really help when executives are not realistically aware of their own strengths or weaknesses.

Comfort with Power and Authority

Many people never reconcile these two sides of the same coin. They chafe when others have authority over them, or they are unwilling to exercise appropriate power when it is called for. Ambivalence about power and authority can render an otherwise capable executive impotent. Willingness to accede to a boss's decisions, even when you think that he or she is dead wrong, is an essential element of a successful career. At some point in each career, the ability to assert power, even when others disagree, is an absolute necessity. Graceful management of these two important scenarios can make or break an executive. To do so requires other qualities found in the healthy person: accurate empathy, a solid sense of self-confidence, and a clear perception of reality.

Energy and Focus

A person's internal forces must be aligned in order for him to accomplish his goals. When they are not, a coach can use psychodynamic principles to figure out what's getting in the way and how to get them back into balance. Sometimes, when an executive can't get going, there is an intrapsychic reason. This is important when an executive seems inexplicably "stuck," or when she is spinning her wheels or is frustrated with a lack of success. This becomes especially important when an executive provokes negative or hostile feelings in others.

More often than not, this is a good time to consider a referral to therapy for such an executive. A clinically trained coach can be of great help in this decision.

Reiteration of Family Dynamics

Sometimes an executive behaves in ways that are easier to understand when family background is known, and often a person can adjust her behavior once she considers the influence that family has had on present behavior. This important aspect of coaching does not, of course, give the coach a free pass to spend lots of time digging away at the roots of a client's family tree, as one might do in therapy. The exploration must be focused, limited, and goal-directed. Connections must be made quickly between the past and the present situation, so that coaching does not get lost in a therapeutic conundrum.

Resistance

Freud observed that humans don't exactly leap at the opportunity to acknowledge and change their behavior. Mostly we *resist* change, because we are doing the best we think we can, and because change is threatening, and because change means that we have to acknowledge that what we are doing now is "wrong." Most people would rather feel *right* than be effective. So, clients will resist change, will resist advice, and will take advice and drop it into the dumpster as soon as they walk out the door, in spite of the fact that they are paying serious money for that advice. Many hard-charging executives and most males *resent* help and advice, and that includes coaching. Psychodynamic theory would say that many people feel ambivalent or even resentful about using a coach, no matter how enthusiastically they behave on the surface. A coach can expect such resistance. Executives can be excruciatingly difficult to schedule, partly because they are very busy, and partly because coaching does not always seem to be of immediate importance (as is an essential customer or board member). Sometimes executives cancel coaching meetings with annoying regularity. There is no need to take this personally or to blame the executive when it happens. It is normal and expectable, but sometimes it is an expression of a natural resistance to change. Change can be threatening. Coaches need to work with resistance and build rapport, so that defenses are lowered, trust is established, and the executive gets himself into a posture that allows the acceptance of help. Occasionally a coach must confront client resistance or ambivalence. This implies that coaches must be trustworthy, both with information and with the important feelings that arise. Sometimes cancelled meetings mean that the coach does not have an effective working contract with the executive client. It can also mean that there are conflicts between the coach and the executive that are unspoken, or that the client is uncomfortable in some way, but has never mentioned the discomfort. Inexperienced coaches tend to get more client cancellations than experienced ones, just as inexperienced clinicians do. This can be remedied with a clear discussion about time and the importance of coaching, along with the simple confidence that comes with experience. Nonetheless, a reasonable cancellation policy, clearly articulated at the onset, is prudent.

Transference and Countertransference

No discussion of Freud would be complete without mention of transference. People bring all of their personality characteristics to every relationship. Therefore, executives will behave toward coaches in the same ways that they behave toward other significant people. In therapy, the clinician exploits this phenomenon. It is noted and analyzed. Coaches don't use transference in the same way as therapists, but they still must be aware of the ways that clients behave toward them, for this behavior provides important clues about the way they behave in important work relationships. Countertransference is also of interest to coaches, who must manage new countertransference reactions and still learn from them. It may be novel for some coaches to find that, instead of treating patients who are in pain or who are ineffectual, they are suddenly faced with executives who are successful, self-assured, powerful, and wealthy. Some coaches may even experience an envy of high-flying executives who earn much more than the coach could ever command. Some coaches might even feel intimidated by the trappings of power, after having left a small clinician's office for a meeting in a CEO's top-floor suite (overlooking Central Park or the Golden Gate Bridge).

On the other hand, it is still true that a clinician's reactions can be instructive, not just to the clinician, but to the executive, as well. The trick is to figure out how to translate a countertransference hunch into a coaching intervention.

Narcissism

Psychoanalysts have contributed a great deal to the understanding of a vexing and complex mix of difficult behaviors called narcissism. Named after the tortured young man who wasted away with love for his own reflection, the narcissist thrives on the attention and admiration of others. At its extreme, it is a personality disorder, but narcissistic forces have driven many effective, powerful, and charismatic leaders. Most of us have some narcissism in our personality. Absent narcissism, we would be drab, meek, and subject to the whims of others to the extreme. Excessively narcissistic executives must manage surging feelings of self-importance, a sense of entitlement (this can be especially dangerous), and a fragile ego. They can be envious. Narcissists often lack empathy and seem only superficially interested in others, usually to the extent that the other can help them. They can be interpersonally exploitive, Machiavellian, and they tend to be "high maintenance" bosses. They require admiration and attention, and they can come across as arrogant (American Psychiatric Association, 1994, pp. 658–662). Narcissists frustrate and annoy others, and if people don't have to put up with them, they won't.

Great leaders probably need some of the qualities of a narcissist, because of the enormous self-confidence (and perhaps audacity) needed to move mountains and take great risk (Maccoby, 2000). They need charisma, and they need vast amounts of energy, some available for vision and some for self-promotion. The coach is invaluable to such a person, but narcissists tend to distrust and devalue mentors, so it is liable to take considerable time and effort for a coach to become a trusted guide for the narcissist. Consistent empathy over extended periods of time seems to be the key. The coach must typically endure an extended series of tests before he or she will be trusted. Even then, narcissists are likely to be exquisitely sensitive to betrayal or misunderstanding throughout the coaching relationship.

The coach's task with narcissism is twofold. First, assess your clients. Decide whether their level of narcissism is appropriate to their career path. (Carefully consider an open discussion.) Second, help them manage narcissistic behavior so that it whisks them along and does not drag them down.

Coaches must also keep an eye on the thoughts and feelings they have for executive clients. Always mull over the question: do those feelings evolve strictly from the relationship at hand, or have I (as coach) brought some "baggage" along? It is the coach's duty to attend to this matter and to keep the present relationship as clear as possible.

Parallel Process

Psychodynamic thinking adds yet one more important idea to the coaching mix, and it comes from the world of psychotherapy supervision. This is the notion that dynamics that occur in coaching mirror the dynamics that the executive client experiences in the regular world of work. In other words, what you experience with your client is likely to be the same thing that others experience when they interact with that client on a daily basis. Therefore, the coach's reactions to this executive are likely to be important and valid clues about this person's work behavior. If you, as a coach, feel intimidated or annoyed or bored with your client it is possible that many others do, as well. Pay attention to reactions like these. They can inform you about necessary adjustments to the coach–client relationship.

On Theory and Application

Psychoanalysis was probably the most interesting thing that I've ever done. I learned an enormous amount about myself. Only problem is, I was more depressed when I finished than when I started. (Anonymous patient)

Psychoanalysis and psychodynamic approaches to therapy have traditionally been long on inquiry and short on implementation. The central assumption, that insight leads to change, is no less true in executive coaching. But the coach has a greater obligation to facilitate action and observable change than does the psychoanalyst, and few business organizations are likely to hire and retain a coach who simply enlightens. Corporations expect to see clear and effective changes in their executives when they spend money on coaching, so the task of the psychodynamically-trained consultant is to translate observations into "deliverables." It is unlikely that psychoanalytic principles alone could possibly be adequate to the challenge.

Summary and Key Points

1. Remember that executive coaching must be results-oriented and positive in tone. Long efforts at introspection are liable to be unattractive in the workplace, as will coaching that is seen as exclusively remedial.
2. Much of what people do and feel is not rational or conscious. Learn how to study people from a psychodynamic perspective, even if you don't often mention your observations or hypotheses.
3. Anticipate resistance. Expect that clients will have ambivalent feelings about being coached, even if they express great enthusiasm. Don't become disappointed or angry when they behave in ways that seem resistant. It is perfectly normal and predictable.
4. Assess the quality and nature of the interpersonal interaction between coach and client. Determine whether it is frank, open, and reasonably honest. Check for distorted interaction such as idealization (i.e., your client treats you as if you were a king or queen or genius). This can be a sign of resistance. It can be a way that clients keep you at arm's length from the matters that need to be addressed. It can be a distraction. The reactions you have to your client are also important clues about how this client affects others.
5. Check to see how capable your clients are at "getting outside of self." Do they only talk about themselves? Are they only interested in themselves or their own concerns? Are they curious about you at all? Do they wonder what others are thinking or feeling? Are they capable of empathy? Are they able to stop talking and really listen? Look for a healthy balance. When that balance is absent, figure out why. Consider confronting your clients about it.
6. Evaluate your clients' ability to accept negative feedback. Are they balanced in their response? Thoughtful? Do they seek it? Or, do they reject it and punish the messenger? Conversely, do they wallow in it, as if they thrive on it while it crushes them? Monitor this capacity and help your clients seek and use feedback in a balanced, productive way.

7. Assess the defenses used by your clients. Are they healthy and appropriate or destructive and rigid? Are your clients aware of them? Teach your clients to observe defenses in key others.
8. Remember that most clinical training in counseling and psychotherapy (especially prior to 1990) contained theoretical and stylistic artifacts of psychoanalysis or psychodynamic psychotherapy (for example, hour-long meetings in the clinician's office, or the stubborn unwillingness of a clinician to answer a direct question with a direct answer). Reliance on this ingrained style can be detrimental to effective executive coaching.

References

Cramer, P. (2000). Defense mechanisms in psychology today. *American Psychologist, 55*(6), 637–646.

Czander, W. (1993). *The psychodynamics of work and organizations.* New York: Guilford.

Hall, C. (1954). *A primer of Freudian psychology.* New York: New American Library.

Harrison, R. (1994). Choosing the depth of organizational intervention (pp. 413–424). In French, W., Bell, C., & Zawacki, R. (Eds.), *Organization development and transformation* (4th ed.). Boston: Irwin/McGraw-Hill. (Original work published 1970)

Kernberg, O. (1979, February). Regression in organizational leadership. *Psychiatry, 42*(1), 24–39.

Maccoby, M. (2000, January–February). Narcissistic leaders, the inevitable pros, the inevitable cons. *Harvard Business Review.*

Macmillan, C. (1999). *The role of the organizational consultant: A model for clinicians.* Unpublished doctoral dissertation, Massachusetts School of Professional Psychology.

Recommended Readings

American Psychiatric Assocation. (1994). *Diagnostic and Statistical Manual of Mental Disorders* (4th ed.). Washington, DC: Author.

Corey, G. (1982). *Theory and practice of counseling and psychotherapy* (2nd ed.). Monterey, CA: Brooks/Cole.

Diamond, M. (1993). *The unconscious life of organizations.* Westport, CT: Quorum.

Freud, S. (1916). *The complete introductory lectures on psychoanalysis.* London: George Allen & Unwin Ltd.

Freud, S. (1951). *Psychopathology of everyday life.* New York: The New American Library.

Goldman, G., & Milman, D. (1978). *Psychoanalytic psychotherapy.* Reading, MA: Addison-Wesley.

Hirschhorn, L. (1997). *The workplace within: Psychodynamics of organizational life.* Cambridge, MA: The MIT Press.

Kernberg, O. (1978, January). Leadership and organizational functioning: Organizational regression. *International Journal of Group Psychotherapy, 28*(1) 3–25.

Kets de Vries, M. (Ed.) (1991). *Organizations on the couch: Clinical perspectives on organizational behavior and change.* San Francisco: Jossey-Bass.

Kets de Vries, M. (1995). *Life and death in the executive fast lane: Essays on irrational organizations and their leaders.* San Francisco: Jossey-Bass.

Kline, P. (1972). *Fact and fantasy in Freudian theory.* London: Methuen.

Levinson, H. (1972). *Organizational diagnosis.* Cambridge, MA: Harvard University Press.

Levinson, H. (1996). Executive coaching. *Consulting Psychology Journal: Research and Practice, 48*(2), 115–123.

Shapiro, D. (1972). *Neurotic styles.* New York: Basic Books.

Tobias, L. (1990). *Psychological consulting to management: A clinician's perspective.* New York: Brunner/Mazel.

Behavioral Concepts

People have used rewards both knowingly and unknowingly, since the beginning of recorded history.

— Martin & Pear (1978, p. 34)

Behaviorism has a long and honored place in the history of psychology and psychotherapy. It is a powerful way to understand human behavior, yet it is widely misunderstood and routinely misrepresented. Behavioral psychology offers powerful tools to the executive coach. This chapter reviews the basics, clears up myths and misrepresentations, and outlines ways that the methods of behavior therapy can be effectively used in executive coaching.

The forces studied and described by Pavlov, Watson, and Skinner influence us all the time whether we acknowledge them or not. In fact, if something happens to you repeatedly, with regularity (even though you say that you don't like it or understand it), you are probably reinforcing it in some way. It makes sense, then, to explore and understand the cues and contingencies that serve to maintain our behavior, as well as the behavior of those with whom we work. The central theme of this point of view is that *behavior is a function of its consequences*. This chapter focuses on the environment which stimulates one reaction over another, and the consequences that maintain or promote behavior. A careful study of those specific forces can help a coach and client take charge and make change. Often, attention to a few simple principles, at little or no cost, can turn things around. Alternatively, it is possible to make things progressively worse through well-intentioned efforts that misuse or fail to incorporate the principles described in this chapter. Ignore behavioral principles at great peril.

History: From Rat Mazes to Cubicles

Ivan Pavlov

Ivan Pavlov, the Russian scientist, explored the reflexive reactions we have when a physician taps us below the kneecap or when we flinch because someone puts a finger near our eye or when we hear a loud noise. He called these automatic responses "respondent." He showed that we can pair a previously neutral stimulus with the loud noise and eventually elicit the reaction without the original noise itself. The automatic response he used in his experiments was drooling. He paired the drooling with various sounds and was able to cause his dogs to drool when he rang a bell. This is called classical conditioning. The ability of living things to develop such associations is adaptive; that is, it helps us survive. We don't have to eat bad food after one bad experience. We can simply smell it and feel repulsed. The things that we pair up with reflexive responses, however, are not always good for us. Sometimes they get in our way. For example, consider the person who has a humiliating experience the first time she speaks in public. It is common to have a debilitating reaction whenever a public speaking situation arises; in fact, many people feel dizzy at the *thought* of speaking in public. Their heart races, their breathing changes, and their sweat glands start pumping. Naturally, they then avoid such situations, the reactions become more powerful, and they never learn to speak in public. Respondent conditioning is not something to be trifled with.

John Watson

The "father" of modern behaviorism was John Watson, who insisted that human behavior be studied and measured objectively and scientifically. He translated Pavlov's ideas for practical human use and insisted that we attend to *observable matters* rather than internal psychological states and abstractions (such as egos or anxieties). If it couldn't be counted or measured, it didn't matter. He was personally interested in how to use behavioral principles in child rearing and in industry. He eventually left academia to pursue a career in advertising. Modern business practitioners share his insistence on measurability.

B. F. Skinner

The best-known and most controversial modern behaviorist was B. F. Skinner (1948, 1971, 1976), who was as much a philosopher as he was a psychologist. He took Pavlov and Watson's ideas, and refined and expanded them to come up with something he called "operant" conditioning. He observed that most of human behavior could not be explained as reflexive reaction, and he focused on the contingencies of behavior. Things that happen after we do something have an impact on whether we do it again. Or, as the early behaviorists explained it, behavior followed by something perceived as pleasant is more likely to recur; and behavior followed by something unpleasant or uncomfortable is less likely to recur. This concept is known as *reinforcement*, and it forms the basis for modern behavioral techniques. Skinner was able to teach pigeons to do amazing things using well-shaped reinforcements, and he advocated careful use of behavioral principles to make society better. His central idea was this: "If you want people to be productive and active in various ways, the important thing is to analyze the contingencies of reinforcement" (Evans, 1968). He experimented with and refined most of the ideas described in this chapter.

Albert Bandura

Stanford psychologist Albert Bandura (1969, 1977) added observational or "social learning" to the mix in the 1960s. Watson and Skinner's views were too mechanical and narrow for Bandura, who observed that people don't always need to experience reinforcement contingencies themselves in order to learn. You can watch your big sister touch the stovetop and learn not to do it yourself, without having to personally get burned. You learn the contingencies socially. Bandura added rehearsal and modeling to the behavioral repertoire, both of which were internal or cognitive events associated with learning. He also added the obvious but complicating observation, that reinforcement goes both ways. We reinforce each other in a process he called reciprocal influence. When you yell at your kids, they stop jumping on the furniture. This rewards your yelling behavior, so you tend to do it again in the future.

O. B. Mod

Most of behavioral psychology was housed in the psychology departments of academia until Fred Luthans (Luthans, 1998; Luthans & Kreitner,

1973, 1984, 1985) began to apply it to organizations and management practices in the 1980s. He termed his early ideas Organizational Behavior Modification or "O.B. Mod" for short. He translated the work of behaviorists into management models and language, and his books are listed in the reference section of this chapter.

Usefulness in Coaching

There are two general ways that a coach can use behavioral principles. First, the coach can use the laws and methods of behavior therapy to help clients understand themselves and change (as people and leaders). Second, the coach can teach clients how to use behavioral methods to manage and improve their own organization. Thoughtful application of behavioral principles ought to form the foundation for any healthy and productive organization. Both of these applications will be discussed in this chapter.

Behavior therapists honor Occam's Razor, the principle of parsimony, and this is a good thing for corporate coaches. It says that "one should never employ a more complex explanation when a less complex one will do" (Craighead, Kazdin, & Mahoney, 1976, p. 13). When something as simple as reinforcement explains someone's behavior, there is no sense embarking on a complex intrapsychic wild-goose-chase.

Another element of behavioral thinking is important for executive coaches: Behavior therapy is experimental. "Research is treatment and treatment is research" (Thoresen & Coates, 1978, p.5). This means that each effort to work with a coaching client is viewed as an experiment. Interventions are used with goals in mind. Progress toward the goals is checked, and the experiment is adjusted, based on the measured progress. This method fits well into modern organizations that are interested in continuous quality improvement.

Basic Principles

Principles from the world of behavior therapy must be considered. They explain much of what happens to us from moment to moment, yet, most people don't think about them very often. Many managers misuse these principles, and they work to the disadvantage of those who are ignorant of them. What follows is a review of the basic forces and relationships that behavior therapy makes available to the coach.

Reinforcement

Reinforcement is a powerful influence, whether you notice it or believe in it or not. Many people feel as if they are swimming upstream, against the flow all the time, and it is because they are doing what Steven Kerr (1975) has called "the folly of rewarding A, while hoping for B."

A functional definition of reinforcement is *anything that increases the likelihood or strength of a response or tends to produce repetition of the response.* In plain English this means that a reinforcement is anything that, when it follows a behavior, tends to strengthen that behavior. Reinforcements are only known through systematic observation. You can guess at what they are, but you will be wrong some of the time, because a reinforcement is not always what people assume it is. Some things that people think might be a reinforcer turn out to be merely "rewards," which are different. Rewards are *desired* by the person who is behaving. The person likes the rewards, but he or she doesn't reliably produce repeat behavior. Reinforcers produce more behavior, whether they are liked or not. If you want A, you must reinforce A with something that has demonstrable power to produce more of A. It is crucial that patterns of reinforcement are not random. Random reinforcement patterns wreak (mystifying) havoc in an organization. Contingent reinforcement gets the results we desire.

Reinforcements are all around us, readily available, and powerful, and people rarely get tired of them. There are varieties of kinds of reinforcements, and distinctions must be made between them so that you can get the results you really want.

Intrinsic and Extrinsic Reinforcement

The first set of distinctions is between intrinsic reinforcers and extrinsic ones. Although the behavioral literature is not completely clear about this distinction, the best way to think about these is as follows: *Extrinsic* reinforcement comes from outside of us and is a little "artificial." Money is a classic extrinsic reinforcer. It doesn't mean anything by itself, but people quickly learn to work hard to get it. Bonus miles, given by the airlines, are another example of extrinsic reinforcers. The airlines are trying to get people to repeat the choice of their company. The miles don't mean anything themselves, but people quickly learn to associate them with something good.

Intrinsic reinforcement comes from within. It takes place within the person, in his or her mind or value system or feelings. Intrinsic reinforcements are unique to each of us. An example of an intrinsic reinforcer is the good feeling you get when you accomplish a difficult task or when you have solved a problem that others can't seem to solve. Even without verbal praise, the internal feelings are reinforcing, as they are liable (for most people) to cause you to do more of this kind of problem-solving in the future. The act of learning a new skill can be intrinsically reinforcing. Some reinforcers can be both intrinsic and extrinsic. A certain look on someone's face can act as an extrinsic or intrinsic reinforcer, depending on what it means to the person who reacts to it.

Research is equivocal about the power and implications of these two types of reinforcers. Many think that intrinsic rewards are superior, because the person experiencing the reinforcement is more likely to take credit for the behavior, while those reinforced extrinsically might just attribute the behavior or learning to the external reward system (e.g., "I did it for the money"). Some also say that extrinsic rewards can "wear out," while intrinsic ones never do. One never tires of doing something deeply satisfying.

Primary and Secondary Reinforcement

Another distinction has to do with whether the association between the behavior and the reinforcer is natural or learned. A *primary* reinforcer is innately reinforcing, while a *secondary* one must be "figured out." The connection between the behavior and the reinforcement must be repeated until they are associated or "learned." The thrill of a kiss is primary; the absence of a kiss (as negative reinforcement) is secondary, as it must be learned. Cash bonuses in the workplace are secondary; the smile of a boss is primary.

It is not always essential to create a new, extrinsic, or secondary reward structure in an organization or coaching situation. There are many "natural" primary reinforcers in the work environment, most of which are available for thoughtful use. Most cost nothing to apply. Some examples are (Luthans & Kreitner, 1985):

- simple greetings ("good morning!" and "how are you?")
- simple attention (Listening to someone is generally reinforcing. It may also be specifically reinforcing of the speaking behavior)
- informal recognition of an employee
- recognition of an employee at a meeting
- compliments ("That report you gave today was excellent.")
- praise ("That was a terrific meeting you ran.")
- a "visit" to someone's office to say hello or get information you could have gotten over the telephone

- asking for advice from someone you want to reinforce
- a smile in the hallway
- a friendly and encouraging telephone greeting ("I'm glad you called.")
- taking someone out for coffee or lunch

Positive and Negative Reinforcement

The difference between positive and negative reinforcement is widely misunderstood. Negative reinforcement is often confused with punishment (a verbal or physical spanking, for example).

Positive reinforcement takes place when something satisfying follows a desired (or "target") behavior. You do something I favor, so I tell you that I am impressed. Negative reinforcement happens when I withdraw something aversive when you do what I want. If I stop giving you the "silent treatment" when you clean up your office, I am using negative reinforcement. The classic laboratory example is that of animals in a cage with an electrified floor, an uncomfortable environment. When they push on the correct lever, the electricity stops, along with the discomfort. This is called negative reinforcement. You make the bad thing stop by performing the target behavior.

Punishment

Punishment is different from negative reinforcement, and is just what it sounds like. When you do something undesirable, you receive a punishment, something that is aversive to you. When you say something indiscrete at a staff meeting, your boss gives you a dirty look. This is punishment. It is also called punishment when you stop applying a pleasurable reinforcer when someone does something you don't want repeated. Taking away privileges in response to poor performance is an example of this type of punishment. Punishment tends to get immediate results, but it has serious negative side effects. Research indicates that when punishment is used as the primary vehicle for learning, two things happen. First, learners are more likely to attribute the learning to the teacher (or setting) rather than to himself or herself. Second, learners are less likely to enjoy the learning process and might even develop resentments related to the teacher. They may then avoid the teacher and the learning environment. Also, punishment often creates an uncomfortable atmosphere, where people are tense or anxious as they struggle to perform. This clearly creates an undesirable outcome in the workplace.

Punishment can become confusing and difficult to control, and the attention one gets when being yelled at can (paradoxically) turn out to be a positive reinforcement to them, which then serves to strengthen the undesired behavior. Sometimes negative attention is better than no attention at all. The way to decide whether this is happening is by looking at the results. Is punishment working? Is behavior changing in a desired direction? Sometimes people yell and cajole, only to complain that behavior never changes. That only means that the contingencies are incorrectly arranged or applied.

The other intriguing problem with punishment, as mentioned earlier, is that it can be rewarding (and reinforcing) to the punisher. The person administering the punishment can feel rewarded, either by the feeling of power that accompanies yelling or punishing, or by the fact that the behavior they find objectionable ceases immediately (but only temporarily).

Reinforcement Schedules or Patterns

The chart below, Table 3.1 (which, in one form or another, can be found in many behavioral textbooks including Luthans, 1985) pictures the relationships between applying and withdrawing something pleasurable or undesirable.

Timing is crucial in the application of reinforcement, and poorly timed rewards or punishments can inadvertently strengthen behavior patterns we dislike. For example, imagine that you have asked an employee to clean up his desk. He does so, and then proceeds to "surf the net." You walk by and tell him "Great job!" It is quite possible that, instead of strengthening the target behavior (desk clearing), you reinforce web surfing. Reinforcement must be immediate and clearly understood by the receiver that it is reinforcing of the desired behavior. *Clear* and *immediate* are the keys.

Behavioral researchers have worked hard to explore the timing of reinforcement, and they have established a literature on reinforcement

TABLE 3.1. Types of reinforcement

	Something nice	Something noxious	Nothing (no response)
Apply it	Positive reinforcement	Punishment	Extinction
Withdraw it	Punishment	Negative reinforcement	

"schedules," or patterns. The use of one pattern or another effects the speed and power of reinforcement and learning.

Fixed Ratio.   Positive reinforcement is applied on every *n*th iteration of the desired behavior. The ratio could be 1:1 (reinforcement is given each time the desired behavior occurs) or 1:*n* (where reinforcement is applied every nth time the desired behavior is seen) and it is not true that a one-to-one ratio is the most powerful. A fixed ratio is a steady and predictable pattern. It tends to be powerful, and it is generally comfortable for the person being reinforced. Piece rate incentives are an example of this schedule. When the reward goes away, the behavior stops pretty quickly.

Variable Ratio.   Positive reinforcement is applied in an unpredictable ratio, given an average *n*. So, if the set reinforcement rate is 1 to 10 (reward is given, on average, every ten times the person produces the target behavior), the reward might come after the 2nd response, then after the 12th response, then after the 7th. Rewards are irregular but consistent in amount over time (on average, every 10th). The classic example of this schedule is the slot machine. People will sit in front of those "one-armed bandits" and pull the lever all night long, while the house knows exactly how much it will pay out over an extended period of time. Variable ratio reinforcement produces a powerfully learned response and great persistence, but tends to be less comfortable for the worker. (Perhaps the cheap drinks in Las Vegas are designed to take the edge off the experience, as well as lower inhibition!)

Fixed Interval.   Rewards are time-based in this schedule. A reward is given after a consistently-set period that the person worked or produced the target behavior. Hourly pay, a salary, and a monthly paycheck are examples of a fixed interval schedule. This schedule is comfortable for the worker, but tends to produce clock-watching behavior. It is not known for producing high volumes of work. A monthly check is hardly immediate enough to influence day-to-day effort. It does, however, create an organization where everyone tends to show up on time and hang around. It can also produce uneven effort, perhaps stimulating better work just before the time for annual evaluations.

Variable Interval.   This occurs when you provide reinforcement at irregular periods, and the person has no idea about the schedule. The worker has no idea when the next reinforcement might come. This produces powerful and resilient behavior, but tends to be uncomfortable for the person being reinforced. Most of life's natural and social reinforcers operate on this schedule. For example, we know that there will be another earthquake in California; we just don't know when it will come. So, we retrofit buildings and feel vaguely uncomfortable while we wonder about the next one.

Individual Differences

It is also important to understand the perceived reinforcement structure of those you want to influence. A reward to one person is aversive to another. A trip to the big league ball game might seem like a great reward to a father, but to a young child it can mean a long car ride, a boring walk through the parking lot, exposure to loud crowds, hot sun, and a situation that is impossible to understand (the rules of the game and what is going on).

The Premack Principle

David Premack described this effect in 1962. The principle says that you can use a high-probability or frequently occurring behavior to reinforce a lower-probability behavior. For example, if you know that you are going to run the disk defragmenter on your computer at some point in each day, you can make a rule that you won't run it until you get at least one project done first. This is especially useful if you prefer one of your routine tasks to the others. You simply use the more attractive task as a reinforcement for accomplishment of the other tasks. If you enjoy checking your e-mail, you can make that contingent upon completion of some of the difficult tasks that you face. You can use the e-mail as a "reward" for accomplishing the other tasks. This is the opposite of what most people ordinarily do when they prefer one task over the other, as they usually start with the task that they like the best (and the less attractive task may never get done).

Leaders can use the Premack Principle organizationally. For example, you can reward high performance with promotion to a job with more responsibility (a more difficult job). You can reward positive behavior with the opportunity to work on pet projects. The possibilities are right there in the workplace. Remember individual perception, of course. The new job must be viewed as attractive by the person being promoted.

Successive Approximations and Shaping

When the target behavior is so difficult or different that it seems out of reach, gradual small steps can be devised and rewarded in order to build up to the desired response. For example, when teaching a child to ride a bicycle, it does not make sense to reward the child when she rides the two-wheeler successfully the first time. So, we take the child through smaller, successive approximations of the end behavior, rewarding her for small successes along the way. Start by rewarding the child when she simply asks about the bicycle. Then offer praise for getting on the bike, then for rolling along while we hold on and guide her, then for small periods when we let go. Then we start the child off and let her ride to another adult. Gradually the child's behavior is "shaped" by rewarding closer and closer successes.

Successive approximation is useful, for example, when a coaching client needs to learn how to make an important speech in front of a large number of people. The task is broken down into many small parts. Each part is rehearsed and learned and rewarded. Eventually, the parts are integrated into the entire speech and it is finally presented in front of the actual audience. This event is (hopefully) immediately followed by applause!

Stimulus Control

Reinforcement is something that is applied *after* the behavior occurs. There is another way to control behavior, and it occurs prior to the behavior itself. It is also important to attend to those things that *precede* behavior and have a probabilistic controlling effect. Factors in the environment that make it more or less likely that a target behavior will happen are called *stimuli*, and skillful arrangement of them is called stimulus control or stimulus management (arrangement of reinforcement is called "consequence management"). We examine the environment and arrange the cues so that the behavior we desire is more likely to occur. A simple example: If you want to lose weight, surround yourself with exercise equipment, not bowls of candy. And change your route so that you don't walk by the donut shop on your way to work.

Effective stimulus management involves analysis of the environment and an examination of how things increase or decrease the likelihood that we will behave in the way that we wish. We remove those things that are likely to retard progress and replace them with stimuli that are likely to help us. We limit our exposure to those that we cannot remove.

All parties must be involved in stimulus management. Those who work in an environment must have input to the way that the environment is arranged.

Table 3.2 shows the relationship between stimulus control and reinforcement in the management of behavior.

TABLE 3.2. The A-B-Cs of behavior management

Antecedent	Behavior	Consequent
Things that precede the behavior of interest. They increase (or decrease) the likelihood of the behavior in the near future.	The behavior we are interested in changing or eliminating or increasing.	Things that happen right after the behavior that tend to increase (or decrease) its chance of happening again.
Example:		
Provide "hot" leads for sales people, along with encouragement.	Sales calls are made; sales happen.	Commissions are paid. Sales people are praised privately and publicly.

Social Learning

Albert Bandura's Social Learning Theory adds much to the behavioral mix by including social and mental events in the process. He pointed out that covert events, things that can't be seen with the eye, serve as cognitive mediating processes in learning and motivation. Humans can learn through vicarious reinforcement, and they don't have to experience the reinforcement personally. Observational learning is usually more efficient (and less painful) than the process of direct trial and error experience. He also advocated self-control, the application of behavior modification procedures to self, and the use of covert processes. Here are some of the methods he introduced to the behavioral literature.

Modeling

This is sometimes called "imitative learning." Humans can learn by observing what happens when someone else learns. It may even be true that imitation is built into our genetic fabric. We imitate without even realizing it. Think about how fashion trends grow in organizations. Powerful people are emulated, and when the boss wears a certain kind of clothes, others follow suit. (Think about how long it took for male CEOs to start wearing those dark colored shirts with white collars after the first few "important" ones led the way.) We observe the contingencies, see how the reinforcements work, learn about the model's emotional responses, and figure out the rules without having to experience any of the pain or discomfort. Research indicates that it is important to choose the right model; that is, someone who is similar to us but is better than we are at the task in question. Coaches and executives benefit by choosing a good model and using him or her as a way to learn a new skill or combination of skills.

There are three basic modeling processes that can help the coach and the manager (Luthans & Kreitner, 1985). They are: 1) learning from imitation (you watch and then do the same thing that was successful for someone else). This happens when you carefully observe someone who is expert at something you want to learn. When new sales people follow a great salesperson around before they take on their own accounts, this kind of modeling is at work; 2) learning from the consequences of others (you discern contingencies). When you notice how a coworker is punished (or does not get a promotion or good assignments) and you can see how the punishment relates to his or her behavior, you are the beneficiary of this type of learning; and 3) using the behavior of others as a cue for your own behavior (the behavior of others tells you when to initiate behaviors you have already learned). It is also important for the leader and manager to understand that all members of the organization are watching to learn about how contingencies operate in the environment. When one employee is reprimanded, everyone else learns about the contingencies of punishment in the organization. Leaders must remember this when they decide to reward or punish managers or employees. It has an "instructive" impact on the rest of the organization.

Rehearsal and Covert Rehearsal

Once a strategy has been chosen it is often useful to rehearse and practice new behaviors or parts of new behaviors. When learning how to speak to someone in a new way, executives can benefit by practicing this behavior with the coach first. Coaches can then provide feedback, and the practice can continue in a non-threatening situation. Once the skill is well learned in this setting, the executive is in a better position to take it out into the real world. An even better approach to using rehearsal of new skills is with audio or videotapes. Clients can practice phone or interpersonal messages on tape first, then review them with a coach. Executives can also leave practice messages on voice-mail for a coach's review and feedback. Videotape is, of course, a powerful way to get feedback about how one looks, speaks, and behaves. Every executive coach should be prepared to use videotape as an assessment and rehearsal tool. It is essential to coaching.

Covert rehearsal, which is covered in Chapters 5 and 10 of this book, is also a useful skill that coaches can teach to executives. There is ample evidence that a mental rehearsal before a performance can provide much of the benefit of a "real" rehearsal. You simply run a mental movie of yourself performing (better and better) the behavior in question. This is useful in preparing for sales calls, important meetings or transactions, or for confronting someone about a difficult matter at work. The more vivid and detailed the "movie" the better. Remember that some people seem to lack the capacity to make mental images, but they can still find a way to rehearse in their mind. Work with them to figure out a process that they can use.

The Token Economy

Sometimes the best way to manage an organizational situation is to set up an artificial reinforcement system and use tokens instead of actual extrinsic rewards. In this system, explicit goals are established and agreed upon. Values are set for specific behaviors to be encouraged. A point system is used, and tokens (or points) are awarded when small goals are met. These tokens or points can then be "cashed in" for real rewards, such as money or trips or public recognition (e.g., sales person of the month).

Care must be taken to establish clear rules that all participants understand and to which they can agree. The goals must be achievable to all, and tokens have to be awarded fairly and evenly according to the rules. It helps when the system is public and visible to participants.

The Organization as Conditioning Agent

In a way, the organization itself acts like a token economy, reinforcing behavior in powerful patterns. The patterns can be intentional (at best) and random or at odds with the espoused goals (the worst). They can even be inhumane (the absolute worst). A behaviorally conscious coach can help clients analyze actual reinforcement patterns that exist in the organizational environment and advocate for deliberate management of them. It makes no sense to ask for behavior A but reward behavior B, which is often the case (Kerr, 1975). It is confusing and demoralizing, as well.

Sometimes the organization just doesn't provide enough reinforcement for the things that it strives to promote. Sometimes high-performing executives, managers, and employees yearn for simple acknowledgment from the organization, but just don't get it, and it takes the wind right out of their sails.

Praising and giving direction to employees can't be left to the goodness of managers' hearts. And it can't be a sometimes thing, saved for the annual performance review. It has to be made part of the corporate culture. (Carol Hymowitz, 1999, *Wall Street Journal*)

Using a Behavioral Approach to Counseling

A five-step process can serve as a basic map for behavior change. Discuss the steps with your client ahead of time and develop an over-all plan that includes goals, smaller objectives, and benchmarks that tell you whether you are on track. Set modest goals, and remember that if the desired changes were easy, they would have been made long ago. It is likely that existing patterns of cues and reinforcements serve to maintain the present behavior.

We will use the case of B. F. Token as an example. Token was recently promoted to the position of Manager of Corporate Engineering at an aircraft company. He has worked hard and effectively over the years as an engineer, and he is not entirely comfortable with his new leadership responsibilities. His vice president complains that he does not seem passionate or confident, and that he doesn't have a strong presence at division meetings. The VP has no problems with Token's technical expertise, but is worried about his leadership potential in the company. He wonders if coaching can help Token.

Step 1. Choose Your Focus

Identify the critical variables or factors. Start large and move toward smaller, contributing factors. For example, you can start with the task of enhancing the overall efficiency of a client. Then identify specific factors that make up the concept of "efficiency," such as time usage, task prioritization, assertiveness with others (e.g., saying "no" when appropriate), management of mental attention, and specific skills required to get specific tasks accomplished. Then break each of those factors into even smaller parts like amount of time spent sitting at a computer versus time spent in meetings. Then pick a small number of the smaller factors as a starting point.

In the example of an ineffective sales force, the sales manager must begin by identifying the factors that control sales. This might include the number of times a sales person calls a new prospect, the number of miles a person drives each day, the number of hot leads each one is given, or the number of meetings each sales person has with a potential customer each week. It might include sales people's scores on a test that measures how well they know their products or how well they know their customers' businesses. Decide whether to focus on one market or another. Be as specific as possible and choose measurable factors. Get the sales force involved in this discussion.

In the example of B. F. Token, the impassive new manager, the coach helps him decide on specific factors that contribute to his boss's perception that Token is ineffectual. The coach conducts a 360-degree evaluation. The results point to several important contributing factors, including the way that Token dresses, the seats he chooses at meetings, the way he sits, the tone of voice that he uses, his lack of eye contact, and the perception that he never disagrees with the VP or offers an alternative view.

Step 2. Conduct a Behavior Audit

Systematically measure and collect data on the factors you have targeted. There is a way, if you think about it, to measure almost anything, including thoughts, daydreams, feelings, time spent checking e-mail, number of e-mails answered in an afternoon or week, number of phone calls answered or returned, number of interruptions in a given day, amount of time spent walking the hallways, number of requests a person turns down in a week, or level of discomfort (highs, lows, averages) at meetings with direct-reports. Collect data first, and do not attempt to fix things yet. The key questions are: *how much?, how many?,* and *when? (not why)*. Use tally sheets, charts, wrist counters, palm pilots, pagers (to catch the client at various times of the day and remind her to self-assess), and confederates to help collect the data. Go with sales people as they do their work. Observe them in the field. Observe Token as he takes on this project, and be ready to provide feedback on a regular basis. Be creative. Make it interesting and amusing.

In the Token example, the coach accomplishes this in two ways. First, he shadows Token at various work activities, including important division meetings and meetings with the VP. Second, he videotapes Token as they meet together. You and Token decide to focus on eye contact, tone and volume of his voice, seating at meetings, and the offering of alternative viewpoints by Token (including disagreements with the VP).

TABLE 3.3. Functional analysis of Token's baseline beahvior

Antecedent	Behavior	Consequent
Sits in the back of the meeting room.	Says nothing at the meeting.	Feels safe, relieved that she did not have to embarrass herself.
Feels not respected.	Says nothing at meeting.	Maintains consistent self-perception.

Step 3. Do a Functional Analysis

Use an A-B-C (antecedent-behavior-consequent) chart to discern how it all "works." Remember to include stimulus control, the factors that precede the target behavior. Without spending energy on the question of "why" things happen, map out the contingencies. What happens under what circumstances, and what appears to reinforce it all?

As an illustration, Table 3.3 is the chart that Token and his coach prepare to help them understand the operational contingencies in his situation.

As can be seen, antecedents increase the likelihood of the behavior in the middle box, while consequents increase the likelihood that the behavior will happen again, next time. This chart helps Token and his coach learn about how the behavior is persistently maintained. It also directs them in their change efforts. They must focus on changing the antecedents and consequents if they want the behavior to change.

Step 4. Develop a Change Strategy or Action Plan

Start small. Go for modest changes at first and get some successes under your belt. This enhances confidence and provides energy for the difficult changes and the long haul. Reinforce, support, and encourage the desired changes (as well as the effort itself). Build on the smaller changes. Once smaller changes are in place, leverage them to make the larger ones. Token and the coach practice and rehearse new meeting behavior using successive approximations. They rehearse scripts for the big meetings, including examples of bright, important contributions that only Token could make (due to his specific area of

TABLE 3.4.

Antecedent	Behavior	Consequent
Sits in the middle of the meeting room.	Says two things at the meeting.	Feels safe, relieved that she did not continue dangerous pattern, that he is making important changes.
Feels respected.	Says more at next meeting.	Maintains new self-perception.

expertise). Then they sit in the actual meeting room, around the large and imposing table, and videotape Token saying things. They start with a video of him purposely saying something silly or stupid. Then they watch it and laugh. They rehearse as he practices saying something simple, direct, and meaningful. They tape him as he does the same thing. Then they watch and critique the tape. Token watches the tape several times to become familiar with the scene. He goes through a mental version of the tape at home, while relaxing in the back yard.

In Token's case, they decide that they will experiment with different seating at important meetings. Seats at the rear are "off limits" to Token from now on. He decides to check with several key players at these meetings, to let them in on his efforts and to make sure that it is OK for him to take "their seats." They encourage him to do so, and this makes him feel safe about this experiment. He also decides that his previous feelings of safety after meetings (in which he had not spoken up) were, in fact, not safe. He reframed the situation so that he could feel "safe" only if he had spoken at least two times in each meeting. So, the A-B-C chart (Table 3.4) now looks like this.

Step 5. Collect More Data

When you do not see the desired result, measure some more of the important variables. Support positive results and problem-solve. Recycle through Steps 1 through 4. Remember that this is an iterative process. One cycle through the steps is usually not enough, and the evaluation step is used to shift the focus after an initial run-through. Perhaps the goals need to be re-thought. Remember: If the desired changes were easy, the client would have accomplished them by himself or herself, long ago. Change requires tenacity, and it is the coach's job to support (and normalize) tenacious effort. The coach can also sit in on some of the meetings to check progress.

Myths and Misconceptions

Ethical concerns have historically been raised in objection to behaviorism, and those concerns are typically related to the problem of manipulation or control. Most people resent the idea that others could control them, and they view behavior modification as an inhumane control mechanism. The main misunderstandings about behaviorism have to do with its perceived power. Behaviorism frightened people when Skinner popularized it because it was seen as potentially manipulative. It could be used to control people without their consent. It has also been criticized because of its disinterest in motives or internal explanations that people offer about their behavior.

Both of these problems are eliminated when clients are involved in the development of the change process. Behavioral self-control is a better way to think of behaviorism in the coaching setting. Internal events, such as thoughts and feelings are integrated as antecedents and reinforcers. Encourage all members of the organization to be involved in a behavioral audit of the environment. As a group, check the contingencies and reinforcements. Advocate non-random reinforcement structures and align rewards with self-selected goals.

The larger argument for behavioral thinking has to do with its inevitability. Behavioral contingencies are operating powerfully everywhere, whether you choose to take a head-in-the-sand view or not. The power of reinforcement and its importance in the workplace cannot be ignored.

> Informed that Margaret Fuller, after much thought, had decided "to accept the Universe," Thomas Carlyle exclaimed, "By gad, she'd better!" (Thomas Allen, 1978)

Strengths and Weaknesses of the Behavioral Approach

Strengths

Behavioral approaches offer several advantages to the coach. First, they encourage measurement and metrics, something that many modern organizations trust and value. With behavioral methods, you can offer a manager a plan for change that includes quantified goals and measurable outcomes. Companies are much more likely to spend money when they can be assured of observable positive outcomes.

Second, behavioral approaches are powerful when small changes are important to highly functioning people. Healthy, active, motivated people tend to make good use of behavioral methods.

Third, when you treat each client situation as an experiment, you have a greater chance of eventual success. When your early efforts don't succeed, frame it as part of the process that leads to new information about how the problem "works." Then adjust your plan and move forward in a different way.

Weaknesses

The greatest difficulty associated with behavioral approaches has to do with the problem of identifying and quantifying specific target and approach behaviors. Sometimes it is hard to isolate the specific reinforcers or the important sub-parts of a large behavior in question. When someone is having trouble because, for example, he or she doesn't seem enthusiastic or doesn't possess the social skills required of a leader at the next level, it can be difficult, at first, to break the larger behavior down into small measurable behaviors. But it can always be done. It just requires a bit of serious, creative thinking and a coach with some experience.

Summary

1. Contingencies of reinforcement are the key to understanding how behavior "works." Examine the environment to see what behavior it encourages and discourages. Pay attention to the patterns of reinforcement, the naturally existing ones, and those you have established. Remember that you can tell when something is a reinforcement by how it works, not by what people say about it or what you might think should be reinforcing (or even by what has been reinforcing in the past, or with other people). Don't hope for A while reinforcing for B.
2. Set measurable, achievable goals. Start small and build. Measure everything. Make the measurement process creative, and find new and interesting ways to assess matters on a regular basis. Make sure that the measurement process is supportive rather than punitive,

and create a measurement system that is simple enough and easy enough to be sustained over time. Conduct each coaching assignment as a small experiment and make adjustments when you get data.

3. Involve people other than your client in the change process. Discuss the reinforcement contingencies with them and get their cooperation. Sometimes the most important factor in a change process is the inadvertent reinforcement of a boss. This process is, of course, up to the client, but a coach can strongly influence the process, and it helps to act as if involvement of the boss, spouse, coworkers, and others is a completely normal way to conduct effective coaching.

4. Use audio and videotaping liberally. These are powerful change technologies that can be used to enhance successive approximation to difficult learning tasks.

5. Teach all coaching clients about reinforcement so that they can use it to enhance their team and organization. There are inexpensive ways to powerfully enhance any organization through thoughtful application of reinforcement principles. There are many effective natural reinforcements available (in addition to financial rewards for good performance). Use them with clients and teach your executives to use them, as well. All organizations can use a periodic reexamination of the overt and covert operational reinforcements that exist.

References

Allen, T. (1978). On the reinvention of the wheel, the franchising of science, and other pastimes. *The Counseling Psychologist, 7*(3), 37–43.

Bandura, A. (1969). *Principles of behavior modification.* New York: Holt, Rinehart, & Winston.

Bandura, A. (1977). *Social learning theory.* Englewood Cliffs, NJ: Prentice-Hall.

Craighead, W., Kazdin, A., & Mahoney, M. (1976). *Behavior modification: Principles, issues, and applications.* Boston: Houghton Mifflin.

Evans, R. L. (1968). *B. F. Skinner: The man and his ideas.* New York: E.P. Dutton.

Kerr, S. (1975). On the folly of rewarding A, while hoping for B. *Academy of Management Journal, 18*(4), 769–782.

Luthans, F. (1998). *Organizational behavior Ed.* (8th ed.). New York: McGraw-Hill.

Luthans, F., & Kreitner, R. (1973, May/June). The role of punishment in organizational behavior modification. *Public Personnel Management, 2*(3), 156–161.

Luthans, F., & Kreitner, R. (1984, Autumn). A social learning approach to behavioral management: Radical behaviorists "mellowing out." *Organizational Dynamics,* 47–65.

Luthans, F., & Kreitner, R. (1985). *Organizational behavior modification and beyond: An operant and social learning approach.* Glenview, IL: Scott, Foresman.

Martin, G., & Pear, J. (1978). *Behavior modification: What it is and how to do it.* Englewood Cliffs, NJ: Prentice-Hall.

Premack, D. (1962). Reversibility of the reinforcement relation. *Science, 136,* 255-257.

Skinner, B. F. (1948). *Walden two.* London: Macmillan Press.

Skinner, B. F. (1971). *Beyond freedom and dignity.* New York: Alfred Knopf.

Skinner, B. F. (1976). *About behaviorism.* New York: Random House.

Thoresen, C., & Coates, T. (1978). What does it mean to be a behavior therapist? *The Counseling Psychologist,* 7(3), 3–21.

Recommended Readings

Baldwin, J. D., & Baldwin, J. I. (1981). *Behavior principles in everyday life.* Englewood Cliffs, NJ: Prentice-Hall.

Hersen, M.., & Barlow, D. (1976). *Strategies for studying behavior change.* New York: Pergamon.

Hymowitz, C. (1999). Hard workers often can feel starved for recognition. *San Francisco Examiner & Chronicle.* September 19, CL 31 (Excerpted from the *Wall Street Journal).*

Krumboltz, J., & Thoresen. (Eds.). (1969). *Behavioral counseling: Cases and techniques.* New York: Holt, Rinehart & Winston.

Thoresen, C., & Mahoney, M. (1974). *Behavioral self-control.* New York: Holt-Rinehart.

Whaley, D., & Malott, R. (1971). *Elementary principles of behavior.* Englewood Cliffs, NJ: Prentice-Hall.

Whitely, J. (Ed.). (1971). The behavior therapies—circa 1978. [Special Issue]. *The Counseling,* 7(3).

4

CHAPTER   Alan Hedman

The Person-Centered Approach

The therapeutic relationship, then, is the critical variable, not what the therapist says or does.

—Corey (1982, p. 90)

Carl Rogers, the originator of the person-centered approach, was a defining spokesperson for humanistic psychology for nearly 50 years. His ideas provided a dominant methodology in counselor education and have widely influenced both individual and group counseling during the last half of the twentieth century. Although it is not widely known, a main feature of his therapy has been the empirical testing of the core conditions associated with personal change in high-functioning individuals. This would seem to make the Rogerian approach an obvious choice for executive coaches, but for some reason it has not gotten much attention. In the world of executive coaching literature, Doctor Rogers receives about the same level of respect as Mister Rogers!

Len Sperry (1996), for example, has written extensively about translating and extending clinical expertise to the dynamics of organizational settings. Although he considers the psychodynamic, cognitive, behavioral, and family systems literature, he makes no reference to the extensive contributions of Rogers. The *Consulting Psychology Journal* (Spring 1996) dedicated an entire issue to Executive Coaching as an "Emerging Competency in the Practice of Consultation." A distinguished group of authors in the coaching field reviewed the literature and attributed exactly one reference to Rogers.

There are probably a number of reasons for this consistent slight. Many professionals see Carl Rogers in the way that they see Mister Rogers: kind and well meaning, but simplistic and clearly out of touch with the hard realities of the business world. If they gave a thought at all to his theoretical contributions, they would likely dismiss them as being too obvious or irrelevant to the work of executive coaches. This lack of attention and respect does a profound disservice, not only to Rogers, but also to the executive coach who is working to improve his or her core competencies. Current research by Goleman (1995, 1998) and others in the application of emotional intelligence in the work-place should help restore some luster to the person-centered approach, as does the work of Stephen Covey (1989). His "Habit 5" addresses this matter directly and in-depth ("Seek First to Understand, Then to Be Understood; Principles of Empathetic Communication").

Robert Cooper (1997) has worked extensively with business leaders and organizations, and he suggests that trust is one of the driving forces for competitive advantage. He quotes a former leader of the Ford executive team, who says,

> Emotional intelligence is the hidden advantage (in business relation-ships). If you take care of the soft stuff, the hard stuff takes care of itself. (p. 31)

This so-called "soft stuff" (trust, loyalty, communication skills, and commitment) has consistently been shown to produce gains, innova-tions, and accomplishments by individuals, teams, and organizations.

Similarly, in his book *If Aristotle Ran G.M.: The New Soul of Business* (1998), Tom Morris states that "relationships rule the world." His working principle is: "People first; projects second. If you have good relation-ships with people, the projects will come." He suggests that the single most important factor in business leadership is relationship.

> What used to be called the "soft issue" of business will increasingly be the differentiators of substainable excellence of every industry in the world. (p. 199)

The well-known dental practice consultant L. D. Pankey advised his clients to "Never treat a stranger," meaning that doctors should get to know their patients before they put an instrument in their mouths (Wright, 1997). Other giants of organizational consulting, including Tom Peters (Peters & Waterman, 1982) and W. Edwards Deming (1986), have repeatedly stated that while technique and technology are im-portant, *trust* is the key issue when working with an organization. The words of these modern-day gurus of organizational consulting sound surprisingly similar to the mostly forgotten or abandoned concepts of

Carl Rogers. Beginner coaches as well as seasoned professionals will find the work of Carl Rogers important. The following questions are key to this approach and are examined in this chapter:

- What core competencies are required for successful executive coaches?
- What are the necessary ingredients for a successful executive coaching program?
- What factors contribute to negative coaching outcomes?
- How can the principles and concepts of the Rogerian, person-centered approach assist the executive coach in being more effective?

Historical Background

Carl Rogers received his Ph.D. in Clinical Psychology from Columbia University in 1931. By the 1940s, Rogers had grown increasingly frustrated with the behaviorist and psychoanalytic approaches dominant at that time, and he was especially bothered by the accepted role of the therapist as the directive expert. He began writing and developing what was then known as nondirective counseling or client-centered therapy. Rogers created a furor by challenging the basic assumption that, "the therapist knows best," as well as the validity of commonly accepted therapeutic procedures such as advice, suggestion, persuasion, teaching, even diagnosis and interpretation.

The person-centered approach is both relationship-oriented and experiential, growing out of the existential tradition in philosophy. Its underlying humanistic vision can be captured metaphorically by considering how an acorn, if provided with the appropriate nurturing conditions, will automatically grow in positive ways, as its potential pushes toward actualization (in this case, as a very large tree!).

Roger's basic assumptions about people and the therapeutic process are distinctly American: pragmatic, optimistic, and believing in unlimited potential. People are essentially trustworthy; they have vast potential for understanding themselves and resolving their own problems without direct interventions by the therapist. They are capable of increasing growth toward self-direction if they are involved in a healthy therapeutic relationship. In his writings from the 1940s until the 1980s, Rogers consistently emphasized that the attitudes of the therapist as well as the quality of the client–therapist relationship are the prime determinants of the outcome of therapy. At its core, Rogerian theory requires that the therapist listen with acceptance and without judgment, if clients are to change (Heppner, Rogers, & Lee, 1984). The therapist's knowledge of theory and techniques were relegated to a secondary position in the Rogerian approach, behind non-judgmental acceptance of the client.

View of Human Nature

A consistent theme underlies most of Rogers' writing: deep faith in the tendency of people to develop in a positive and constructive manner if a climate of respect and trust is established. He had little use for any system based on assumptions that people could not be trusted or must be directed, motivated, instructed, punished, rewarded, controlled, and managed by others who are in a superior or "expert" position.

He maintained there are three therapist characteristics for a growth-promoting climate in which people can realize their inherent potential:

1. Congruence or genuineness
2. Unconditional positive regard and acceptance
3. Accurate empathic understanding

Congruence or Genuineness

Of the three characteristics, congruence is the most important. Congruence means that thought, feeling, and behavior are all aligned. The therapist must be real, genuine, integrated, and authentic. Rogers always distrusted any therapeutic facade. He believed that through authenticity the therapist serves as a model of a human being struggling toward greater "realness." Therapists must "be themselves" during the time they are counseling. They must be able to put aside all facades and roles during the counseling process. This naturally may require the counselor to engage in self-disclosure from time to time.

Unconditional Positive Regard and Acceptance

Therapists need to communicate a deep and genuine caring toward their clients. This caring is unconditional in that it is not evaluative or judgmental of the client's thoughts, feelings, and behaviors. It is an attitude of "I'll accept you as you are" rather than "I'll accept you when. . . ." It is also important that this caring be nonpossessive. According to Rogers (1977), research indicates that the greater the degree of caring, accepting, and valuing, the greater the chance that therapy will be successful.

Accurate Empathic Understanding

A main task of the therapist is to demonstrate understanding of the client's experience and feelings as revealed in the therapeutic interaction. The therapist strives to understand the client's subjective reality; trying to "walk in his shoes" by reflecting, with sensitivity and accuracy, a therapeutic understanding of what was said as well as the meaning and feelings underlying the words. Accurate empathy goes beyond the recognition of obvious feelings to those less obvious feelings, the ones that are only partially recognized by the client. This deeper subjective understanding of the client can only come with patience and careful, caring listening.

If these three therapist attitudes are communicated to the client, Rogers postulates that the client will become less defensive and more open to necessary therapeutic changes. The success or usefulness of the counseling process depends upon these qualities. For a more complete description of these core qualities, see Cormier and Cormier (1985).

Basic Characteristics and the Core Premise

Rogers did not present the person-centered theory as a fixed or complete approach to therapy. Rogers and Wood (1974) describe the characteristics that distinguish the person-centered approach from other models. Two of these distinctions are: The person-centered approach focuses on client responsibility and the capacity to discover ways to encounter reality more fully. This approach emphasizes the phenomenal world of the client. *That is, the primary intent is to comprehend the client's internal frame of reference and focus on the client's perception of self and the world.* The person-centered approach is not rooted in a set of techniques or dogma. Rather, it is best seen as an attitude and belief system demonstrated by the therapist. It is both a way of being and a shared journey in which therapist and client reveal their humanness and participate in a growth experience.

The Process: Therapeutic Goals

The underlying aim of therapy is to provide a climate conducive to helping the individual become a healthy and fully functioning person. The person-centered approach places the primary responsibility for the direction of therapy on the client. The general goals of therapy are as follows:

1. Openness to experience (less defensive, more aware of reality).
2. Achieving self-trust.
3. Internal source of evaluation (looking to oneself for the answers).
4. Willingness to continue growing. As can be seen, specific goals are not imposed on clients; rather, they choose their own values and goals.

Therapist's Function and Role

The role of the person-centered therapist is grounded in a way of being, in an attitude, not in theory, knowledge, or techniques designed to get the client to "do something" or to change. Basically, the therapist creates a climate that allows the client to grow. First and foremost, the therapist must be willing to be real in the relationship with the client. The therapist does not diagnose or label, nor does the therapist give advice.

Rogerian counseling places demands on the counselor, and a coach should pay heed to these requirements, as well. A person-centered approach requires a counselor who is able to be "present" in the counseling relationship. The counselor must be able to be fully engaged with the client, undistracted by personal agendas or roles, so that he or she can accurately experience that client. He or she cannot be an agent of the company, attempting to mold their client according to company needs or the dictates of a boss. The counselor must also be able to demonstrate *unconditional positive regard* for the client, establishing no conditions for acceptance. The counselor must take a nonjudgmental attitude and communicate this to the client. He or she must be able to achieve *accurate empathy*, to sense the client's private world as if it were his or her own. These are simple but uncommon qualities, and because they are not easy for most people to learn, many psychotherapists have spent years practicing and honing them.

Relationship Between
Therapist and Client

The person-centered approach emphasizes the personal relationship between client and therapist. It is an active partnership. Rogers summarized this basic hypothesis (in 1961) in the following way:

> If I can provide a certain type of relationship, the other person will discover within himself the capacity to use that relationship for growth and change, and personal development will occur. (p. 33)

In later writings, Rogers (1967) hypothesized in a fairly radical observation that "significant positive personality change does not occur except in a relationship."

The contributions of the person-centered approach, however basic and self-evident they may appear, have had a profound effect on the helping professions. Its core skills (active listening, respecting clients, and adopting their internal frame of reference) should also be the fundamental tools for the effective executive coach. This will become clearer with a closer look at the basic ingredients for a successful executive coaching program.

Basic Ingredients of Executive Coaching

It is curious to look at the current literature on executive coaching and see the striking similarity to many of the ideas and concepts of Rogers. Sperry (1996), although he never makes direct reference, surely sounds Rogerian when he discusses executive coaching and consultation. The consultant's role is one of listener, confidant, and personal adviser. Essentially, the consultant serves as a sounding board and as an objective and trustworthy source of feedback. Such consultation sessions consist of directed discussions initiated by the executive/client who sets the agenda.

David Peterson (1996), in discussing the art of one-on-one change in executive coaching, has clearly been influenced by Rogers. He describes the first phase as "Forging the Partnership." The coach must build trust and understanding so that people will want to work with you. A partnership requires that coaches earn the trust of people they coach, so they can provide the right amounts of challenge and support throughout the process. If a coach fails here, people will discount the coach's perspective and will resist taking risks or experimenting with new behaviors. To build trust, coaches must learn how people view the world and what they care about. He even quotes Carl Rogers on this last point: "The best vantage point for understanding behavior is from the internal frame of reference of the individual" (Rogers, 1961, quoted in Peterson, 1996, p. 79). This strategy requires effective listening skills, patience, and an understanding of the dynamics of human behavior.

Richard Diedrich (1996) from The Hay Group also sounds very Rogerian when he discusses feedback in the coaching process. To be effective, feedback "needs to be two-way, engaging, responsive, and directed toward a desired outcome." One of the most important elements in this process is empathy, which builds trust when expressed through listening and the active sharing of perspectives.

Peggy Hutcheson (1996) proposes tips for coaches that will help them move along the continuum from wanting to control the results to wanting to empower others by helping them take responsibility for change. That sounds like something directly from the Rogerian Handbook for Executive Coaches! Her specific tips include:

1. Accept that the coach is not in control.
2. Listen.
3. Pay attention to what is not being said as well as to what you hear.
4. Coach, don't judge.
5. Guide the other person to his or her own solutions.
6. Suspend your expertise.

When Kilburg (1996) discusses negative coaching outcomes, as in "insufficient empathy for the client" (the coach did not truly care about the client's well-being or future), his debt to Rogers is obvious. When Witherspoon and White (1996), discuss four distinctly different executive coaching roles: 1) coaching for skills, 2) coaching for performance, 3) coaching for development, and 4) coaching for the executive's agenda, each is premised on the Rogerian concept of establishing an equal working partnership between coach and executive.

Rogerian Applications to Coaching

Rogers' ideas have always been thought to be ideal for high-functioning, mentally healthy people. From this brief review of current literature, it should be obvious that Rogerian principles are central to the success of an executive coaching program.

A coach using these ideas should aim to accomplish two tasks with most clients. The first task is the general application of the Rogerian principles: (a) Create a genuine, authentic, one-on-one relationship with the client; (b) Achieve accurate empathy through unconditional positive regard and acceptance; (c) Really hear the client and fully accept him or her as he or she currently is; and (d) Reflect what you hear back to the client so that he or she can fully appreciate their situation as it is.

The second task deriving from Rogers is useful with most coaching clients, but not all. (Those clients who are excellent listeners are the exception.) Teach clients how to listen. Listening is a prerequisite for any effective relationship. People will allow themselves to be influenced by a person *after* they decide that they have been heard and understood. Plus, people who do not listen are not interesting. They are not taken seriously. Yet, in these fast-paced times, many executives lack solid listening skills, and an effective 360-degree evaluation often points this out. Use active listening with clients and show them how to do it. Active listening includes the following:

- **Restatement**. Teach clients how to repeat or summarize what someone says before responding with new information.

  "Let me make sure that I've got this right. You think that finance is not allocating enough resources to your project. Is that what you mean?"

  This serves to clarify things and demonstrates that they are interested and they accurately grasp what the other person has said. This implies respect for the speaker, and it becomes even more important as business speeds up.

- **Paraphrasing**. Teach clients how to summarize what another person has said, so that an important aspect of the message can be emphasized and explored.

  "You seem to be saying you have second thoughts about the Acme project."

- **Reflection.** Clients can learn to reflect back feeling states to speakers. Coaches can model this and then teach it. It can be very effective on occasion.

  "You don't sound very confident about the timeline."

- **Summarizing.** Teach clients how to take several statements from a speaker, tie them together into a theme, and check them out with the speaker to see if the meaning is accurate.

  "All right. So, on the one hand, you think there is a clear opportunity here, but on the other hand, you are worried about whether we can convince the board to fund the project fully enough to make it work. Am I understanding you correctly?"

- **Physical listening.** Help clients with their posture and physical mannerisms so that they give the clear impression that they are paying attention. Give them feedback about their eye contact, and the way that they appear when they are listening.

- **Listening for feelings.** Even when your client is not going to mention the emotions that a speaker has for a topic, it is important to *notice* what people seem to be feeling as they speak. This technique has an added benefit: It makes conversations more interesting. Obviously, talk about emotions is not always appropriate in the business setting, so discretion is important here.

- **Giving feedback on specific listening skills.** When your client interrupts, call his or her attention to it. When clients change the subject without attending to what the previous speaker has said, mention it to them. When they go on and on without noticing the impact on the listener, tell them. Catch them when they argue unnecessarily or when they judge too quickly or when they seem disinterested. Better yet, *show them* on a videotape that you made while they were listening or speaking.

- **Giving clients feedback on the impression they make on you.** Notice your own feelings as a coach and as a person. Think carefully about this, and when it is appropriate (when it will contribute to your clients' development, and is not a manipulation) share your reactions with them. The principle is this: If you have a certain strong reaction to them, it is likely that others have a similar reaction.

- **Coaching clients on authenticity.** Assess their level of genuineness, including how personally they engage listeners. Discuss this with them and work on achieving just the right amount of personal engagement in each interaction. Some clients may be too personal, revealing much too much about themselves, while others reveal nothing. Some people grew up in cultures where it is considered impolite to ask personal questions or reveal personal matters, especially in a business situation. To others, however, this can seem stiff and disinterested.

Strengths of the Approach

The person-centered approach provides profound insight into how an executive coach should be with a client. Active listening, respecting the client, and adopting the client's internal frame of reference can provide clients with the opportunity (so rare in the busy-ness world) to be really listened to and heard. The power of these so-called soft attributes should never be underestimated as they help build trust, commitment, and loyalty to the executive coaching process. Many business leaders lack empathy and listening skills, and the coaching process can provide a living model for empathic listening when done from a person-centered view. This can be a huge advantage for a leader.

Although these Rogerian attitudes are important throughout the entire coaching process, their greatest strength lies in the beginning stages related to "forging the partnership." Unless trust is established, and attitudes of respect, care, and acceptance are communicated, most executive coaching interventions will fail.

The Rogerian approach is useful in executive coaching because pathology is rarely, if ever, the issue at hand. Executive clients are typically high-functioning, mentally healthy people who need to explore their current working situation and make adjustments or learn new skills. The person-centered way allows for quick rapport and accurate assessment of the coaching situation.

Occasionally, clients are referred for coaching (by a boss or by the organization), but they are not "on board" with the coaching process and do not welcome or trust it. They may superficially cooperate, even though they feel resentful or disdainful. A fast-moving plan for change can be disastrous in such a case, as the executive client is not likely to put much sincere effort into the process. At worst, a client sabotages the process, and everybody loses. A Rogerian approach, from the beginning, has the best chance for success, for accurate empathy will require the coach to figure this out, without judgment, defensiveness, or blaming. The coach and client can start with the "truth" (that the client resents the coaching or is afraid of it) and go from there to the possibility that coaching can become a positive experience.

Limitations

The Rogerian approach is not a good "stand alone" theory. This approach is an excellent place to begin a coach–client relationship, but is not a good place to remain as the coaching process develops. Content knowledge, assessment skills, and motivational techniques all have an important role in executive coaching. The insights from other theoretical perspectives, particularly cognitive-behavioral, family systems, and psychoanalytic theories are necessary to compliment the core conditions described by Rogers.

Coaching Examples

Two very different examples will help exemplify how best to apply the person-centered approach in executive coaching.

The Case of Bill

Bill is a 40-year-old V.P. for Human Resource Management in a mid-sized, non-profit organization. He has been required to attend coaching sessions by the new CEO who finds Bill to be good on "rules and regulations" but lacking in people skills, namely an ability to show warmth and understanding. Bill was esteemed by the former CEO, who appreciated his in-depth knowledge of complex administrative procedures.

Bill represents a typical senior executive, as described by the KRW International Group (Kiel, Rimmer, Williams, & Doyle, 1996), someone who scores one or two standard deviations above the mean on measures of dominance and need for control. He is not "psychologically minded," and may hold distrust or disdain for the "soft" side of leadership. Therefore, planning for resistance is extremely important with this type of client. We can assume that the coaching process will be "bumpy."

It became clear that Bill was highly resistant to coaching. He did not think the present CEO really understood him and was dubious that anything helpful might emerge from the coaching process. The Rogerian perspective was extremely useful in helping the coach forge a partnership with Bill. Rather than immediately proposing a game plan or rushing to develop a training technique, the coach spent the majority of the first few sessions listening intently in order to see the issues from Bill's point of view. Generally speaking, working for understanding is more productive than direct confrontation with resistant clients. Gradually, Bill began to see the coach as an ally who could help him. After establishing trust, the coach developed an anger management and communication skills program, and Bill was able to work with him on developing these skills. The process of empathy; that is, the way that the coach learned to see things through Bill's eyes, was essential. It caused Bill's resistance to melt. There was then little to resist.

The Case of Betty

Betty, age 35, was considered a budding superstar for a large recreational management corporation. She was being groomed to assume more managerial responsibilities, but was encountering difficulty. Her boss noticed that she was very uncomfortable with conflict and often avoided such situations. Betty had many years of successful independent job experience, but limited experience in managing other people. She was also a perfectionist who had great difficulty in dealing with perceived failure.

Betty had initially reported being both "excited and scared" about the possibility of a coaching program. A previous (directive) counseling experience made her wary of another similar venture. Knowing that she was primarily in charge of the direction of the current coaching program, she participated, but without enthusiasm. Here again, the Rogerian approach helped Betty get past her wariness and hesitation. The coach's willingness to listen, his attitude of caring and respect, helped establish the trust necessary to begin working on her problems with conflict and perfectionism. The coaching began with efforts at accurate empathy. The empathy led to an understanding of the way that Betty felt. A coaching program was developed, along with an action plan after Betty decided that she was being met and heard by a genuine person who understood what she thought and felt. Once her initial resistance diminished, she was able to engage in coaching on her own behalf. She figured out what needed improvement and development, and got going. Her coach encouraged honest and direct communication during the coaching process and used it as a bridge to the use of more direct communication in the work place. The coach encouraged Betty to confront difficult situations in a direct manner, and they rehearsed the interactions together. They worked on establishing and valuing authentic communication. Betty learned some of the Rogerian listening skills and practiced them, so that they would be in place for difficult moments or conflicts in the workplace.

Her coach also listened carefully to Betty's concerns about perfection, reflecting back and paraphrasing, so that Betty could hear and think about what it all meant. Gradually, Betty began to accept herself in greater proportions, giving up the need to feel perfect in order to engage projects and people.

Summary and Conclusions

1. The person-centered approach can be viewed as the sine qua non (or ultimate prerequisite) for the successful executive coach. It is a threshold skill. It must be in place before other interventions are attempted. Without it, other coaching interventions are unlikely to make a difference. The core skills described by this approach are demanding, but they constitute a core competency for coaches. This approach is essential for the development of a working relationship with clients. The ultimate power of the person-centered approach is realized when it is used in eclectic combinations with other powerful theoretical interventions.

2. Brush up on Rogerian skills, if necessary. Review basic listening techniques and actively work on your own interaction skills as a coach.
3. Teach listening skills to your clients. With their permission, give them extensive feedback on the way that they listen and the impact that they have on you and on others.
4. Relentlessly strive to understand things from the point of view of your client.

References

Cooper, R. (1997, December). Applying emotional intelligence in the workplace. *Training & Development*, 31–38.

Cormier, W., & Cormier, L. (1985). *Interviewing strategies for helpers: Fundamental skill and cognitive behavioral interventions.* Monterey, CA: Brooks/Cole.

Deming, W. (1986). *Out of crisis.* Cambridge, MA: NIT Center for Advanced Engineering Study.

Diedrich, R. (1996, Spring). An iterative approach to executive coaching. *Consulting Psychology Journal*, 61–66.

Goleman, D. (1995). *Emotional intelligence.* New York: Bantam.

Goleman, D. (1998). *Working with emotional intelligence.* New York: Bantam.

Heppner, P., Rogers, M., & Lee, L. (1984). Carl Rogers: Reflections on his life. *Journal of Counseling & Development, 63*, 14–20.

Hutcheson, P. (1996, March). Ten tips for coaches. *Training & Development*, 15–16.

Kiel, F., Rimmer, E., Williams, K., & Doyle, M. (1996, Spring). Coaching at the top. *Consulting Psychology Journal*, 67–77.

Kilburg, R. (1996, Spring). Toward a conceptual understanding and definition of executive coaching. *Consulting Psychology Journal*, 134–144.

Morris, T. (1998). *If Aristotle ran G.M.: The new soul of business.* New York: Henry Holt.

Peters, T., & Waterman, R. (1982). *In search of excellence: Lessons from America's best-run companies.* New York: Harper & Row.

Peterson, D. (1996). Executive coaching at work: The art of one-on-one change. *Consulting Psychology Journal*, 78–86.

Rogers, C. (1961). *On becoming a person.* Boston: Houghton Mifflin.

Rogers, C. (1967). The conditions of change from a client-centered viewpoint. In B. Berenson & R. Carkhuff (Eds.), *Sources of gain in counseling & psychotherapy.* New York: Holt, Rinehart & Winston.

Rogers, C. (1977). *Carl Rogers on personal power: Inner strength & its revolutionary impact.* New York: Delacorte.

Rogers, C., & Wood, J. (1974). Client-centered theory: Carl Rogers. In A. Burton (Ed.), *Operational theories of personality.* New York: Brunner/Mazel.

Sperry, L. (1996). *Corporate therapy & consulting.* New York: Brunner/Mazel.

Witherspoon, R., & White, R. (1996). Executive coaching: A continuum of roles. *Consulting Psychology Journal*, 124–133.

Wright, R. (1997). *Tough auestions, great answers. Responding to patient concerns about today's dentistry.* Carol Stream, IL: Quintessence Books.

Recommended Readings

Corey, G. (1982). *Theory and practice of counseling and psychotherapy* (2nd ed.). Monterey, CA: Brooks/Cole Publishing Co.

Covey, S. (1989). *The seven habits of highly effective people.* New York: Simon & Schuster.

Cognitive Psychology and Cognitive Therapy

Men are not moved by things, but the views they take of them.

—Epictitus

Sometimes executives can benefit by changing the way they think, especially when their thinking limits their success. Coaches armed with cognitive methods can be of great help when this happens. This is true because of the special role that coaches play. A coach can (and should) tell you that you are thinking poorly, while few others can do this. Your spouse can't, your colleagues can't, and your boss can't, either. A coach can teach you how to improve the quality of your thinking.

Case Example

Barney Smith, a bright, ambitious operations manager has gradually made his way up the corporate ladder, through hard work, energy, and effort. He's likable, has good intentions, and he knows operations inside and out. But he seems to have hit a ceiling, and this perplexes him, because he is willing to do whatever it takes to continue to succeed. He can't seem to figure out what is wrong. He puts in more hours than anyone else and usually takes work home with him, as well. There always seems to be too much on his plate, and he feels like he is doing the work of three people. His most recent evaluation sticks in his mind, when he was told that he needs to delegate more. He doesn't feel comfortable delegating, he has never done much of it, and has chosen to do almost everything for himself, except for the clerical tasks done by his secretary. In short, he is a prolific individual contributor masquerading as a leader. Aware that delegation is likely to become increasingly important as he moves to positions of greater responsibility, he decides that he must learn how to delegate. He takes a seminar and reads some self-help management books, but things don't change. He still can't seem to delegate effectively, and he's not sure why. Barney is committed and sincere, working as hard as he possibly can, putting in long hours and still making sure that everything is done in exactly the right way. He has his hand in virtually everything in his department. But he feels frazzled at times, and his employees don't seem as committed as those in other departments.

What do we do about Barney? Can we help him change this pattern of behavior? What is the best way to approach him? What does cognitive psychology have to contribute?

The Theory

Cognitive psychology is the study of the mind, its ways, and patterns. In this view, the mind is the product of the brain. The study of cognitive psychology is typically a university-based endeavor, and it has been around since about 1955. As one might imagine, it is a complex area of study, having to do with intellectual processes such as memory, perception, language formation, and the roles of various brain functions.

Cognitive *therapy* is younger and simpler, and it has very practical potential in the workplace. Its core concept is this: people can learn to notice and change their own thoughts with powerful emotional and behavioral benefits. Its central idea breaks with earlier theories in that it focuses on conscious thinking rather than unconscious processes. It is relatively simple to explain and to teach and, with the right people, can make a quick and profound difference in the way that we feel and behave.

History

There are two key figures in the development of cognitive therapy. Albert Ellis was a highly energetic and prolific psychologist who broke with Freudian tradition in the 1960s to forge his own psychotherapy based upon the relationship between conscious thought, emotion, and happiness. He observed that psychoanalysis (which focused on complex unconscious processes) seemed ineffective and found that patients did better when he actively taught them specifically better ways to think.

Aaron Beck (1967, 1976) studied profoundly depressed people at the hospital of the University of Pennsylvania at about that same time. He experimented with structured programs that taught new thinking patterns to people who felt hopeless about themselves and their lives. He concluded that "automatic thoughts" (repetitive thoughts that were wrong in systematic ways) were responsible for depression and anxiety, and he aimed therapy at changing the mental "rule books" of hospital patients.

In 1965, a cognitive experimenter named Lloyd Homme came up with the idea of a "covert operant," and this turned out to be a key to the application of Ellis's and Beck's experiences. Homme observed that conscious ideas could be treated in the same way as overt behaviors; that is, they could be observed, manipulated, and managed. Jealous thoughts need not be conceived as the product of unconscious processes. They could be observed and changed directly through deliberate and diligent effort using behavioral techniques such as reinforcement and shaping.

Although these ideas were resisted in the clinical psychology arena for many years, the persistence of Ellis, Beck, and others, as well as the intrinsic practicality of the approach eventually won its place in the therapeutic toolbox.

Philosophical Basis

In order to understand cognitive therapy it is useful to consider the thoughts of two philosophers. The first is from the stoic Epictitus:

> Man is not disturbed by events, but by *the view he takes of them*. [emphasis added]

The second is from the old Kantian koan:

1. I see a Tiger.
2. I think I'm in danger.
3. I feel afraid.
4. I run.

The core idea is that Kantian statement 3 (as well as 4) derives from statement 2, *not* from statement 1, as most people assume. The way that you feel does not come from your surroundings or from the things that are happening to you or even from your direct perceptions. The situation can't make you sad or crazy. It is a matter of thinking: What you choose to think determines what you feel and what you do next. If you are thinking poorly, you will feel bad and you will make poor decisions. This is an extraordinarily powerful and useful principle, one that has not gone unnoticed by motivational speakers. Thinking mediates emotion. Specific thoughts create and control feelings. If you think you are in danger, you are likely to feel afraid. If you feel afraid, you are likely to run. But what if the tiger is in a cage? What if you are a tiger tamer, and you've been around tigers all your life? Simply seeing a tiger does not cause fear and running. You have to *think* you are in danger before those other things happen. As in the caged tiger example, our first thought in a challenging situation is often not the optimal thing to think. Luckily, we are not stuck with that first thought or instinct. Thinking is, largely, under our control. Humans are capable of observing their own thinking and even capable of changing what they think. Most people make the mistake of assuming that the events of life, the tigers, make us feel bad or good. This is a problem, because we cannot control most of the important things in life. Life is too big and too mysterious, and it tends to do what it wants, independent of what we think we would prefer. The basic premise of the cognitive approach is: W*e can't control life, but we can control how we think about life*. By controlling our thinking we are then able to manage our emotions and behaviors.

Coaching with Cognitive Approaches

There are three cognitive areas of interest available to coaches who want to use cognitive methods, and each involves a different aspect of client thinking: 1) general style of thinking, 2) specific thinking patterns, and 3) specific thoughts. These methods, along with the use of imagery, are described below.

General Styles of Thinking

Beck described four problematic patterns that he observed in depressed people, and David Burns translated his work for the lay public in a book titled *Feeling Good* (Burns, 1980). These four patterns need to be examined, challenged, and changed. Beck (1967) called them "depressive distortions," which are shown in Table 5.1.

TABLE 5.1.

1. **Arbitrary Inference.** A conclusion drawn in the absence of sufficient evidence (or of any evidence at all). For example, you conclude that you are worthless because it is raining on the day that you host an outdoor party.

2. **Selective Abstraction.** A conclusion drawn based on *one* of *many* elements of a situation. A worker blames herself entirely for the failure of a product to function, even though she is only one of many people who have produced it.

3. **Overgeneralization.** An overall sweeping conclusion drawn on the basis of a single, perhaps trivial event or bit of evidence. A student regards his poor performance in a single class on one particular day as final proof of his worthlessness and stupidity.

4. **Magnification and Minimization.** Gross errors in performance evaluation. A woman believes that she has completely ruined her car (magnification) when she sees that there is a slight scratch on the rear fender. A man still believes himself worthless (minimization) despite a succession of praise-worthy achievements.

From Davison & Neale (1978, pp. 197–198).

Specific Thinking Patterns

San Francisco psychologists McKay, Davis, and Fanning (1981) contributed 15 patterns of thinking that cause problems on a reliable basis. Table 5.2 is a paraphrasing of their list.

Specific Thoughts

Ellis, on the other hand, developed a list of 10 specific thoughts that must be recognized, evaluated, challenged, and changed (see Table 5.3). He called them "Irrational Ideas" (Ellis & Harper, 1961). According to this approach, it is rigid and thoughtless adherence to these specific ideas that cause us problems, not life itself.

The tables shown above list examples of the styles, patterns, and specific thoughts that cause negative emotions and problem behavior. The task for the coach is to help clients become aware of these thoughts and patterns and then to substitute effective ones for the negative and irrational ones. Improved executive effectiveness is sure to follow, especially when the new pattern is repeated diligently until it replaces old thinking patterns and feels "natural."

TABLE 5.2. Styles of distorted thinking

1. **Filtering.** You take the negative details and magnify them while filtering out all positive aspects. Sometimes people have a characteristic theme for their filter, such as *danger* (safety), or *loss*, or *injustice*. They view and evaluate everything through that lens.

2. **Polarized Thinking.** Things are black or white, good or bad. You have to be perfect or you're a failure. There is no middle ground. Things are either awful or they are terrific. They are right or wrong. There is no realistic gray area. This is particularly important in how people judge themselves or others.

3. **Overgeneralization.** You come to a general conclusion based on a single incident or piece of evidence. If something bad happens once, you expect it to happen over and over again. If someone lets you down once, you assume that they are incompetent, and that you could never trust them with anything important again.

4. **Mind Reading.** Without their saying so, you know what people are feeling and why they act the way they do. In particular, you are able to divine how people are feeling toward you. You think that your assumptions about what others are thinking are true.

5. **Catastrophizing.** You expect disaster. You notice or hear about a problem and start "what-ifs." What if tragedy strikes? What if it happens to you? You immediately assume the worst possible outcome. This is your style.

6. **Personalization.** You think that everything people do or say is some kind of reaction to you. You compare yourself to others, trying to determine who's smarter or better looking. You tend to relate everything around you to yourself.

7. **Control Fallacy.** If you feel externally controlled, you see yourself as a totally helpless victim of fate. You don't believe that you can effectively influence the important outcomes. They are out of your control. Or, conversely, you feel excessively responsible. Everything depends on you, and if things do not go well, it is all your fault. The fallacy of control has you responsible for the pain and happiness of everyone around you. This is a sizeable burden.

8. **Fallacy of Fairness.** You feel resentful because you think you know what's fair, but other people won't agree with you. Fairness is a big standard for you. You think everything should be fair, even though there is insufficient evidence to indicate that life is particularly fair. When things go poorly, you are liable to respond with, "That's not fair. It's just not fair. It shouldn't be that way."

9. **Emotional Reasoning.** You believe that what you feel must be true . . . automatically. If you *feel* stupid and boring, then you must *be* stupid and boring. Your feelings are the truth.

TABLE 5.2. (*Continued*)

10. **Fallacy of Change.** You expect that other people will change to suit you if you just pressure or cajole them enough. You need to change people because you feel that your hopes for happiness depend entirely on them. Some of your relationships are based on the premise that you can change the other person. You talk about how they should change quite a bit. You give them advice.

11. **Global Labeling.** You generalize one or two qualities into a negative global judgment. If you have one bad interaction with someone in a department, you tell others that the whole department is "a bunch of jerks."

12. **Blaming.** You hold other people responsible for your pain or take the other tack and blame yourself for every problem or reversal. When something goes wrong, someone is surely to blame. It is how you respond to difficult situations or errors.

13. **Shoulds.** You have a list of ironclad rules about how you and other people should act. People who break the rules make you angry and you feel guilty if you violate those rules. Your shoulds are perfectionistic. No one could really meet these standards.

14. **Being Right.** You are continually on trial to prove that your opinions and actions are correct. Being wrong is unthinkable, and you will go to any length to demonstrate your rightness. This makes you defensive, and you have to hang onto your opinions and justify what you have done.

15. **Heaven's Reward Fallacy.** You expect all your sacrifice and self-denial to pay off, as if there were someone keeping score. You feel bitter when the reward does not come. You work extra hard and sacrifice, and do the right thing, expecting to get a lot of credit later. Often, it doesn't come, and this upsets you.

From McKay, Davis, & Fanning (1981, p. 26), with material added for coaching.

Imagery

Cognitive therapy also makes use of images. Mental pictures of things and other kinds of imagery can both hurt and help people. Frightening images constrain us; comforting images soothe. Most, but not all people, visualize and are capable of manipulating the images they see. The first step in using imagery is to make an imagery (capacity) assessment. Coaches must check to ensure that their client makes mental pictures and that they can call up one image or another when asked to do so. If you discover that your client does not easily visualize or is not capable of imagery, this approach should probably be

---

TABLE 5.3. Ellis's irrational thoughts

Irrational Idea 1. It is a dire necessity for an adult to be loved or approved by almost everyone for virtually everything he or she does.

Irrational Idea 2. One should be thoroughly competent, adequate, and achieving in all possible respects.

Irrational Idea 3. Certain people are bad, wicked, or villainous and they should be severely blamed and punished for their sins.

Irrational Idea 4. It is terrible, horrible, and catastrophic when things are not going the way one would like them to go.

Irrational Idea 5. Human happiness is externally caused and people have little or no ability to control their sorrows or rid themselves of their negative feelings.

Irrational Idea 6. If something is or may be dangerous or fearsome, one should be terribly occupied with it and upset about it.

Irrational Idea 7. It is easier to avoid facing many life difficulties and self-responsibilities than to undertake more rewarding forms of self-discipline.

Irrational Idea 8. The past is all-important and because something once strongly affected one's life, it should indefinitely do so.

Irrational Idea 9. People and things should be different from the way that they are, and it is catastrophic if perfect solutions to the grim realities of life are not immediately found.

Irrational Idea 10. Maximum human happiness can be achieved by inertia and inaction or by passively "enjoying oneself."

---

discarded. A small number of people simply do not seem capable of noticing images or pictures in their minds. For them, a foray into this world can be frustrating and demoralizing, unless you are able to help them use a vague "sense of things" (in place of imagery) to accomplish this work. Most people, however, are quite familiar with their own image-generating process, and some are extremely facile. Imagery manipulation can be very useful to such individuals.

Begin by assessing the specific images that come to mind when your client is working. In Barney Smith's case, for example, as his coach, you could help Barney figure out what images he associates with delegating. Next, you would ask him to imagine delegating a task to someone specific. Then have him notice which images pop up. If none come to him, ask him to let an image evolve. Instruct him to observe the image in great detail, and then assess the image and its meaning. Finally, encourage him to make changes in the image and help him practice changing the old image to the new one. The task is to shift from dysfunctional images to ones that are more useful.

Rian McMullin's *Handbook of Cognitive Therapy Techniques* (1986, pp. 272–276) lists many such helpful images for this purpose, and Chapter 7 on Hypnotic Communication in this text describes 10 useful imagery techniques.

Application

The best way to make use of these ideas is to start at the bottom of Kant's paradigm and work backwards, as shown below in Table 5.4.

Begin by teaching your client the cognitive model, its assumptions, and principles. Then observe client behavior or emotion and connect those to the precipitating thoughts. Assess whether behavior is effective, compared to desired behavioral goals or objectives. Identify discrete problematic behavior. Size up negative emotions and feelings. When and under what circumstances does the negative emotion occur, and what problems does it cause? Then—and here is the key step in this method—connect the behavior and feeling back to the specific thoughts, patterns, or styles (from the lists above) which produced them. In this model, the thoughts *produce* the feelings and the behaviors. Once you have identified the thinking that produces problematic feeling and behavior, the task is to challenge and dispute it. A person's own distorted thinking patterns are rarely obvious to himself or herself. Outside help is usually needed in this process, and it is often necessary for the helper to be tenacious. Most people prefer to be "right" rather than effective or happy. Feedback of this sort requires some authority or rapport on the part of the consultant, manager, or outsider, but it is *the* essential step in the change process. This

---

TABLE 5.4. Kant's paradigm

4. I run.	(behavior)
3. I feel afraid.	(feeling or emotion)
2. I think I'm in danger.	(thinking or cognition)
1. I see a Tiger.	(perception)

feedback step also requires skill and finesse, for it can easily be perceived as simple criticism, or worse: rejection.

Once problematic thinking has been identified and challenged, it must be adjusted or replaced. If a simple cognitive adjustment is possible, an easy, elegant intervention can be the result, especially if the interaction can be framed in a positive way. If replacement thinking is necessary, care must be taken to come up with a thought, pattern, or style that is more "true," more realistic, and more effective than the old one. And the thinker must buy into the new thinking.

The last step is evaluation. Success is judged with the same model. If feelings are good, if behavior has changed, then thinking has improved. Effective thinking leads to powerful positive feelings and effective behavior.

Application: Barney Revisited

A coach who uses the lessons of cognitive therapy might work with Barney using the six-step program outlined below, taking into account the following keys to success. The six-step program is as follows:

Step One: Gather Data

First, we need Barney's cooperation and commitment. We start by exploring the problem to figure out what is happening. We don't necessarily accept Barney's diagnosis or view of the problem. We might use a 360-degree evaluation, a standard procedure in executive coaching described in Chapter 1. We ask for input from the people to whom Barney reports, the people who report to him, and from his peers. We ask Barney to provide the names of the people for the 360-degree evaluation, and when the feedback comes in, we correlate it into relevant themes. In Barney's case, the assessment information indicates that people above Barney in the organization view him as bright and hard working, but in a little over his head. They wonder how he could ever take on more responsibility. They cannot put their finger on the source of this impression, but it does seem that Barney is not a "big picture" guy, as one vice president reports. Barney's coworkers confirm his busyness and the frazzled demeanor. He seems pulled in many directions, and it appears that it's always tough for him to have everything done on time. He always appears to be struggling, and he does not seem comfortable, happy, or fun to be around. He often seems distracted and vaguely worried. They acknowledge that he is competent, but he comes across like he's struggling, and they can't say exactly why. Barney's subordinates are very helpful in diagnosing the problem. Although they like Barney and they even admire him, citing his work ethic and integrity, they are annoyed with his apparent lack of confidence in them and his inclination to micro-manage. They report that they have tried to give him feedback about this, although no one has been very direct with it. They cannot understand why he doesn't see it himself, and they don't want to hurt his feelings or get themselves into any trouble. He just doesn't seem to trust them to do anything really important, and he tries to do it all himself. Some of his employees would prefer to see themselves as "team members" (a term that Barney often uses) but they feel more like caddies (sticking with a sports metaphor) or assistants to him, rather than full players. Some workers are quite annoyed, some really don't care, and some report having "given up," and have quit taking responsibility for projects. They just wait for detailed instructions from Barney and do what he tells them, step by step. They feel that he doesn't have much faith in them, so they don't take any initiative, to speak of. Most report that theirs is not a very exciting or gratifying place to work, yet they really like their boss and think he's a good person.

Step Two: Study the Data and Develop an Understanding of the Problem

In this step, we sit down with Barney and go over our information in great detail, remembering to protect the people who gave it to us, while managing Barney's defensiveness or hurt feelings. Few people really like negative feedback, even when they ask for it and know that it will be good for them. Sometimes feedback needs to be dispensed in small, well-framed doses. Raw data need to be processed and translated into usable, acceptable information. The communications skills and accurate empathy of the executive coach are important in this step.

Here's what we would discover about Barney's thinking patterns:

1. He has a deep-seated notion that it is important to work really hard, harder than anyone around him. Barney's sense of personal worth and integrity derives from the amount of sheer effort he applies to work tasks on a daily basis. Delegation seems lazy to him, as if he were shirking his real work. When you mull this over with him, he acknowledges that such a fundamental view of work might make it hard to delegate anything important to anyone else.

2. He thinks that he is the only one who can do things properly. "If you want it done right, do it yourself," is something he remembers his father telling him. He also figures that it takes more time to show others how to do things than it takes to simply do them himself. It seems more efficient, from his present point of view, to just get on a task and get it done.

Step Three: Develop a Plan

The plan we develop will be based on Kant's paradigm (I see a tiger, I think I'm in danger, I feel afraid, I run), meaning that we will focus any efforts on Barney's flawed thinking patterns. The eventual goal will be to help Barney think differently about some aspect of his work so that he can change his behavior.

We go over Beck's distorted patterns, Ellis's self-defeating thoughts, and McKay et al.'s problematic thinking styles. Barney acknowledges some attempts he has made to delegate, as well as his perception that the results weren't satisfactory. He also acknowledges that he has given up on the process, for the most part. He deeply believes Ellis's thought number 2 (One should be thoroughly competent, adequate, and achieving in all possible respects.) This thought causes him problems when it is time to delegate, because he really thinks that good people ought to do things themselves rather than ask someone else to do them. When he asks others to do things that he could do himself, he gets a vague sense that he is shirking, that if he were really strong and adequate he could (and should) do them himself, rather than "push them off" on someone else. He also thinks that he's the only one who can really do things properly, the best way, the way he would like to see them done. He's even concerned about the steps that someone else might take to get to the same end result. He is concerned that they might not do it his way. He is deeply concerned about what he would say if he were to delegate tasks and end up unhappy with the results. What would he say? How could he tell someone that what they have done does not meet his high standards, especially when he could have simply done it himself in the first place? It just seems easier to do it himself, and it would thus be done properly, and he would avoid all this messiness. Then Barney could feel like a hard worker, deserving of his pay and of the respect of others.

Barney's inability to delegate also stems from his tendency to use two of McKay et al.'s problematic styles of thinking. The first is number 7 on their list, "Control Fallacy." He has trouble delegating because he would have to give up some control, and this is not in his cognitive style. He has no experience with letting go of control, he doesn't trust others enough to let go of some control, and he doesn't trust others enough to assume they will evaluate him properly (generously) if things don't work out in the best possible way. He's afraid others will blame him if the tasks he delegates don't work out perfectly. It all seems too risky because of his control fallacy style. Also, he uses the thinking style called "Heaven's Reward Fallacy" (number 15). He deeply believes that hard work and effort, even lots of small efforts will get one into "heaven." (He doesn't literally believe in "heaven," but does feel a powerful, if vague, sense that it is important to do a lot of good work.) Therefore, it would be a mistake to "palm off" any work to others. One simply stays longer at the office and does it oneself. Eventually this behavior will be rewarded.

Cognitive therapy would say that these thinking errors need to be spotted, labeled, and discussed. We would clearly describe for Barney the flaws they contain along with the expectable results. We would then solicit examples from Barney's real life behavior, and discuss them with him in a neutral way, avoiding blame and seeking humor.

Step Four: Actively Dispute Problem Thinking

The next step in this approach involves active and relentless disputation of the problem thinking. We would work with Barney to begin to actively catch each instance when his thinking is hurting his performance. The key to this effort is to work backward through Kant's model. Examples of ineffective behavior lead to an exploration of what Barney was feeling at the time, and to what Barney was really *thinking* which led to the poor decision. We would teach Barney to notice what he is thinking when it comes time to delegate or do things himself. As a part of this process, Barney can set delegation goals for himself, picking appropriate tasks and times and people to whom to delegate. That way he will be able to pick specific situations for self-study. "What was happening when you were supposed to pass off the telecommunications project? Let's go back over it and review what you were thinking and feeling at the time," we might say. This all must be done in a neutral style. Blaming is banished, so that freedom of expression and exploration are maximized.

Here are some examples of how to dispute Barney's problematic thinking. First of all, Barney needs to be helped to understand that he does not add value to the company (at his level) by taking care of details. He thinks that, by taking care of lots of small and difficult tasks, he is doing the right thing. But this is precisely the *wrong thing*, because his time and skills are needed in other areas, specifically in leadership activities such as coordination, motivating others, strategizing, and reinforcing. He adds value by preparing and supporting others as they accomplish day-to-day details, and this becomes even more important when factoring in the learning that takes place when the people he manages figure out how to accomplish new tasks. Barney needs to grasp that when he rolls up his own sleeves, he actually *subtracts* value from the company because he is not taking care of leadership tasks and is actually undermining the efforts and morale of those whose job it is to take care of the details. Second, he must come to see that when he takes care of the detail work himself, thinking that he can do it best, he deprives others of the opportunity to learn.

Step Five: Replace Problematic Thinking with New Thinking

In this step Barney and the coach work together to develop new thinking to replace the old. This new thinking must meet several criteria:

First, it must be more accurate and true in real life than the old thinking. This is not a Pollyanna approach. We do not try to think things that are not true. When we carefully examine the old, we can usually discern that the old thinking was, in fact, irrational. New replacement thoughts must pass the tests of truthfulness and accuracy. If Barney can't accept them as true, the system won't work. Why should he take on the task of thinking something that he really doesn't believe?

Second, the new thinking must be reasonable and achievable. Grandiose or extremely radical new thinking isn't likely to work. People rarely change their thinking in radical ways (outside of cults), and when they do, we must wonder about their sense of self. Radical change probably won't last. Thought changes made in this setting must be relatively small and not significantly incompatible with the rest of Barney's cognitive map. If large-scale changes in belief seem warranted, a longer-term plan must be adopted, and it should include small steps to get there.

Third, the new thinking must be acceptable to Barney. If it violates Barney's core values or religious views, it probably won't last, even if Barney says it will.

Here's an example of replacement thinking. Barney must learn that he can still put in many hours, and he can still work very hard. But, in order to add value to the company, he must behave like a leader: He must engage in the activities of *leadership*, such as directing others (to leverage Barney's skills), coordinating the work of others, teaching others the skills they need to do the job as well as Barney can do it, and motivating. This is how Barney gets into "heaven." This may require that Barney overcome some fear or resistance to the learning of difficult leadership skills, as well.

Step Six: Reinforce and Sustain New Thinking

The new ways of thinking must be rewarded and supported in the real world of work behavior. Behavior change is usually uncomfortable at first, and the coach must support changes in thinking and in behavior. It may be useful at this stage to enlist the active involvement of others in the process of supporting and rewarding Barney's new behavior, especially if others are to benefit from it. The old ways of thinking are likely to be resilient and can easily bounce back before new thinking is solidly entrenched. The coach's job at this stage is to cheerlead and to point out the benefits of new thinking to Barney.

Keys to Success

Early on, the coach must discover the best way to influence Barney. There are three possibilities. First, Barney might allow the coach into his mental world because the coach is viewed as some sort of authority. Perhaps Barney perceives the coach as smart or in possession of some special expertise. Second, perhaps Barney figures that it is in his own best interest to listen and take the coach seriously. Barney sees the benefit. The third avenue is through rapport. The coach uses interpersonal skills to develop a trusting relationship that allows the coach to remark candidly about the effectiveness of Barney's thinking. Resistance is minimal in each of these three circumstances, but it cannot be taken for granted. It is easy for clients to nod their head and act like they are going along with the program while secretly feeling criticized or not understanding the process.

Using a cognitive approach will be most effective if Barney is the kind of person who can notice or "hear" his own thoughts. Not everyone seems capable of this. Some people, no matter how hard they try, cannot seem to discern their own specific thinking; cognitive methods do not work well with them. Other people have the capacity to listen to their thinking, but are not tuned in. They are not used to this kind of introspection, but can learn how to do so with a little instruction and practice. This is a valuable life skill in any context. The question for them is: "What am I telling myself?" or "What was I thinking when I felt that way or when I said that?"

Evaluation

This can be conducted in two ways. First, specific, measurable goals can be established at the beginning of the process. These can be examined at several points subsequent to the coaching. Second, another brief 360-degree evaluation can be conducted. Supervisors, direct-reports, and peers can offer feedback regarding specific areas of progress, and this can be done over the telephone, or via voicemail. Written, measurable forms of evaluation are crucial at some point, as well. The value of coaching must be clear to those paying the bill. Clear results are also important when the time comes to sell more coaching work in the future.

Strengths and Weaknesses of the Approach

At best, this approach can work wonders in a short period of time. Some people can rapidly learn to notice and label their thinking and then change it to great benefit, especially when they are motivated. Most people can learn this technique with relative ease and can implement significant changes that are sustainable when someone, such as a coach, consistently reminds and reinforces these changes over a period of several months. Some people are able to make rapid changes when new ideas are presented in the "cognitive" format by an "expert" (the coach), even though others have presented the same ideas, in different forms, on many previous occasions. A related advantage is that this approach allows the coach to make direct corrective comments without labeling the client "bad" or "crazy." Everybody's thinking needs adjustment from time to time, and the right cognitive adjustment can produce immediate rewards.

This method is readily adaptable to the business and corporate environment. It is direct, straightforward, and results-oriented. It is easy to explain and managers can quickly see the point and the potential benefits.

Even so, humans tend to slip back into old patterns, and it helps to have reinforcement available for extended periods of time. This can include simple reminders like small signs around the office, a note posted on the refrigerator, a regular journal with a commitment to long-term change, or ongoing intermittent phone calls with a coach.

It is useful to recruit team members and coworkers to help with the process, if it can be done without embarrassing the client.

Limitations

There are two main weaknesses or cautions associated with the cognitive approach. First of all, not everyone seems to be able to notice the way that they think. Their own thinking styles, specific thoughts, and distortions are not readily available to them. Some of those folks can *learn* to access their own thinking, but others don't seem able to do this at all. If a coach approaches all managers or clients in the same way, assuming that they can easily observe, reveal, and catalog their own thinking, the coach runs the risk of frustrating or even humiliating a client unnecessarily. A good first step is to ascertain the extent to which a client can access various forms of his or her own thinking. This is easy to do, and can be accomplished by asking simple questions:

- Are you able to notice and tell me about your own thoughts?
- Do you think in words or sentences or language at least some of the time?
- If I ask you to think about what you are going to do tomorrow, what *form* does the thinking take?
- Is it in pictures, or words that you see or hear?
- Do you just get a *sense* of things, or do you get feelings?

Many people use pictures for one kind of mental task or activity, words or visualized words for another, and a sense of things for other mental purposes. Some people talk to themselves all day long. Others never do. Start by helping your clients figure out their own mental style. Assume no mental way is better than any other. If your client really doesn't seem able to access any recognizable forms of thinking, use some of the other approaches in this book. Cognitive approaches can lead to a long, frustrating goose-chase when attempted by those who are not good candidates.

This approach seems to work best with people who can quickly tell you what they are thinking and feeling from moment to moment. It's not that others can't learn to identify these internal states and processes, it's just that a referral to a counselor might be the best place for such foundational learning. Conversely, this approach works better when the coach is also a person who is able to notice and manipulate his or her own thinking, as well. Some coaches may not find this method to their liking because they, themselves, don't have a mental style that is well suited to noticing their own thinking. This makes it difficult to explain it all to others.

Packaging Cognitive Therapy

A second cautionary note is related to the way that this approach is presented to clients. Many people feel insulted when their thinking is challenged. This is not hard to appreciate. Nobody really enjoys being told that the way they think is wrong. It is important to package cognitive methods in a positive frame, so that they are not interpreted as "You think stupidly. Let me tell you how you should think." Such an approach is bound to be met with resistance. This challenge is no small task, and some form of positive rapport is an essential prerequisite. Rapport can take many forms, but it must be established, quickly or slowly. The danger of rejection, depending on the social dynamics of the situation, is profound. The presentation of this approach must be tailored to the unique personality characteristics of each client in each workplace situation.

Bear in mind that this is an approach that has been designed to work with individuals, one at a time. There is no reason that it might not work in groups or with work teams, but not much has been written to describe that process. It might involve a coach who teaches cognitive principles to a work group, which then discovers its own problematic and irrational group thinking. The process could be fun and productive, especially if all members buy into the endeavor with minimal defensiveness.

Summary and Key Points

The cognitive approach can be extremely useful in management and executive coaching. It requires a manager or executive who can notice and describe his or her own thinking relative to a perceived behavioral or work place problem. The coach spends several hours on a one-on-one basis with the manager so that the method can be taught and learned. The specifics of that manager's cognitive map are carefully discerned, and changes are made in the specific ways that he or she thinks about an important work-related set of problems or skills. Changes are implemented by the manager, reinforced by the coach, and supported in the work environment.

1. Ineffective behavior patterns can be quickly and reliably enhanced by examining and changing specific underlying thoughts. These thoughts are reviewed and challenged by coach and client.
2. Cognitive approaches are not for everyone. If the client or the coach is not able to learn how to notice specific things that she is "telling herself," the process is unlikely to be effective.

3. Coaching is conducted like an experiment. Cognitive data are collected, analyzed, and a change effort is untaken. Information from the evaluation of results is fed back into the process.
4. Cognitive change does not often take place after one single iteration of the process. Repetition is usually necessary.
5. When thinking changes, feelings and behavior follow suit.

References

Beck, A. (1967). *Depression: Clinical, experimental, and theoretical aspects.* New York: Hoeber Medical Division (Harper & Row).

Beck, A. (1976). *Cognitive therapy and the emotional disorders.* New York: International Universities Press.

Burns, D. (1980). *Feeling good: The new mood therapy.* New York: Signet/New American Library.

Davison, G., & Neale, J. (1978). *Abnormal psychology* (2nd ed.). New York: Wiley.

Ellis, A. (1973). *Humanistic psychotherapy.* New York: McGraw-Hill.

Ellis, A., & Grieger, R. (1977). *Handbook of rational-emotive therapy.* New York: Springer.

Ellis, A., & Harper, R. (1961). *A guide to rational living.* New York: Institute for Rational Living.

Homme, L. (1965) Perspectives in psychology XXIV: Control of coverants, the operants of the mind. *Psychological Record, 15,* 501–511.

McKay, M., Davis, M., & Fanning, P. (1981). *Thoughts and feelings: The art of cognitive stress intervention.* Oakland, CA: New Harbinger Publications.

Recommended Readings

Emery, G. (1981). *A new beginning: How you can change your life through cognitive therapy.* New York: Simon & Schuster.

Emery, G., & Campbell, J. (1987). *Rapid relief from emotional distress.* New York: Fawcett.

Goleman, D. (1985). *Vital lies, simple truths.* New York: Simon & Schuster.

Johnson, W. (1946). *People in quandaries: the semantics of personal adjustment.* New York: Harper.

McMullin, R. (1986). *Handbook of cognitive therapy techniques.* New York: Norton.

Ornstein, R. (1986). *Multimind.* Boston: Houghton-Mifflin.

Postman, N. (1976). *Crazy talk, stupid talk.* New York: Dell.

Seligman, M. (1991). *Learned optimism.* New York: Alfred Knopf.

Serban, G. (1982). *The tyranny of magical thinking.* New York: E. P. Dutton.

Wegner, D. (1989). *White bears and other unwanted thoughts.* New York: Viking-Penguin.

Zastrow, C. (1983). *Talk to yourself; using the power of self-talk.* Englewood Cliffs, NJ: Prentice-Hall.

Family Therapy and Systems Thinking

In short, knowledge of cause and symptom is not very productive. Rather, knowledge of the system, its parts, their interrelatedness, the communication feedback between the parts, and the system's homeostatic functioning is far more useful to an understanding of the problem and a search for its resolution.
—Brown & Christensen (1986, p. 14)

General systems theory and the family therapy approaches that evolved from them have a good deal to offer the executive coach. They provide specific techniques and an overarching, integrative viewpoint that can be extremely useful. Corporate culture has received considerable recent attention, especially as companies merge. "Culture" can best be understood using the tools of systems thinking. Corporate organizations follow the very same general rules that other groups do, and the dynamics of families are usually quite relevant to work groups.

Many of the core components of family therapy are an ideal fit for executive coaching and the business environment. Coaches will find that corporate clients take to these approaches with ease and comfort, and they are likely to grasp their usefulness immediately. Since family therapy's methods approximate those of organizational development, translation of therapy methods into business coaching is relatively easy. Some of the pioneers of family therapy even thought of themselves as family *coaches* rather than therapists. Those who coach in family businesses often describe succession planning as a type of family therapy. Of course, the language of family therapy must be transposed carefully, as the language of family life could confuse or alienate business clients, and the application of family systems interventions can be quite tricky at times.

Family Therapy and Business

There are several reasons why family or system thinking is so relevant. First, family therapy is built on a cybernetic view, a view that imposes the concepts of complex mechanical control processes and feedback cycles onto communications theory. This necessarily places the emphasis on context rather than person. It parts ways with older therapy models, which take a linear, direct, cause–effect stance. The individual's behavior is understood in the context of organizational dynamics. When a client behaves a certain way, it is understood as a function of the organizational system. Behavior is a response to the demands of the system. The way someone behaves may be a maneuver to influence or protect the system or a reaction to organizational stressors. This view avoids blaming the coaching client, and it is not likely that clients will confuse it with traditional psychotherapy. This makes it useful in dealing with teams of executives. It offers a clear advantage, and gives the coach credibility. For example, when a manager starts too many new projects and finishes too few, the problem is located (in this view) in the organization, not in some personal flaw of the manager. More precisely, it is seen in the interaction between the manager and the organization. Second, family therapy tends to be present-moment oriented, and this is good, because practitioners are unlikely to show much interest in a client's personal psychological history. This view fits well in the corporate world. Immediate change is a reasonable goal, and many business people find this goal attractive when their resources are on the line. A business coach who spends much time wondering about the past or seems too interested in the client's developmental history is in danger of being labeled a "shrink." Third, family systems and organizational systems are typically quite similar. A useful intervention derived from family therapy can often be applied to a business organization as well (Darou, 1995). And fourth, since individual behavior is seen as a function of the dynamics of the organization, the company itself is considered "fair game" for examination and intervention. This point of view opens the door for coaches to have a positive influence on the organization in a more substantial way, and to sell more work, as well.

Background and History of the Approach

The family therapy paradigm began to take shape in the late 1940s and early 1950s in the United States (Goldenberg & Goldenberg, 2000). Norbert Weiner developed cybernetics, the study of feedback systems and how they control machines and computers. Cybernetic systems use continuously self-regulating feedback mechanisms to correct deviations and restore stability. This way of thinking represented a paradigm shift from the older view of linear causality. The British anthropologist Gregory Bateson took Weiner's ideas and applied them to human communication and interaction. He focused on the relationship between stability and change, and gradually, the focus shifted from individual to context, from content to process, and from linear causality to circular (or reciprocal) determinism. Each of us influences the behavior of others, all the time, in a back-and-forth way. The questions of interest shifted from *"why"* to *"how"* and from *"what is wrong with this person?"* to *"how does this person's behavior make sense in relation to its context?"* The study of cybernetics led to a post-modern, second-order cybernetics which added the observer to the system. In this view, any observer, or coach, cannot remain outside of the system. A coach becomes a member of any system he or she coaches. We are not able to stay outside of the context; we necessarily become a part of it as we participate. This factor can be a great help or can become a significant liability to the coach. Coaches are then influenced by the same factors that influence clients. This is helpful when you get a feel for how people really behave and respond, but it's a liability when you become constrained by the same organizational dynamics that influence your client. It also becomes a liability when you lose your neutral or unbiased view. When you consult to an organization for extended periods, it is nearly inevitable for you to become a member of the system or organization, yourself. This then means that the rules of the system will change to incorporate you; you are then controlled by those rules. You will behave (in part) in response to the rules of the system you are studying.

Family therapy represents a paradigm shift in counseling theory. As family therapy has evolved and matured, various divergent perspectives emerged within the paradigm, and there are several diverse models within family therapy. One such model, Strategic Therapy, which is based upon complex ideas about communication and influence, will be reviewed in Chapter 7, Hypnotic Communication. Useful concepts that are common to most other family therapies are described in this chapter.

Review of the Basics

There are four relevant overarching concepts that can serve to orient the coach's work with an executive client. This is a review of some of the operating principles of systems thinking, applied to the task of executive coaching.

Concept 1: Focus on the Present

A systems approach insists that the coach study the present rather than the past, since it is the relationships and dynamics of the present organizational system that control and maintain the behavior of individual members. Don't worry too much about how things got to be the way that they are, and don't go on long, wild-goose chases down the path of "how-I-got-to-be-this-way," or worse: "if-only-I'd-have-done-something-differently." The answers are right here, right now, in the present system. They are right in front of you and all around you. Stay in the present moment.

Concept 2: Process Over Content

The systems-thinking coach will focus on process more than content. The actual content of a message is of less interest than how it is communicated. The details are of less interest and less importance than the *way* that it all happens. Process is about *how* things happen, how things take place, who talks to whom, when, and in what way. Who never speaks directly to whom (as if prohibited)? What happens before and after what other things, in predictable fashion? What things happen, and under what circumstances? What happens under stress, when deadlines are near? What kind of behavior is normal at some meetings and unacceptable at others? The coach is interested in the interaction norms. When something happens at one level of the organization, what tends to follow at others? We are not particularly interested in *why* they seem to happen, for the answer to that question is likely to produce "reasons," and reasons don't get us anywhere. Reasons tend to be abstractions, intervening explanatory variables that we can't do anything about. They often lead to blaming and finger pointing, excuse making, and rationalization. Sometimes they distract us from action. Concern is focused on redundant patterns of interaction, and the repeated use of the same flawed solutions.

Concept 3: Problem Locus

When something is wrong, family therapists examine the system, not the individual. When one person manifests "symptoms" he or she is identified as the IP, or identified patient, meaning that the family has decided to label that person's behavior (which is a function of organizational pathology) as causative and problematic. This has the effect of permitting the organization to stay the same. As long as the family can blame one person, nothing changes in the system. A systems-oriented approach would lead the coach to examine the system when an "identified client" is having individual difficulties. Human behavior can only be properly understood in its social context. An individual only changes when the system changes, and the system only changes when individuals change. They are interrelated, not independent.

Concept 4: First-Order and Second-Order Change

This is an important distinction for the coach and the client, not to be confused with second-order cybernetics, which has to do with the way that the coach becomes a part of the system. First-order change occurs when an individual member of a group makes a change in behavior that does not influence the way that others function. It is often a form of individual compromise (or growth). Second-order change occurs when the organization cannot accommodate a change made by an individual and must, therefore, make an adjustment in its structure. The rules change, and the organization is transformed. A significant change in the behavior or functioning of one key person can precipitate a second-order change in the organization, and organizational discomfort and resistance usually accompany it. Such individual behavior is thought to "unbalance" the existing system.

Useful Ideas for Intervention

Once a coach and client grasp those four overarching concepts, several specific ideas and terms can be used to coach effectively.

Homeostasis

Groups, organizations, and their members strive to maintain homeostasis, to keep things the same. Even a poor homeostasis is generally preferred to frightening or disorienting change. This implies that the group will resist or even sabotage changes that an individual might make, even as they praise the change effort. The thermostat is a classic metaphor for system homeostasis. When the temperature in a room drops below a set point, the thermostat sends a signal to the furnace to switch on and produce heat. When the heat in the room reaches the set point, that same thermostat sends another signal for the furnace to turn off. The temperature of the room remains constant within a certain acceptable range of comfort. Groups and organizations are the same way. There are two ways that this model explains ineffec-tive behavior. On the one hand, methods that people use to maintain equilibrium can be problematic. On the other, even positive, well conceived changes made by a client are likely to be met with resistance, for change is often experienced as a threat. Many corporate programs, or "management fads-du-jour" fail due to the force of organizational homeostasis. It must be accounted for in change efforts.

Equifinality

You can start anywhere in the system or organization and come to the same conclusions and understandings. There are many ways to "skin the corporate cat," and since all of the parts of the system serve to maintain the system, you can use multiple paths to get to the same destination. Eventually all the road signs point the same way. Often a coach is permitted limited access to parts of an organization. Start with the part that is available, since it is usually possible to get to where you want from there.

Because of another key concept called "wholeness," a change in one part of a system will necessarily cause changes in the other parts. The metaphor often used to illustrate this aspect of systems life is the mobile, the free-balancing little work of art that is hung over a baby's crib. It seeks and finds its own unique balance, and if you pull on any single part, all of the other parts go out of balance. When one person in an organization has trouble, it is a sign that there is something out of balance in the organization or that the organization has found a dysfunctional balance point. For example, when one person is stressed beyond the breaking point, it usually means that something else about the system is unhealthy. Operations cannot function without effective finance. Marketing cannot operate without coordinated information technology, which cannot make it without HR. This applies to the (more important) informal dynamics of the organization, as well.

Systems and Subsystems

Every large group (e.g., a company) is made up of many smaller groups; each is organized in some way for some purpose, with its own set of rules and norms. Boundaries exist between subsystems, and those boundaries can be rigid, flexible, or permeable. These boundaries dictate when and how members participate and communicate. Subgroups must be understood and boundaries respected. While all organizations create a formal mechanism for transmission of information, the most important messages often move along informal channels. This is true of the formal business arrangements, too. In fact, the modern view of marketing as the central hub of a business organization depends upon the effective integration of numerous subsystems (e.g., sales, IT, customer service, and engineering).

Rules and Norms

Members or participants in each system or subsystem are expected to behave in certain ways. Sometimes it takes an outsider to notice the rules and norms. Sometimes they are not obvious. But they are crucial, and are often considered as part of office "politics." Some are tantamount to commandments (to be violated at great cost or risk), while others are often ignored. Notice which are overt and which are unspoken (and why). Who can break which rules? Which norms violate a formal organizational creed? Who sets standards, and why? Organizations are often influenced by powerful personalities who are not formally empowered in the organization. For example, when you look carefully at most organizations, there are a few people who possess much more institutional power than their title would indicate. Everyone seems to understand these people's power and accept it. It is an unwritten rule. Who are these people and what is the source or basis of their power?

Myths and Mystification

Companies, like families, collect essential images and stories which serve to define and protect the group during times of stress or uncertainty. These myths are often nearly sacred, and they are rarely challenged, as most members of the group take comfort in them. Many organizations, strong or weak, have stories to tell about their founder or leader. These stories can be very instructive. They can also hold us captive, especially when the realities that created them no longer prevail. The stories of the De Pree family of CEOs at Herman Miller, Inc.—the Zeeland, Michigan, furniture company—provide a great example of the power of myths and stories. Those stories are detailed in Max De Pree's 1989 book, *Leadership Is an Art*.

Roles

The systems coach is interested in roles that people take on in organizations. A role is a set of consistent expectations about behavior and reaction. What roles do various people play? What would happen if they stopped playing them? How do these roles serve to keep things the same (the homeostasis function)? After a while, people expect others to continue to behave in the way they always have, and they become uncomfortable when people do not behave consistently with their formal role in the organization. Is it dangerous to behave out of role? One person who holds onto a formal role in the organization can define it by the way that he or she behaves, and it can be difficult for a new person to take over that formal role. For example, tasks are usually not evenly distributed in logical alignment with the company's organizational chart. People have taken on roles over the years that have nothing to do with their position in the formal structure.

Family Roles

It can also be useful to examine the "family" roles or types that adults seem to take on in the workplace. These roles include: star, blamer, hero, rebel, martyr, scapegoat, distracter, cheerleader, jester, invalid, placater, favored son, mascot, saint, and skeptic and most are familiar as remnants of families of origin (Blevins, 1993).

Here are brief descriptions of the above mentioned roles people take in organizations. They are taken on to accomplish something in response to the organizational structure and interpersonal system. Homeostasis applies. When the system changes, people occupying these roles resist the change, but eventually adjust their role behavior.

> **Star:** This person is accorded star status in the organization. He or she is treated as special, and he or she generally performs at a very high level. Inadequacies are minimized and mistakes are ignored. The star's future is assumed to be quite bright.

Blamer: This person always seeks to blame someone for everything that goes poorly. When things don't come out the way the organization wants, someone must be to blame. This person reliably points this out.

Hero: This person's job is to "save the day." Whenever the organization is in a tight spot, he or she gets involved and makes things work out. The hero makes the big sale or gets the team through an accreditation or inspection.

Rebel: These people don't quite fit in. They are highly autonomous, and they usually don't follow the rules. They dress differently, think differently, and behave differently, and they get away with it, for the most part. Top management finds them annoying, but they are often good at what they do.

Martyr: This person endures constant suffering on behalf of the organization or its members, typically to get and keep a certain kind of attention.

Scapegoat: This person bears and accepts the blame for the team when things go poorly.

Distracter: This person does things that take attention away from the team's problems or difficulties. He or she finds other things to which the team should attend.

Cheerleader: This person stays on the sidelines most of the time and encourages others to take action. He or she does not take risks or get directly involved in anything difficult.

Jester: This person creates humor compulsively. Jokes and laughs distract the team from difficulties and problems. This can be delightful and it can be annoying.

Invalid: This person is often sick or damaged or impaired in some way, so that he or she cannot always take on or complete difficult assignments. Additional stress is too much for the invalid.

Placater: This person can be counted on to appease people when things get difficult. He never confronts things. He always backs down.

Oldest/Favored Son: This person is given special treatment and has extra responsibility. He or she often serves as a trusted go-between for leadership and other layers of an organization. He or she gets subtle benefits and opportunities that others don't get, but is expected to take some responsibility for the behavior of the "younger siblings."

Mascot: This person is kept around for good luck. Mascots are treated as if they were cute and somehow good for the team, but they are not actually expected to contribute much of substance.

Saint: These people never think, say, or do anything wrong. They are above it all, and behave virtuously, even when such behavior is not completely appropriate or realistic. They behave as if they are better than others. People treat them this way.

Skeptic: This person can be relied upon to cast doubt, especially when optimists or creative people come up with new ideas for the team. The skeptic will throw cold water on them every time.

The coach must remember: The person is not the role. This is true of formal organizational roles as well as remnant family roles. Some of the difficulties that people experience are the result of inflexibilities and some come about because the role-related behavior of one person places demands on others. Fixed role expectations, inflexible rules that are not discussible, rigid hierarchies, and well-established coalitions need to be examined and flexed if individual behavior is going to change, because individual behavior is seen as a reaction to these role problems within the organizational system. Table 6.1 is a blank chart for use by coaches and clients to track and figure out which members of the organization fulfill various family roles.

There is also role strain, role overload, and role conflict with which to contend (Carlson, Sperry, & Lewis, 1997). All three of these problems are prevalent in the corporate world, and are likely to become more widespread as American work life evolves and speeds up. American workers are increasingly expected to serve in multiple roles in a downsized, super-efficient, and nimble organization. Role overload happens when one person is simply assigned too many different and demanding roles in an organization. Role strain occurs when the expectations of many different roles pull a person in several directions at once, especially when "team play" is expected. This often happens to people who are hard working, reliable, and unwilling to say "no" to new requests. Role conflict occurs when assigned roles are intrinsically incompatible. Appropriate but inexpressible hostility is likely to result, and people behave in all sorts of strange ways under those conditions.

Pseudomutuality

Families often act nice, make nice, and behave politely, even though members are in a state of grave conflict or cannot actually stand one another. This pseudopositive pretense allows them to stay the same and to avoid embarrassment or open conflict. Companies do the same thing, for the exact same reasons. A coach can often say things that could never be spoken by employees or team members, but when the

TABLE 6.1. Role tracking chart

Role behavior:	Member							
Star								
Blamer								
Hero								
Rebel								
Martyr								
Scapegoat								
Distracter								
Cheerleader								
Jester								
Invalid								
Placater								
Favored son or								
Oldest son								
Mascot								
Saint								
Skeptic								
(add your own)								

coach speaks to them, they can then be heard and acknowledged, and no insider has to take the blame.

Triangulation

This occurs when coalitions evolve outside of the formal hierarchy or structure (Kerr & Bowen, 1988; Segal, 1997). In families, for example, a mother and a son may form an alliance that excludes the husband-father. Information flows (or is kept secret) based upon the coalition. Some people are accustomed to triangulation and can become exceptionally skilled at establishing these unhealthy alliances. They are typically used to manipulate power and information in an unbalanced system. They can be treacherous. They can be used to exclude someone or gang up on him or her. They encourage secrets and discourage open communication. They sabotage trust. Sometimes it is the coach's job to tactfully call attention to these triangles and to obvious, but unspoken, arrangements.

Rites and Rituals

There are customary ways that things are done in families and in groups. Some things are always done at certain points in time or in response to other things. These "ways" can ossify and become rituals, unspoken and sacrosanct, to be violated at great risk. They make up a substantial part of the group culture. A simple example is the way that people predictably sit at meetings. In many organizations, people sit in the same seats, meeting after meeting, week after week. No one can say why people sit in the same spots, but it would make everyone uncomfortable if someone sat in the "wrong" seat.

Directives

An intervention used in strategic family therapy has the therapist issue direct prescriptions for change. The therapist then observes. If the client makes the change, all the better. If the client or the system resists, a learning opportunity emerges. This event sheds light on the relationship between the behavior in question and its functional meaning within the system. Ordeals are a subset of directives, and they ask that the client perform something quite difficult as a way to learn about the current problem. The ordeal is usually designed to make the original problem behavior seem small in comparison. For example, if there were a good reason, a coach could ask a client to sit in a different seat at a staff meeting or ask a client to disagree with someone they had never disagreed with before.

Family Life Cycle

Various family systems theoreticians have observed that the structure and behavior of families evolve in developmental cycles, and the management literature includes a similar view of businesses. Behavior that suits a company at one stage is counterproductive at other stages in the life cycle. Clients must occasionally take a hard look at how well they fit the current organizational cycle and then adapt, move, or leave.

Applications

The family therapy model requires us to abandon linear thinking. It is foolish, from this viewpoint, to try to understand the behavior of a person in isolation from the system in which he or she functions. It is counterproductive to attempt to use personal history to understand someone's current behavior. People are best understood in terms of the role they play in their organization and in the way that things stay the same. The unit of study is the team, the work group, or the entire organization. We constantly influence each other, and we are constantly influenced. All of us play roles in the group homeostasis. Although people are usually unaware of the role they play, sometimes they are vaguely aware, and occasionally they have a clear understanding of their role and its function. It never hurts to entertain a discussion about roles and the way that they work on a team.

This way of viewing things creates limitations as well as opportunities for the executive coach. On the one hand, the entire organization opens up as subject matter. On the other hand, if the coach does not have permission to interact or intervene at a group level, it is possible to feel stuck or helpless within a sick or problematic organization. Interaction with others in the organization runs the risk of violating (or appearing to violate) a client's confidences.

What follows are seven ways to use family system concepts and thinking in executive coaching. These options must be customized to fit the client organization. More than one option can be used at a time.

Option 1. Teach the Family and Systems Point of View to Your Client.   Introduce the key concepts as a way to evaluate and understand what is happening to them. Decide how much of a "family" vocabulary to use. Some clients will welcome, or even introduce, the language of families, including terms like parents ("dads" or "moms"), kids, older siblings, family arguments, family business, and parental subsystems. Some companies talk about a "divorce" (divestiture) or about "expecting Dad to solve the problem" (waiting for the CEO to fix everything). Others may find such a vocabulary to be odd. When this happens, simply use a "systems" point of view (homeostasis, cybernetics) that makes little reference to families, per se. Once this model is on the table, many options become available.

Option 2. Observe Important Process Variables Within Your Client's Organization, or Better Yet, Teach Your Client to Do So.   Start with the behavior of team members at meetings. This is the easiest venue for process observation. Below is a checklist that can be used to study meeting behavior in an organization. List those present at the meeting across the top of the page and simply tabulate the number of times each person does the things listed in the left-hand column, as shown in Table 6.2

Once you or your client have collected these data, analyze them for patterns and meanings. This will not be difficult, as your client will probably have clear ideas about the implications. You can then decide what to do with this new and valuable insight, plus, you have alerted your client about the importance of process variables and how they function (They are often much more powerful than the content of a meeting, and they usually go undiscussed.). Once they get into the habit, clients can learn to observe process patterns without the help of the chart.

Option 3. If a Client Is Interested and Willing, Explore His or Her Family-of-Origin Experiences.   Most of us currently use behavior that was forged in our families; we act out roles, we handle conflict, and we view ourselves in ways that have roots in that era of our development. Most people can derive useful insight from such an examination. The danger in this option is that it may remind a client too much of the worst aspects of psychotherapy, implying that he or she is "damaged" or in need of therapeutic assistance or cannot do anything now about the way that they have been formed.

Option 4. Help Your Client Examine His or Her Current Organization as If It Were a Family.   This family metaphor may help clients understand how their behavior fits in, how they are accepted and treated, and how they can adjust in order to become more effective. In this model, your client's behavior makes sense in relation to what it accomplishes or how it reacts to the organizational system. Assess the availability of components of the system, meaning: Figure out how willing others are to participate in the coaching of your client. Is the larger organization willing to participate? Would they consider changes if that's what it would take to improve your client's situation? How much can you push them and how much can you expect from them? Are they off-limits?

For example, help your client understand the roles that he or she is expected to assume. Most executives have never undertaken such an inventory. Examine how they feel about the expectations and duties

TABLE 6.2. Process observation checklist

People at the meeting ⟶					
Behavior to be noted:					
Silent					
Introduces topics					
Clarifies					
Draws others in (solicits)					
Arrives late					
Interrupts					
Asks questions					
Appears disinterested					
Keeps group on task					
Takes group away from task					
Expresses feelings					
Disagrees					
Leaves the room					
Agrees, supports					
Summarizes					
Suggests					
Proposes options					
Tests for consensus					
Pleads for special interest					
Speaks to one person					
Elephant-in-the-room comment					
Engages in side conversations					

Note: The "Elephant-in-the-room" comment in the chart above refers to a remark about something that is glaringly obvious to most members of the group, but is previously unspoken (because it seems dangerous or embarrassing or too difficult to tackle).

associated with those roles (formal and informal), as well as how they are expected to behave in them. (Are they expected to act like they love the role? Are they expected to behave as if they are burdened, but do it for the good of the group?)

Each family has a characteristic communication pattern, and one must understand that pattern in order to communicate within it. Communicating against the flow is liable to be met with resistance and confusion. Each work group has its norms, and they must, at the very least, be acknowledged, if not respected. Some families are perfectionistic, some use humor in healthy and unhealthy ways, some have an angry flavor, and family members usually play expected roles. The contributions of some members are more valued than that of others. Some are permitted to speak in some situations and others are not. Families treat outsiders in characteristic ways, and a coach might expect different treatment by different work groups. Some families wall themselves off from the rest of the world so that they can operate without criticism or resistance, and most families have "unspoken issues" which are essentially off-limits for discussion. Success and failure are treated differently in different families, and mistakes are handled quite differently in different companies and industries. Consider the way that mistakes are treated in the medical community compared to the way they are handled in airlines. In the airline industry, mistakes are routinely examined in the open, with the expectation that such an examination will prevent future error. In the hospital industry, error is denied, hidden, and rarely discussed in the open. Doctors are expected to be perfect (Leape, 1994). Families are usually composed of subgroups, and information is not uniformly shared across these groups. Power or control of various group functions is unevenly assigned to one subgroup or another, and people become uncomfortable when members cross boundaries or step out of roles. Alliances are formed and maintained between various members for various purposes and at differing times.

Option 5. Give Directives.   Ask your client to do something different. If organizations function as systems, any disruption of current patterns of behavior should be instructive. Using the equifinality principle, we should be able to start anywhere in the system to make a change, assuming that the rest of the system will resist the change or change itself to accommodate the new pattern. If your client never attends a particular weekly meeting, for example, instruct him or her to do so. Watch to see if he or she complies or resists or sabotages, and help your client observe the larger system or work group. If your client does not complete the directive, work together to figure out how it happened that the directive was not carried out. What emotions accompanied the situation? What did your client actually do? What images or expectations does your client have about what might happen? What needs to change in order for him or her to complete the directive? If your client carries out the directive, examine the system. Look for system resistance or disapproval and learn from that. New or novel behavior is always instructive in the context of a system.

Option 6. Provide Direct Skills Training.   In family therapy, specific communications techniques are often taught to one member or all members of the family. Teach your client specific skills such as active listening, assertion, and public speaking. Videotaping is often a powerful intervention when visual feedback will help.

Option 7. Explore the "Miracle Question" (de Shazer, 1991). Ask your client what would happen if, one night while sleeping, a miracle happened, and he or she is now significantly more productive and effective. What changes would that bring? What would it be like? What would it feel like? Who would notice; who would care? How would your client have to behave now? What would he or she do?

Option 8. If You Have Permission, Take Action (or Help Your Client to Take Action) on the System Itself.   Facilitate second-order change. This is likely to involve discussions with key players in the organizational structure, and requires that they see such discussions as being in the organization's interest. You or your client can make the following presentation: "We have discovered, as part of the coaching, that our group could benefit from a discussion of how we interact. We would like you to take a look at this with us." Ask others the question: "What would happen if Joe Client did this or that? What would change? What would you do?" Remember that each group has characteristic ways that it handles "outsiders," and that once you begin to operate within a group you, as coach, lose your outsider status and become a part of the system itself. Remind all parties that change is usually uncomfortable and is predictably met with resistance.

Strengths

Family and system approaches are different enough from traditional and stereotyped ways of doing psychotherapy to make them compatible and acceptable to business clients. Most companies are leery about turning a psychotherapist loose in the boardroom. Coaches with a systems point of view behave and think much like a traditional organizational development consultant. They are concerned with the organization, its structure, its behavior, its effectiveness, and health. Family therapists give directives, and most business clients welcome that from a consultant. Some even figure that if they are getting directives, they are getting their money's worth. Active listening, restatement and reflection, and accurate empathy (in spite of their undeniable value) are occasionally viewed with skepticism in the corporate consulting arena.

At the same time, focusing on the organization has the advantage of deflecting blame from the coaching client. As mentioned earlier, coaches must take care to avoid becoming limited to the role of "doctor" who fixes losers or broken employees. When that happens, no one wants to work with you. You become the proverbial "Angel of Death" or last resort before an executive goes out the door. This is why it is important to avoid becoming the company "shrink."

Occasionally, a systems focus can precipitate a shift in the view of who the client actually is. Instead of an individual client, the organization may, instead, choose to view the organization or a part of the organization as the "client," causing the coach to shift role and focus.

A second advantage is that systems approaches can lead to enhanced client understanding of the organizational and political environment, and while this is always a plus, it is of particular value with two types of clients: those who are politically naïve or inept and those who do not value political shrewdness. It is virtually impossible to succeed in a modern organization without attention to the local political environment.

A third advantage is that a systems approach often opens the door to the rest of the organization, where a coach can make a more significant difference and, for what it's worth, create more business for himself or herself in the future.

Weaknesses

First, systems approaches can be complex, depending upon which variation you choose. Some of the available interventions are complicated to grasp and to put into action. It is possible to make a mess if a complex system manipulation goes awry. Some of the family interventions described in textbooks seem to have been invented on the fly, and are appropriate only for the old master who invented them. Some systems therapists like to seem mysterious or impenetrable. This may work, but it might backfire, depending upon the coach's personality and the expectations and egos of clients.

Second, this approach can leave coaching clients in a powerless position if they decide that they are part of a dysfunctional work system that is unlikely to change. This might cause a client to consider leaving the organization (which may or may not be a good idea, both from the point of view of the client and company), or might cause him or her to simply feel bad. Nonetheless, it is always better (for clients as well as coaches) to possess an accurate understanding of the organizational situation.

Third, your client or their organization may not care for the family metaphor. It can be a turn-off in the corporate world, and the way that the model and methods are presented is crucial. If you are going to use this approach, it will be important to find a way to present it so that it will be embraced. A trusted consultant, particularly one who has delivered valued results in the past, can present almost anything and find a responsive audience. A new coach must be somewhat more careful at first.

Summary and Key Points

The systems viewpoint is extremely powerful, and the ideas presented in this chapter are likely to be familiar to the organizational consultant. They can be implemented in two ways. First, clients can learn about the family systems model and its key concepts and can apply these to his or her own situation, on the assumption that such an understanding will enable them to make changes in their own approach to things. Second, clients can take these concepts and target second-order change, by behaving differently or by overtly requesting system change. Discomfort and resistance are to be expected as the organization strives to stay the same. But, like a mobile that becomes weighted differently, a new organizational homeostasis is just around the corner, and the changes are usually worth it.

1. Organizations can usefully be understood from a systems point of view. This means that the principles of family systems therapy can be fruitfully applied to executive coaching. Such principles are likely to be welcomed in most business organizations (depending upon how they are packaged).
2. Individual parts of a system (clients) can only be understood in the context of the organization (the larger system). Behavior is controlled by the system, and behavior changes the system. Circularity replaces linear thinking in this view. Interventions can focus on the client or on the organization with the same end result.

3. Systems (and organizations) tend toward equilibrium. When pressure is brought on them to change, they respond with feedback mechanisms to get things back into balance.
4. Clients and others often take on roles of which they are only vaguely aware. It is often helpful to discuss and clarify role-related behavior and its meaning and function in the organizational system.
5. Clients can learn to use process observation and systems principles to understand the organization and to make changes in their behavior in order to productively influence the organizational system.

References

Bateson, G. (1999). *Steps to an ecology of mind: Collected essays in anthropology, psychiatry, evolution, and epistemology.* Chicago: University of Chicago Press. (Original work published 1972).

Blevins, W. (1993). *Your family yourself.* Oakland, CA: New Harbinger Publications.

Carlson, J., Sperry, L., & Lewis, J. (1997). *Family therapy: Ensuring treatment efficacy.* Pacific Grove, CA: Brooks/Cole.

Darou, W. G. (1995). Family systems and organizations. *The 1995 annual: Volume 2, consulting.* San Diego: Pfeiffer & Company.

De Pree, M. (1989). *Leadership is an art.* New York: Dell.

Goldenberg, I., & Goldenberg, H. (2000). *Family therapy: An overview* (5th ed.). Monterey, CA: Brooks/Cole.

Kerr, M., & Bowen, M. (1988). *Family evaluation: An approach based on Bowen theory.* New York: Norton.

Leape, L. (1994). Error in medicine. *JAMA, 272*(23), 1851–1857.

Segal, M. (1997). Murray Bowen: Emotional Systems. In *Points of influence: A guide to using personality theory at work.* San Francisco: Jossey-Bass.

Recommended Readings

Brown, J. H., & Christensen, D. N. (1986). *Family therapy: Theory and practice.* Monterey, CA: Brooks/Cole.

Davis, K. (1996). *Families: A handbook of concepts and techniques for the helping professional.* Pacific Grove, CA: Brooks/Cole.

De Shazer, S. (1991). *Putting difference to work.* New York: Norton.

Haley, J. (1991). *Problem-solving therapy.* San Francisco: Jossey-Bass.

Hoffman, L. (1981). *Foundations of family therapy: A conceptual framework for systems change.* New York: Basic Books.

Schultz, S. J. (1984). *Family systems therapy: An integration.* New York: Jason Aronson.

Sherman, R., & Fredman, N. (1986). *Handbook of structured techniques in marriage and family therapy.* New York: Brunner/Mazel.

7

Hypnotic Communication

You know what charm is: a way of getting the answer "yes" without having asked any clear question.

—Albert Camus

If linear communication and injunctions were effective, there would be little work for executive coaches. When people are *able* to respond to direct suggestions for change or improvement, they do. They take feedback, make an adjustment, improve, and move on. This happy scenario, however, is rare. More often than not, people resist feedback and resent it when they get it. Even when they accept feedback, it is often true that they cannot seem to do anything useful with it. They cannot translate the feedback into effective and lasting action. These sad observations are well known to anyone in the personal change business. Humans have a hard time with change. We say we want to be different, we make New Years' resolutions, we go on diets, and we vow to do better. People know that they would be better off if they maintained a clean desk or if they submitted their expense reports in a timely manner. They know how to exercise, and they know that they should communicate more effectively with their team. But sometimes, they just cannot get themselves to do it.

Influence and Resistance

It is also true that attempts by one human to influence another create resentment along with resistance. "Who does he think he is?" is the unspoken reaction to suggestions to be different. We don't like people who try to change us, and divorce courts are brimming with couples that suffer from the curse of interpersonal influence gone wrong. "If I change, that means he was right, and I am wrong," is another underlying source of difficulty.

Most humans resist injunction ("You do this."). We resist being told what to do. We resent it, partly because it means that someone else is smarter or better than we are, and partly because it means that we are not presently doing it properly, and partly because it represents a loss of control. We resist out of habit. Once you have done something for a long period of time in the same way, it seems uncomfortable or even weird to try to do it a different way, even when you tell yourself that you should change.

This chapter is for those coaching situations when well-conceived change attempts are not working, when clients are stuck and coaches are stalled, and when behavior is refractory to good advice. Such situations are common and frustrating to all involved. They also represent opportunities for the coach to make his or her "mark." One successful intervention in a situation that previously seemed impossible can help establish a reputation that is valuable, indeed. Organizations are willing to pay for help that they cannot provide from within. The ability to break a logjam is the coach's *inimitable competitive advantage*. This is why they will call you back.

Hypnosis and Communication

A single accepted definition of hypnosis has, so far, proved elusive.
—Lynn & Rhue, 1991

At first, the relationship between hypnosis and business communication may seem mysterious, and it requires some explanation. How could trance be used in corporations? The answer is found in an understanding of hypnosis; what it is and how it works in its broadest sense.

Hypnosis has a long and storied history and it has been practiced by shamans and stage performers over many years. Mysterious figures used trance states to cause witless victims to do strange and embarrassing things. It is these types of images that have contributed toward hypnosis being misunderstood by the public.

There are several ways to define and understand hypnosis, both with and without obvious trance states. Single-factor theories describe hypnosis as a "state." One view is that we are always in and out of trance, or that we are always in one kind of trance state or another, that life consists of a continuous series of overlapping and changing trance states. This view was captured by the late Sidney Jourard:

> We begin life with the world presenting itself to us as it is. Someone— our parents, teachers, analysts—hypnotize us to "see" the world and construe it in the "right" way. These others label the world, attach names, and give voices to the beings and events in it, so that thereafter, we cannot read the world in any other language or hear it saying other things to us.
>
> The task is to break the hypnotic spell, so that we become undeaf, unblind, and multilingual, thereby letting the world speak to us in new voices and write all its possible meanings in the book of our existence.
>
> Be careful in your choice of hypnotists.

In this view, hypnosis represents the larger trance states that we live in, the ones that define and shape our reality, the fish's water, and the bird's air. This view is explored by the constructivists (and cognitive therapists, as well). We live the world of our own personal perceptions and are limited by the boundaries of that perceptual world— boundaries that we have put in place ourselves. Watzlawick, Bleavin, and Jackson's 1967 exploration of paradox in patterns of human communication led to several of the interventions described in this chapter, as well as a basis for some of what cognitive psychotherapists and systems therapists do in their therapy offices. Milton Erickson spent fifty years exploring the ways that hypnosis could be used to communicate, and Jay Haley (1967, 1986) and others (Gordon & Meyers-Anderson, 1981; O'Hanlon, 1987) have documented his complex legacy in detail. There are other theories of hypnosis, referred to as "Socio-Cognitive" (Lynn & Rhue, 1991) that are contextual and social in nature. Coaches are well advised to do their homework in this literature, as it is difficult to describe (especially in a brief chapter), and the necessary patterns begin to take hold only when one samples several of the available sources over a period of time. The readings are fascinating and well worth the time. Examples are listed at the end of this chapter.

Principles and Attitudes

The hypnosis literature contains a variety of useful viewpoints for coaches. Several come from observations of Milton Erickson (Haley, 1986; O'Hanlon, 1987). Some of these ideas can be found in the book *Change* by Watzlawick, Weakland, and Fisch (1974). For example:

1. Human change is nonlinear. The present does not directly lead to the future, and efforts to direct change in a linear way are doomed to failure. The past did not directly lead to the present situation, and efforts to explore the past (as a vehicle for change) are futile. Paradox is at least as likely to prevail as sensible logic. Study the patterns if you want to understand how to change.

2. It is impossible to not communicate. All behavior is communication (Watzlawick et al., 1967). Many ways to communicate do not involve talking or talking about "the problem."

3. People have (within them) what they need to evolve, to change, and to improve. It is rarely necessary to actually teach them anything but specific skills. They can figure the important things out for themselves in their own unique way. It is more important to study a person's ways than to try to teach them something. Start from your client's point of view. The way that someone already does things is the path to growth or change. Study, in particular, the ways that people stay the same and to keep things the same, even as they declare the need to change. How do they do it? Most limitations are systematically self-imposed.

4. It is often easier to influence through implication than injunction. People listen hard for the implications of things and are curious about them, even when they don't realize they are doing so. They are also more open to implication than injunction. People like to figure things out for themselves and don't like to be told what to do.

5. More of the same will not produce a new result. (*Plus ça change, plus c'est la même chose.*) You cannot keep doing the same thing and expect to change. Effective solutions are often "strange" ones. They are also often uncomfortable to initiate. The only solution to difficult problems is often of a "second-order" nature; that is, the solution changes the rules of the system.

6. The map is not the territory. Things are not the way we explain them, nor are they the way that they seem. The explanation is not the reality.

7. The more flexible person gets her way. It is inflexibility that constrains us, not simply a lack of information, or lack of skill, or bad habit. All of those problems can be resolved if we can be flexible and persistent. Encourage and support more choice rather than less. Offer choices to people as often as possible, even when the choices are somewhat illusory. Most parents understand how to do this with their children: "Would you like to take out the trash first, or would you rather pick up your room?" is an example. This is called the "illusion of alternatives." People respond well to the perception of choice, even if the choices aren't so hot.

Several of these ideas eventually led to what business people have come to refer to as "out-of-the-box thinking."

Hypnosis Without (Obvious) Trance

A view of hypnosis that is limited to trance is of little use to an executive coach, and much of the work of post-trance thinkers is complex enough to be problematic. But there is a way to define hypnosis that makes it extremely useful to business coaches. Much of what hypnosis has to offer coaches has this definition in common: *Hypnosis is communication that bypasses critical-analytic thought.* We use hypnotic communication when we influence each other without making a direct request. There are many ways to do this, and some people devise ways to influence without realizing it. You may know someone who naively does this—a favorite teacher, an uncle, your mother, or even a local community leader. Somehow these people are influential, and you can't quite put your finger on why that is.

Some "Practical Magic"

Here are some techniques that come from the world of non-trance hypnosis. Most of them derive from multiple sources, and when a single source is known, it has been cited. Those sources can be found in the readings at the end of the chapter. (Many of these ideas came from a lecture by Paul Watzlawick at the San Francisco Academy of Hypnosis in February of 1988.) People who make their living in sales might find them familiar.

Indirect Suggestion

You can suggest things without directly suggesting them, and sidestep the resistance that accompanies injunction ("you do this"). Indirect suggestions involve a creative process, and there are many ways to do them. The key is to plant an idea or set up a situation that causes someone to do something without being specifically asked or told to do it.

For example, one way to make an indirect suggestion is to "wonder" about something. *Wonder* is a strange and powerful word. It tends to predict the future in a positive way and seems to direct energy and an open mind to the effort. It opens the door to possibilities. *"I wonder what would happen if we didn't go to market by the 30th?"* is entirely different from "We need to get to market by the 30th." "I wonder what it would take to develop a new product to do this?" "I wonder how we could get to know someone inside the Acme Company?" "I wonder how you establish contact in a country like Viet Nam?" These are not injunctions or even requests, but they plant an idea in a gentle, positive way. To plant an idea is to use indirect suggestion.

You can make indirect suggestions by saying *things to someone else.* Let's say that you want to suggest to your client that he enhance his appearance in the business setting. Instead of saying it directly to your client ("You dress poorly and should dress differently") and creating resistance or resentment, you could (carefully) say it to someone else while your client is present. "If my client weren't listening, I would tell you that he would be a lot better off if he wore a white shirt when he has marketing meetings. I think people would take him much more seriously." While this is certainly a "tricky" way to communicate, when done skillfully it can become a powerful way to say things that could not be spoken directly.

Similarly, you can make your messages more powerful by pre-empting them; that is, prefacing them with information that makes them paradoxically seem more important. For example, "You know, I'm really not supposed to tell you this, but . . ." is a way to make your message very powerful by indirect suggestion. Another way to pre-empt is to begin your message with "I know that this is going to sound kind of stupid, but. . . ." Yet another way to say something by not saying it is to start out with "If you tell anyone I said this, I'll deny it, but. . . ."

You can also create a "straw man" of the possible resistance by beginning your suggestion with "I don't know, the thing that you want would require an awful lot of work. . . ." The possibility of extra work is the straw man, easily knocked over by your client who responds, "I don't mind work! I like hard work." You can substitute many other desirables for the word "work" in the equation, such as: effort, time, attention, listening skills, or money.

You can use comparisons to your advantage. For example, you can offer that "A lot of people don't seem to understand this next part . . ." (you've suggested that it is difficult or complex and further, that an average person can't understand it). This challenges many people to focus their attention and to work hard to get your message. You can also use the indirect effect of comparisons in the following way. Choose a kind of client who is attractive to your current client. Then you can say, "You know, I once worked with a client who was a (insert "Rhodes Scholar," for example), and she picked up on this concept right away. You wouldn't believe how hard she worked at improving." Conversely, you can choose a kind of a client who might be unattractive to your client and say, "I once worked with a _____ (prostitute, drug addict, drug dealer, etc.) when I was working as a psychologist, and he never seemed to be able to get better at this." Your present client, not wanting to be grouped with this unattractive kind of person then works hard to be different. You have set up an indirect suggestion to work hard at something without actually having asked for it.

Specific Language

Certain words have the power of implication built into them and should be used carefully or should be avoided. For example, the word *try* has failure built into it. Failure is implied in the word itself. When you "try" to do something, you are not saying that you will get it done. Rather, you are saying that you will make efforts and attempts that will likely fall short. *Can't* is another such word, as it implies that something is impossible. Often a more accurate word is "won't." Won't carries entirely different connotations, and the connotations are powerful and instructive. *Yet* is a very useful and powerful word, as it can be applied to action that is desired in the future: *"You haven't learned how to do this yet"* is a way of planting the suggestion that you will learn how to do it in the future. *Right now* is a similar phrase, and it can be used in much the same way: *"You aren't putting in the time right now."* *As* is another such word, and it implies that you can do something. *"Notice how things change as you learn how to listen to your team members."* The word *need* is a strange and powerful one, in that it implies necessity, even when people don't think they are using it that way: *"I need more time and resources"* implies that you could not exist without them and that it would be disastrous if you didn't get them. It is entirely different to say, "If I can get enough time and resources we could finish the project in 90 days. Without them it would take much longer and would result in significant market losses."

The power of these specific words is in their shared implication. They say one thing (in common usage) and they imply other things. Sometimes the implication is clear and shared, and sometimes it is not. But it is always useful to observe the use of such words, to calibrate one's own usage, and to align one's implications with one's goals. Listen to clients and help them master these kinds of words and use them powerfully yourself. Pay attention to implication.

Specific Non-Trance Hypnotic Communications

There are many ways that language can be used hypnotically (outside of explicit trance states). The first principle is to be careful with positive and negative linguistic formulations; that is, use positive words and sentence structures rather than negative ones. For example, think about what happens when you hear "Don't think of a rooster." You have to do the very thing that you are being asked *not* to do. You must think of a rooster to try to accomplish the requested task of not thinking of a rooster. It is automatic and unavoidable. Instead, offer the following: "Think of a big green elephant." When you think of the elephant (which is explicit and interesting enough to capture almost anyone's interest) you have to let go of the rooster image. It gets replaced, using a positive sentence structure. The mind is not able to directly respond to negatives. When you use them you complicate things and make action much more difficult. It is analogous to trying hard to relax.

Storytelling

Effective leaders and persuasive people have always used stories to make their points. This is because we use a different part of the brain to process a story than the part we use when trying to follow linear instructions. Stories are full of indirect suggestion, and the plot of a story is often one great indirect or direct suggestion about how life really works. You can make all kinds of suggestions through a good story. Examples are the same way, as they tell people how things work along with what is expected of them. Remember the powerful motivating stories you hear. Write them down and memorize them. If you are a good storyteller, take advantage of this asset. If not, learn how to tell stories. Create opportunities to practice. Make up your own stories, formulated especially for this client or that one. Use previous clients (while managing confidentiality) for relevant anecdotes. Integrate one or two important indirect suggestions (along with an appropriate outcome) into each story. Be careful that you don't repeat your stories, and never explain them. Let your clients figure out what they mean from their own point of view. In fact, ambiguity is often the most powerful way to react to the indirect suggestions that you plant. Clients often feel compelled to fill in the blanks in the most important ways. Sometimes clients fill in the blanks in wonderful ways that would never occur to you.

Often people can "hear" a message in a story that they cannot hear in any other form. When you tell a story about how someone accomplished something, you can access the principle that goes like this: "If it is possible for someone in the world, it is possible for me."

Imagery

Be careful how you imagine yourself to be, because you might become that way.

—Sidney Jourard (Jourard & Landsman, 1980)

We process images differently from other kinds of language forms. Images get us. They are powerful and can really move us when well presented. Notice the difference between the *taste of butterscotch* and a recipe. There's no comparison. The taste always wins. Pepper your language and coaching with sharp, compelling images. Exhort your clients to imagine themselves doing something or experiencing something. Help them imagine what it is like to learn something new or to accomplish something difficult or to complete something satisfying. Help them *feel* what it is like to be in that position. Use images and use the word *imagine* regularly.

Find out how your client handles images. Some people have a stilted imaginary life. Help them grow their imagination, and remember, when the imagination and reality come into conflict, the imagination always wins. This is true when people use their imagination to hurt as well as help themselves. Beware, however, that a small number of people don't seem able to make pictures in their minds. With these clients, help them use images in whatever form is comfortable. Some people can create images without making mental pictures. They somehow use a "sense of things" to accomplish the same tasks that others might do with mental pictures. Begin with an imagery assessment. Discern how they presently use images and what form the images take.

Here are some specific examples of the ways that imagery can be used. Many come from Rian McMullin's 1986 reference listed at the end of the chapter. These are examples of types of images you can help your client develop as resources for growth and change.

Coping or Mastery Images.   Use images that help a person cope with a difficult situation or task. For example, you can help your client create an image of himself or herself successfully asking for a raise or a new assignment. These images can be large, general images or small detailed ones. The detailed images tend to help when one is learning a new skill or attempting something novel.

Modeling Images.   Your client can imagine someone who is already excellent at a desired task or skill. He or she can go through the steps (in his or her imagination) as if he or she were the skilled person. This can serve as a transitional learning experience, making it easier to actually do the new thing when the time comes. "Imagine Bill Smith asking this client for business. See what it feels like to do it if you were him."

Idealized Future Images.   Help your clients imagine how they would like life to be in five years. Where do they want to be, how do they want to be, what do they want to be doing, and how do they want to feel? Help them to use their imagination to *experience* what the future can be like. This can make things more real and can make them more accessible.

A variation on this approach is to imagine yourself at the age of 85, looking back on your life. Is there anything to be learned about the current situation?

Leveling Images.   Use this approach when it is difficult for your client to confront or deal with someone else. Public speakers use this technique to successfully get through (or over) their fears. "Imagine your audience in their underwear." is the classic image used for this purpose. "Imagine your boss in his gardening clothes or in his robe, when he has just gotten out of bed." "Imagine your client with you at a baseball game or at a picnic with all of the kids." Then go through the future interaction, and do it successfully. Eventually move to an image that is exactly like the one you have to confront.

Corrective Images.   You can use this kind of imagery to undo and redo mistakes that you have made. Go back over the same situation and do it again. This time change something significant and see what difference it makes.

Worst-Case Scenarios.   When faced with a difficult or intimidating situation help your clients develop an image of the absolute worst possible scenario. Help them decide whether or not they could stand that outcome (they always can, even though it might involve a very undesirable situation). Then back off a couple of notches or levels and determine what the realistic worst-case might be. Decide how bad that would be and whether some preparation must be made for it. Then go ahead and develop a plan for success, knowing that you can handle any imaginable result.

Ultimate Consequences Images.   Imagine, in detail, what the outcome might be if you actually do what you are now considering. Imagine what might happen if you take another path. "Imagine what a day or a week would be like if you took that new job with the start-up company." Imagine what might happen if you are able to successfully learn what you are striving to learn. What are the benefits? How will life change?

Cathartic Images.   Imagine blowing up at your boss or your team. Just let yourself go in your imagination. See what this is like. Then you won't have to experience it in real life.

Empathy Images.   Imagine yourself in the shoes of an important other. Go through a situation in their position and allow yourself to think what they might be thinking and feel what they might be feeling. This is a great way to learn how to read people better and to become a more cooperative leader or better sales person.

Security Images.   Develop and practice images that make your client feel safe. "Imagine that you are in your back yard, at home, on a warm, sunny day." "Imagine yourself in the presence of someone you trust, someone who makes you feel safe." They can then keep those images around for times when things get difficult.

Metaphor

We also process metaphor differently from "regular" day-to-day language. Metaphors help us to understand and to change. They give us another way to view the same old problems and situations, and they encourage us to engage our intuition. Some of what constitutes great literature is metaphor, as it has no intrinsic meaning or purpose other than to instruct us in larger ways. Metaphors make us think and cause us to notice things that we had never noticed before.

Alice in Wonderland, Kafka's *The Trial,* and Plato's *Allegory of the Cave* are examples. Much biblical material is metaphor. Religious lessons are frequently taught this way. Metaphors are available from Judaism and Christianity, from Asia and India, from science fiction and literature, and even from children's stories. Sheldon Kopp (1971) explored the use of metaphor in his book *Metaphors from a Psychotherapist Guru,* and defined a metaphor as

> a way of speaking in which one thing is expressed in terms of another, whereby this bringing together throws new light on the character of what is being described. (p. 17)

Kopp also quoted Paracelsus by observing that

> . . . the guru should not tell "the naked truth. He should use images, allegories, figures, wonderous (sic) speech, or other hidden roundabout ways." (p. 19)

David Gordon, in a metaphor "cookbook" (1978), makes the point that "Each therapy or system of psychology, then, has as one of its basic constituents a set of metaphors. . ." (p. 8).

Metaphors allow the storyteller to get away with things he or she could never tell us directly. For example, let's say that you are working with someone who dresses inappropriately for the business situation.

The way that she presents herself is ineffective, and some relatively simple changes might cause her to be taken more seriously. It might be difficult to give this feedback directly or it might be hard for the client to hear it in a way that motivates or mobilizes change. This is a time to consider a metaphor or anecdote. Create an example of someone who looked or presented herself in a way that didn't work. For example, Richard Nixon lost debates, and perhaps a presidential election, because his makeup and presentation were poorly suited for television cameras. Often the metaphoric message will come across loud and clear and in a way that won't create hurt feelings or resistance. A coach can always use a metaphor or story first, observe its impact, and give direct feedback later, if necessary.

Metaphors also encourage risk-taking without actually asking for it. Remember how you have felt more daring after having heard a story or gone to a movie with an inspiring message.

Humans are always trying to make meaning out of things. With a metaphor, you invite the listener to make sense of what's in it, to pass it through a personal filter and to find the logic and the "moral." Great teachers, leaders, coaches, and motivators have always known this, so they build their repertoires of metaphors and anecdotes and use them. Moderation is important, of course, and metaphors should be used judiciously. Too much of a good thing can turn a wise teacher into an annoying irrelevancy. "When I ask you to take an aspirin, please don't take the whole bottle," the old golf teacher, Harvey Penick, used to say (Penick & Shrake, 1992).

Modeling

As a coach, turn yourself into a model of positive attitude and action. Do this in your own way, with your own style. As a consultant and "expert," others will read you to determine how things are going. If you are confident and at ease with yourself and the process of coaching, problem solving, and growth, they will read this confidence and feel assured. It is as if you create a small, positive trance state, a set of assumptions about how things are and will be in the future. You don't need to *say* that you know what you are doing, you don't need to *say* that things are going to be all right, you simply behave as if that were true. This creates a powerful suggestion. You are then in a position to "predict the future" by stating that goals will most likely be accomplished. You can state them almost casually. "Oh, I imagine you will learn this quite quickly," you assert with calm self-assurance.

This requires excellence on your part. You must do your homework, learn and know your stuff, and make yourself do the right thing.

When you lack a certain skill, you must go out and learn it. In this way, you can develop the experience necessary to speak with authority and confidence.

Reframing

Much meaning is derived from context. Standing in your underwear means nothing if you are home, alone. But it has a very different meaning if you are at a corporate cocktail party. Watzlawick et al. (1974, p. 95) define reframing in a technical way:

> To reframe, then, means to change the conceptual and/or emotional setting or viewpoint in relation to which a situation is experienced and to place it in another frame which fits the "facts" of the same concrete situation equally well or even better, and thereby changes its entire meaning.

Coaches can help clients shift contexts to derive new and important meanings. The way we feel is determined by the way that we look at things, how we ascribe meanings, and what we see as the context. It all depends on how we look at it. We can help our clients flex up and change the context. We can offer an alternative context, as no context is completely fixed.

There is a great example from the athletic coaching arena, where a coach seems very hard on one specific player. She yells at that player and notes every error, following it with corrective action that sometimes seems punitive. The player finally confronts the coach. "Why do you hate me," she asks? "I know I'm not a great player, but I work hard, and try to do everything you say."

"I don't hate you," replies the coach. "I yell at you because you have potential. Don't worry when I yell at you. Worry if I stop yelling at you."

Ambiguity

Although you may value clarity and precision in your communications, it is not always the most effective way to coach. Intentional ambiguity has its uses, because humans tend to fill in the gaps. When presented with ambiguous stimuli or confronted with words or situations that have multiple meanings, humans are naturally inclined to complete the picture, to connect the dots, to make sense out of abstractions, and to create personal meaning in unclear situations. Clear and complete communications have their advantages, but ambiguous ones require the listener to work, to sort things out, to think.

Sometimes this is exactly what the speaker wants and what the listener needs. Sometimes it's a good idea to let the listener chew on things himself or herself for a while. Often clients will fill the gaps in ways that will surprise. Sometimes clients bring in information that neither the coach nor the client would expect, had they approached the problem from a linear point of view. This is not a recommendation to make things intentionally vague, which can be annoying to the learner, but occasional incompleteness and ambiguity can be powerful.

The "As-If"

In order to learn something new or difficult we have to put ourselves into a position to do the learning. You cannot learn to ride a bicycle unless you are on the bike and moving. This is close to actually riding it. But how do you make the transition from being a non-rider to being a rider? The key is in the *as-if*. You have to behave as if you already know how to do it. This is true in real (grown-up) life, as well. You can't make a sale as a real-estate agent unless you are out there, showing homes and writing up offers. You act like a real-estate agent before you actually are one. This is how you become one. You cannot become a writer unless you write. The as-if is exemplified in the following story told by Paul Watzlawick:

> Three children came to visit their father on his deathbed. Just before he died, he told them that he had divided his estate in the following way:
>   Child #1 gets 1/2 of his worldly goods.
>   Child #2 gets 1/3 of his worldly goods.
>   Child #3 gets 1/9 of his worldly goods.
>   The father then gasps and dies. When the children inventory the father's things, they discover that all he had left when he died were 17 horses. The horses are worthless as meat, so they couldn't "split" a horse. They began to argue, and then to fight, when an old man rode by on his horse. "What's the matter?" he inquired. When the three told him of their plight, he responded, "That's easy to remedy. Here, use my horse." They did, and now having 18 horses, they awarded half to the first child (9), one-third to the second child (6), and one ninth to the third child (2). That added up to 17 horses, so the old man got back on his horse, which was left over, and rode away.

Final Thoughts

The point of all of this, of course, is that there are many ways to "skin a cat," and that direct, linear presentation of recommendations for change are not always the most effective or powerful. A good coach must develop a wide repertoire of influencing strategies, and must know that just because a client shows up to meet with you, it doesn't necessarily follow that he or she is ready, willing, and able to change. Most people resist direct injunctions (such as "You should do this; you must be different than you are.").

These techniques are called "hypnotic" because they influence in a way that bypasses critical thinking, not because they make use of obvious hypnotic trance states.

Many of the ideas in this chapter are creative and some are mildly manipulative. Most are particularly non-linear. They do not move in a direct fashion from point A to point B. They must be used carefully, with respect for your coaching client. Take care to ensure that no one ends up feeling foolish as a result of your interventions, and make sure that you have your clients' best interests in mind.

These "hypnotic" approaches require a special rapport, and they help to build rapport, as well. Take care of that rapport, as it is the glue that binds your client to you and to the change process.

And one more thing: loosen up and have a little fun together. Here's Paul Watzlawick again with the title of his 1983 book:

The Situation Is Hopeless, But Not Serious.

References

Gordon, D. (1978). *Therapeutic metaphors: Helping others through the looking glass.* Cupertino, CA: META Publications.

Gordon, D., & Meyers-Anderson. (1981). *Phoenix: Therapeutic patterns of Milton H. Erickson.* Cupertino, CA: META Publications.

Haley, J. (1967). *Advanced techniques of hypnosis and therapy. Selected papers of Milton H. Erickson, M.D.* New York: Grune & Stratton.

Haley, J. (1986). *Uncommon therapy: The psychiatric techniques of Milton H. Erickson, M.D.* New York: Norton.

Jourard, S., & Landesman, T. (1980). *Healthy personality* (4th ed.). New York: Macmillan.

Kopp, S. (1971). *Metaphors from a psychotherapist guru.* Palo Alto, CA: Science & Behavior Books.

Lynn, S., & Rhue, J. (1991). *Theories of hypnosis: Current models and perspectives.* New York: Guilford.

O'Hanlon, W. H. (1987). *Taproots: Underlying principles of Milton Erickson's therapy and hypnosis.* New York: Norton.

Penick, H., & Shrake, B. (1992). *Harvey Penick's little red book: Lessons and teachings from a lifetime in golf.* New York: Simon & Schuster.

Watzlawick, P., Beavin, J., & Jackson, D. (1967). *Pragmatics of human Communication.* New York: Norton.

Watzlawick, P., Weakland, J., & Fisch, R. (1974). *Change: Principles of problem formation and problem resolution.* New York: Norton.

Watzlawick, P. (1983). *The situation is hopeless, but not serious.* New York: Norton.

Recommended Readings

Camus, A. (1957). *The fall.* New York: Knopf.

Hoorwitz, A. (1989). *Hypnotic methods in nonhypnotic therapies.* New York: Irvington.

Lankton, S. (1980). *Practical magic: A translation of basic neuro-linguistic programming into clinical psychotherapy.* Cupertino, CA: META Publications.

McMullin, R. E. (1986). *Handbook of cognitive therapy techniques.* New York: Norton.

Watzlawick, P. *Ultrasolutions: How to fail most successfully.* New York: Norton.

CHAPTER

Social Psychology and Coaching

How could we have been so stupid?
                    —John F. Kennedy (after the Bay of Pigs invasion,
                                        quoted in Janis, 1971)

Social psychology is the study of social influence—how people influence each other. Although we like to think of ourselves as autonomous and independent, humans don't operate in a social vacuum. The real and imagined thoughts and behavior of people around us have a powerful impact.

The topics of social psychology are directly relevant to executive coaching and the process of interpersonal influence. This chapter describes how coaches can effectively learn social psychology's lessons and apply them to coaching. Social psychology has contributed much to what we know about leadership, persuasion, conformity, influence, and coercion, and has added groupthink, field theory, and cognitive dissonance to the management consulting vocabulary.

A Brief History

If I were required to name the one person who has had the greatest impact on the field, it would have to be Adolf Hitler.
                    —Doren Cartwright (1997, p. 84)

Social psychology is a young science, and its origins are in events related to the Second World War. Most of the early studies were

136

motivated by a desire to avoid another fascist catastrophe, and people who escaped the horrors of Nazi Germany conducted them. The father of social psychology, Kurt Lewin, came to the United States in 1933, the same year that Hitler became Chancellor. Lewin used his research skills to study the consumer behavior of American women to help promote the success of rationing. His own mother and most of his relatives had perished in a concentration camp. Lewin's protégés studied autocratic and democratic leadership and the authoritarian personality, and they generally came to the happy conclusion that democracy was the most effective way to run an organization. However, Stanley Milgram's controversial experiments demonstrated that the vast majority of people would follow simple orders to administer strong electric shocks to others (Milgram, 1963). Solomon Asch showed that people can usually be convinced to conform to the opinion of others, even when it is clear that that opinion is wrong (Asch, 1951). Philip Zimbardo and his associates (Haney, Banks, & Zimbardo, 1973) created a fake prison in the basement of the Stanford psychology department and, in an experiment that got completely out of control, ended up with prison guards (who had been chosen at random) who behaved quite brutally. Social psychologists, like many people in the 1950s, had figured that there was something faulty about the German character, but they learned from laboratory studies that most of us could fall prey to the worst kinds of human impulses if the conditions were just right (or just wrong). Gordon Allport (1954) and Gunnar Myrdal (1944) undertook a comprehensive description of American racial attitudes and prejudices. Robert Rosenthal and Lenore Jacobson (1968) unearthed the "self-fulfilling prophecy" and showed that teachers can virtually *create* performance levels in children based upon the teacher's predisposed expectations for those children, even when expectations were randomly assigned. David Rosenhan (1973) took a group of mentally healthy researchers into a mental hospital, got them admitted, and then couldn't convince authorities that they really weren't mental patients. One researcher was stuck there for seven weeks, because hospital staff interpreted everything he did as confirmation of his mentally ill status.

The Power of the Situation

The main finding that ties together all of these strange and interesting forays into conformity, obedience, and social perception is that *situations* are much more powerful than character, even though we rarely acknowledge that fact. Social psychologists refer to this as the "fundamental attribution error." Humans tend to *overestimate* the importance and power of personality and *underestimate* the influence of the social situation. We attribute things to internal forces such as personality or character instead of social forces in our surroundings. But Milgram's subjects could be made to shock others, Asch's subjects could be made to endorse the obviously wrong opinions of others, and Zimbardo's students could be turned into brutal prison guards by the power of the social situation. Social psychology teaches us that we must pay attention to social influences if we are to effectively lead, manage, and change. Coaches must remember the power of the environment, as clients and the bosses of clients are likely to focus too much attention on personality and character. Often the reasons for the success or failure of a client can be found in the way that the culture or situation is structured.

Advertising professionals and organizational consultants use the lessons of social psychology seamlessly and regularly. This chapter applies some of those important lessons to executive coaching.

Field Theory

One of Kurt Lewin's many contributions is "field theory," and it represents a way to help coaching clients cope with the social environment. Instead of focusing on personal qualities or shortcomings, it forces coaches to pay attention to the immediate social surroundings and pressures.

Lewin's basic theory was that behavior is a function of the person and the environment, or $B = f(P, E)$ as he stated it. In Lewin's view, action and research were one in the same, and he called change projects "action research." Each change project is conducted as a research project. The usual research steps are taken, and this is a great way for coaches to work with executives. The steps are as follows (Krupp et al., 1986):

1. **Identify the problem.** For coaches, this means identifying one discrete aspect of a client's behavior or skill set to work on. It is best to choose a "problem" that can be altered or "fixed," especially at first.
2. **Gather data and analyze it.** Feed data back to the client.
3. **Make an action plan.** Create a plan that has a high likelihood of success. Get "buy-in" from all parties involved.
4. **Implement your plan.** Take action; put the plan into effect.
5. **Collect more data, monitor the situation to evaluate how you are doing.**

6. **Problem redefinition.** Using the data you have collected, make necessary changes in your definition of the problem. Data are used throughout the process to track progress and change or adapt the approach. The question is always: "How are we doing, and how do we need to adjust our focus?" The process is cyclical, and it is important, at the onset, to view the cycling as "normal" and expectable, not as a failure.

Lewin saw things systemically, and believed that in order to change, an existing system must be "unfrozen, moved, and refrozen," and that involves the total picture of influences. Lewin invented the "force-field analysis" (1951), an assessment of all the relevant current social forces. The force-field analysis works like this: Draw a line down the middle of a page of paper. This line represents the present situation and its balance between the forces of change and the forces that keep things the same. On one side of the line, draw arrows to represent the forces for change ("driving forces"). On the other side of the line draw arrows that represent the forces pushing to keep things from changing ("restraining forces"). This diagram tells you where you need to go to work. The forces for change must be strengthened and the restraining forces must be weakened. Lewin observed that it is often easier to decrease the restraining forces than to strengthen the facilitating forces, and the process of weakening the restraining forces is more likely to reduce tension, while a strengthening of enabling forces can increase tension, which makes everything harder (Segal, 1997).

For example, let's say that an executive wants to become a partner in her firm. Table 8.1 illustrates how Lewin's force field analysis is applied.

Once you have completed this analysis it is easier to construct an action plan. Forces for change must be strengthened and forces that tend to maintain the status quo must be weakened or eliminated.

It must be noted that the force-field analysis is not simply a rehashing of the standard problem-solving steps, in that it focuses on the *current* equilibrium situation, and the *present* forces for and against change.

An alternative way (Silberman, 1986) to use a force field analysis is to simply list the following:

1. The situation as it is now.
2. The situation as I want it to be.
3. What will keep the situation from changing?
4. What is the most powerful obstacle?
5. Action steps.
6. Resources needed to make the change.

TABLE 8.1. Lewin's force-field analysis: An example

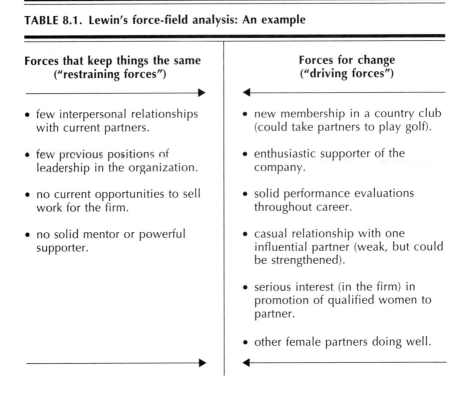

Forces that keep things the same ("restraining forces")	Forces for change ("driving forces")
• few interpersonal relationships with current partners.	• new membership in a country club (could take partners to play golf).
• few previous positions of leadership in the organization.	• enthusiastic supporter of the company.
• no current opportunities to sell work for the firm.	• solid performance evaluations throughout career.
• no solid mentor or powerful supporter.	• casual relationship with one influential partner (weak, but could be strengthened).
	• serious interest (in the firm) in promotion of qualified women to partner.
	• other female partners doing well.

Cognitive Dissonance

A second important social psychology contribution was by Leon Festinger (1957), and it is called "Cognitive Dissonance Theory." This theory states that humans have a need to feel consistent. We are comfortable when our thoughts, feelings, and behaviors are aligned, and we are uncomfortable when they are in dissonance. When uncomfortable, we strive to resolve the inconsistency, either by changing behavior, or, more typically, changing what we tell ourselves about the situation or the behavior. The classic example in social psychology research is from a study by Knox and Inkster, done in 1968. They found that bettors at a racetrack were more confident in their horse *after* they had placed their bet than before. They simply had to make their thinking consistent with the action they had already taken.

Thus, you will be in a dissonant state when you snap at an employee if you generally think of yourself as a "nice" person. How could these two apparently conflicting things both be true? The tension created by cognitive dissonance must be resolved in some way, and if the event has already occurred, you can't go back and erase it, so you tell yourself something that makes it all add up correctly: That employee deserved it. He did something so thoughtless that he required being snapped at. Or, you could tell yourself that, while you are actually a very nice person, you are under an enormous amount of stress right now, and anyone would snap under present conditions. But you must do something to resolve the dissonance between what you think of yourself and your behavior. There are actually many ways to do this. For example, you could discredit a source of conflicting information, you could view problematic information from a different point of view, or you could use selective recall and leave out discordant aspects of the information. But you must do *something*, and what you do is often irrational or illogical. As Cialdini puts it, "we all fool ourselves from time to time in order to keep our thoughts and beliefs consistent with what we have already done or decided" (1985, p. 53).

Social psychologists also point out that there are two very basic human motives that often invite cognitive dissonance: 1) the need to possess an accurate view of things (the need to be right) and 2) the need to feel good about ourselves. Although these two motives are sometimes naturally or easily satisfied, they often cause conflict. Sometimes, if we view things accurately, we must acknowledge that we've behaved poorly or stupidly or, at least, suboptimally.

There are two divergent ways to deal with this problem (Aronson, Wilson, & Akert, 1997). The first is called the "self-esteem approach." Using this approach, we distort things in order to feel right and feel good about ourselves. The desire to feel right is a powerful motive for humans. In fact, many people would rather feel "right" than happy. Sometimes this requires that we justify previous behavior, even though, if we thought about it, we would realize how silly it really was. Sometimes it means that we have to go on making the same old poor choices in order to justify decisions we made before. Sometimes it means that we must sing the praises of something we have suffered for in the past, like a fraternity or sorority that was difficult to break into. For example, companies have been known to continue to use poor software long after it has become clear that the software was no good, simply to justify the decision-maker's judgment. If you switch, you must acknowledge that your original decision was wrong, so you trudge along, trying to find something good about the situation and punishing those who criticize it. This is often the reason that people can't change. If they did, they would be acknowledging that they had been wrong before. We often cling to our views way too long in order to protect our self-esteem and view of ourselves.

This phenomenon causes us to rationalize and justify. Social psychologists have discovered some unexpected patterns in this area. For example, they found that if you want someone to like you, it is better to get them to do something for you rather than to do something for them. Ben Franklin actually seems to have stumbled on this "trick" long before social psychology. He referred to it in eighteenth century writings (Aronson et al., 1997, p. 206). This seems odd at first, but cognitive dissonance provides the explanation. After someone has done something for you he or she has to be able to explain that behavior. One way to make it all fit is for them to decide that they like you, that you are worth it. Otherwise, why would they have done something for you in the first place?

The second approach is called "social cognition" and it comes from the drive we have toward accurate social perception. Most humans possess the desire to get things right, to figure out what is true. We intuitively understand what is at stake, and we try hard to understand the social world around us. But we theorize imperfectly, and social psychologists have described several classic paths to self-delusion. This becomes a problem when we get stuck on being "right," and being right becomes more important than being effective. Remember: Many people would rather be "right" than happy. To them, at the time, it just seems better.

Schemas and the Effects of Expectation

Social psychologists refer to the theories that we use to understand everyday events as *schemas*, and these schemas are both useful and treacherous at the same time. They are cognitive simplifications in the form of thought-rules. We can't live without them, but they routinely trick us, and we resist changing them when new information conflicts.

For example, we see things based upon how we expect them to be. If we have an expectation in advance of an event, we perceive it in alignment with the expectation. If you are told that someone or something is positive and special, you are likely to perceive any ambiguities in a positive light. First impressions work this way. Your first impression of someone has a powerful impact on how you evaluate him or her in the future. Reputation works this way. A person's reputation precedes him or her and is a powerful influencer of how that person is perceived in the present moment. Recency also applies. Your most recent interaction with someone is also more powerful than your long-term opinion. The self-fulfilling prophecy is another example of a problematic human tendency. We treat people in line with what we already think of them, and they behave in alignment with expectations.

These judgmental heuristics are useful, as they allow us to avoid having to think through every step of a decision process hundreds of times each day. Here are some examples:

The Availability Heuristic

We use this shortcut when we make a judgment based upon how easily we can bring an example to mind. We tend to think something is more true if we can bring to mind a good picture of it. You might think that earthquakes are the most dangerous thing about life in San Francisco even though car wrecks kill far more people there. This is the reason that the drunk (in the joke) looks under the street lamp for his keys, even though he lost them across the street: "The light's better here!" he notes. It follows, then, that if you want to make a good point or you want your view to seem true to others, you would do well to paint a picture, use a metaphor, or connect it to something well known.

The Representative Heuristic

This mental device checks to see if a new piece of information matches information in a category and then assumes that the new information is like all the other cases in the category. For example, you are much more likely to be hired as a CEO if you look and act the way that people think "typical" CEOs do. That is why you sometimes get the advice to "dress like the people who already have the job you want."

Anchoring and Adjustment

This heuristic causes us to stick close to the first estimate of a situation. For example, in negotiations, the first offer or bid on the table is a powerful one, because it "anchors" all subsequent perceptions which must "adjust" from it. If the first offer is in the $500 range, it is very hard to move perceptions into the $5,000 range, even though others may actually be willing to pay $5,000. This phenomenon is also called "the dominance of first impressions," and it means that executives simply must get feedback about how they present themselves and must pay attention to the first impression that they make. A recent advertisement by the American Civil Liberties Union makes the disturbing point that Martin Luther King Jr. would have been "75 times more likely to be stopped by the police while driving" than Charles Manson.

This heuristic has many other implications. For example, if a real estate agent wants you to favor an $800,000 house, she might walk you through a more expensive home first and talk about million dollar homes in the neighborhood.

The Perseverance Effect

Numerous studies have documented the tendency for most of us to think in the same ways, over and over again, even when there is no benefit to the tried and true thought patterns. A simple story about this phenomenon, *Who Moved My Cheese?* (Johnson, 1998) sold millions of copies in the past several years. We think the same things in the same ways as a style, not because it is an effective way to process information. We even continue to think in the same way after receiving contradictory feedback. This is an area where a persuasive coach can really earn her fees. If you can bump a client out of an old, worn-out, cognitive rut, you will have made a significant contribution, indeed. People can rarely do this for themselves.

Lessons in Leadership

Social psychology has been interested in leadership since World War II, particularly in regard to the devastation caused by tyrants and dictators of that era. The first major studies in leadership and group dynamics demonstrated that, when compared to autocratic and laissez faire leadership, democratically led groups were superior. They resulted in higher productivity overall, less in-group conflict, more on-task behavior when the leader was absent, and more creativity (Lewin, Lippitt, & White, 1939). Humans clearly do better when they feel that they have a role in the decision-making.

Leadership research has often centered on the "great person theory," which wonders if great leaders possess certain personal qualities that enable them to excel. Not surprisingly, the fundamental attribution error applies here, too, in that no personality or character or intelligence factors have been consistently associated with great leaders. Leaders are only modestly more intelligent than non-leaders, only a little more charismatic, and not consistently more driven toward accumulation of power (Aronson et al., 1997). In a large study of American presidents, one hundred personal factors were matched with historical effectiveness, and only three factors stood out, only one of which was something that the person had influence over himself (Simonton,

1987, 1992). The factors associated with great leaders were height (tall is better), family-of-origin size (small is better), and number of books published before becoming president.

Contingency Theory

Of greater importance is the match between the leader and the situation. Some kinds of leaders are ideal for certain times, while others are a better fit during other conditions. Some situations call for a certain kind of bold charisma while others require cautious leadership and a focus on the details. Sometimes task-oriented leaders (those who tend to pay the most attention to getting the immediate job done) are best and at other times a relationship-oriented leader is better. Prospective leaders would be well advised to look carefully at situational demands to determine what kind of leadership to apply. Many people are simply not flexible enough to make the changes that a difficult situation requires. A coach might be able to guide a leader through a difficult period or even advise a change of leadership or organizational structure to take advantage of an executive's strengths and weaknesses.

Emotional Intelligence

Any modern discussion of coaching, leadership, and executive effectiveness must include the work of Daniel Goleman who points out that IQ and the usual technical ingredients are insufficient (Goleman, 1998a, p. 93).

> Every businessperson knows a story about a highly intelligent, highly skilled executive who was promoted into a leadership position only to fail at the job. And they also know a story about someone with solid— but not extraordinary—intellectual abilities and technical skills who was promoted into a similar position and then soared.

This body of work is mandatory reading for the executive coach. Goleman asserts that it is *Emotional Intelligence* (the "EQ") that makes or breaks leaders, that it is the "sine qua non of leadership," and that it is possible (albeit difficult) to learn the component skills. Goleman defines emotional intelligence as follows (1998b, p. 317):

> . . . the capacity for recognizing our own feelings and those of others, for motivating ourselves, and for managing emotions well in ourselves and in our relationships.

He claims that his research demonstrates that emotional intelligence is twice as important as IQ or technical skills. Intellectual skills and technical expertise are important, but they are only threshold skills. They get you in the door and onto the playing field. It is EQ that enables you to survive and excel. Goleman notes the results of a landmark study on top executives who were "derailed." The study was done at the Center for Creative Leadership in the 1980s and repeated in 1996. It found that the two main reasons that hot careers fizzled were rigidity and poor relationships.

The components of EQ are self-awareness, self-regulation, motivation, empathy, and social skills. These are all natural areas for coaches, and, in fact, Goleman specifically recommends coaching for those who want to enhance their emotional intelligence. Goleman also notes a coming crisis for American corporations and an opportunity for coaches: As IQ continues to rise in children, EQ is on the decline (1998b, p. 11). Coaches are often called on to help executives who have made a name for themselves through years of hard work in front of a computer screen and are now asked to manage or lead people. Goleman provides an "Emotional Competence Framework" for assessment of just such a person. (1998a, pp. 26–27).

Cooperation and Competition

There is a body of work in social psychology that strives to determine the best ways to enhance cooperation when it is appropriate. Competitive or aggressive reactions are sometimes called for, but more often than not, a potential win–win situation is completely missed because one person behaves competitively when a cooperative response would have been far better. When trust has not been established in human relations, people think in terms of a zero-sum game or condition. They figure that any piece of the pie that others get means one less piece for them. This is a condition of scarcity, meaning that there is not enough to go around for everyone. The win–win viewpoint is quite different, and it is predicated on the idea that if we communicate what we desire, there may be a happy fit between what you want and what I want; we might both be able to get much of what we each desire, or we may be able to create more of everything by working together. Such a happy outcome requires honest and open communication, as well as some level of trust.

Social psychologists have used a game called the "Prisoner's Dilemma" to test how people cooperate or compete (with competition referred to as "defection" in the literature). In this simulation two people are arrested and held for interrogation. Each is told that if he will testify against his partner, he himself will be set free. A scoring system is set up to highly reward cooperation (i.e., not ratting on the partner); to reward ratting modestly; and to put oneself in a dangerous position if one cooperates but one's partner rats on him. It is called a "mixed-motive" situation, because participants must decide between total self-interest, trust in others, and benevolent interest in the well-being of others. In this game it is risky (but potentially rewarding) to look out for someone else. Hundreds of studies indicate that people are inclined to become locked into an escalating series of competitive moves, especially if they feel that their trust has once been violated or that they have been taken advantage of. Trust is easy to damage, and it requires ongoing attention. One cannot simply assume that existing trust is stable. It must be monitored and nourished.

It turns out that a strategy called "tit-for-tat" is ideal when tested against all comers in a computerized Prisoner's Dilemma tournament (Axelrod, 1984). In this strategy, the player begins with a cooperative response and then simply chooses the same option that the other player chose on the previous move. This begins by communicating a willingness to cooperate along with an unwillingness to be taken advantage of. Most people probably respect such a strategy, a cooperative stance by someone who is not willing to be exploited.

In any case, the social environment must be examined along the cooperative-competitive spectrum. Competition is best for some things, but cooperation is essential for others.

Interpersonal Influence

Robert Cialdini reviewed the available literature on interpersonal influence and conducted his own participant observation studies in which he and collaborators studied influence in real life situations (Cialdini, 1985). Here is what he learned.

Reasons

First of all, if you want someone to do something for you, it is best to supply a "reason." The reason need not be particularly impressive or compelling. In fact, there is research evidence that the simple inclusion of the word "because" will often do the trick. The nature of the reason doesn't seem to matter much, but the fact that you gave a reason will greatly increase the odds of compliance. Cialdini points out that children discern the power of the word "because" early on, and they often use it to justify behavior. "Why did you do that?" Answer: "Because!"

Repetition

Second, if you really want to accomplish something, repeat a constant and consistent theme. Say it over and over again in a consistent manner. As long as you don't overdo it, this creates the advantage of making what you are saying familiar, and because of the availability heuristic (we tend to believe that which comes easily to mind), what you are repeating eventually gets attention and credibility. The best way to take advantage of the power of the human urge toward consistency is to combine it with commitment. First, get a commitment to do something, then all subsequent behavior must conform to that commitment. This works for self-change, as well. Make yourself state a commitment to something clear and measurable, so that there is no way to weasel out without you (or others) noticing. Then make your behaviors line up with your commitment. This solves the problem of cognitive dissonance.

Owing Favors

Third, the rule of reciprocity calls for us to repay favors. If you do a favor for me, I should try to repay that favor, to balance things out. We are *obligated*. It may well be a good idea to keep everyone in your organization in debt to you for something or another. Powerful political figures are well aware of this phenomenon. Cialdini uses the example of the Hare Krishna's gift of a flower in airports in the 1980s. Many people felt woefully indebted, in spite of themselves, after accepting that simple gift. It is important to note that once you have given a gift you must allow the opportunity for the return of the favor. People deeply resent being put into the position of having received a gift that they are unable to repay in some way.

Following the Crowd

Another, extraordinarily powerful source of influence is the *principle of social proof*. This principle states that, as social animals, we watch each other to see what the trends are, and then we follow them. We use the mass behavior of others to determine what is true, valuable, and important. It is like the zebras on the plain: When the other zebras run, you'd better run too, just in case, even though you have no personal idea of why you are running. The human tendency to follow prevailing social trends and patterns is profound, and it explains things like the Jonestown massacre, fashion trends, and suicides and homicides subsequent to other suicides and homicides in the news. It also explains why television sitcoms still use laugh tracks, even though everyone says that they hate them. In spite of our expressed dislike for this phenomenon, it works. It is especially important in times of uncertainty and ambiguity, and it is most powerful when the people we observe are similar to us. Keep this in mind next time you find yourself laughing at something that is actually not very funny. Keep this in mind when you are making difficult decisions at work. Guard against mindless conformity and what Cialdini calls "pluralistic ignorance." Following trends has its value—it tends to keep us safe—but it has many more liabilities, and helps to explain much strange human behavior. Pay attention to the trend, but don't trust it implicitly. Check things out for yourself. On the other hand, when you need to influence someone else, you may want to point out the prevailing trend in the direction of the point of view you advocate.

Similarity and Other Like Factors

Not surprisingly, we tend to like people and things that are similar to us and familiar. We like people who look and dress like us, and people who are physically attractive have a great edge in life: We tend to believe them and we tend to think all sorts of positive things about them, including the fact that they are "good." This trend is called the "halo effect" in the psychological literature. We also tend to attribute good qualities to people we like, and people who can make themselves liked in the workplace have a clear and powerful advantage. Although this may seem obvious, this interpersonal liking is often overlooked as a force in the workplace. We tend to like people who have a similar background to our own, and it pays to find something in common with someone you are trying to influence.

Choosing Models

The power of similarity is also important in the use of modeling. Modeling is typically found in the repertoire of the behavior therapist or behaviorally oriented consultant, but it clearly involves interpersonal influence. When your client wants to change or learn something new, one great way is to find someone who already knows how to do it, to observe that person carefully, and to copy him or her. The best kind of model for your clients is someone like them. Similarity makes for a more efficient modeling process. Do not choose someone who seems perfect or who is in total mastery of the sought-after skill. Rather, pick someone who obviously had to work at learning it and is in the process of improving. This tends to make the skill more accessible to the learner and the learner more open to the new skill. Research indicates that it is better to choose a role model from the same gender and ethnic group of the client, and someone at roughly the same prestige level in the organization. It even helps if the model occasionally has to struggle with the learning process, has to work at it, and it is terrific when the model can talk about the process to your client. It is difficult to identify with a flawless model. It helps if the model has overcome the same obstacles faced by your client and better if they have similar concerns. Multiple exposures to the model and multiple models make for the best learning experience. And remember to encourage the client to adapt the model's approach to his or her own style; that is, to do what the model is doing in the client's own way (Cormier & Cormier, 1985, p. 311).

Compliments are powerful. We tend to believe praise when it is lavished on us, even when we should know better, and we tend to like the person who is lavishing it.

The phenomenon called "killing the messenger" has its basis in social psychology, as any television weather–person can tell you. They often get blamed for the bad weather they announce. One must be careful about taking the role of bad-news messenger, especially if called upon to do this regularly. It can lead to trouble, for you will become associated with the badness of the events communicated. If there are lay-offs to be announced, think carefully about who will be the one to break the news.

Social psychologists have even provided data for the "luncheon technique" (Razran, 1938). A series of studies have demonstrated that subjects were more likely to give approval to topics when they were presented along with food. It seems that tax deductions for business lunches have a basis in scientific research.

Compliance

Social psychology has studied the ways that people go along with the influence of others. One of the most useful findings comes from a series of studies by Rule, Bisanz, and Kohn, reported in 1985. They created a hierarchy of preferred strategies used to get compliance, and aside from methods that might be called "dirty tricks," they found the following:

1. A simple request is the most preferred tactic, for example, "Would you please . . ."
2. A reason is compelling, and personal expertise or a role relationship makes a request more powerful. For example, "We've been friends for a long time now . . ." or "I really need this because . . ."
3. Bargaining is useful. "If you would do this for me, I will be glad to do that for you."
4. Invoking a norm or a moral principle or altruism works. "It's the right thing to do," or "Everybody else is doing it," or "Other people are depending on us . . ."
5. A compliment works to get compliance: "You are so good at this type of thing . . ."
6. Negative, deceptive, or threatening approaches are at the bottom of the list, along with the use of force. These should only be used as a last resort, if at all.

The optimal way to ensure compliance with your requests is to allow the targets of your request to save face, to help them feel that they are doing a nice thing, of their own volition.

Social psychology has also identified the sources of power that clients have in the workplace (French & Raven, 1959), and it may be useful for coaches to review these sources, outlined below, with clients. How is the client doing in each of these ways to influence? Does he or she rely on one to the exclusion of others? Are they happy with the compliance they get?

Sources of Compliance Power

a. **Coercion**. Based upon the agent's ability to punish or withhold rewards.
b. **Reward**. Based upon the agent's ability to provide rewards.
c. **Expertness**. Based on the target's perception that the agent has important knowledge or ability.
d. **Legitimacy**. Based on the target's belief that the agent is authorized by a recognized power structure that the target answers to.
e. **Referent power**. Based on the target's identification with and attraction to or respect for the agent.

Ideally, coercive power is minimized in a modern organization, but clients must be willing to judiciously use that source if necessary. The use of referent and expert influence, however, is likely to create the optimal working environment, productivity, and creativity.

Summary and Key Points

1. Treat each "case" and client as an on-going field study. Treat it as research. Lewin's action research can be described as "research on action with the goal of making that action more effective" (Witherspoon & White, 1997, p. 19). Talk about it that way. Let your clients in on the research, get them involved. Create an optimistic, non-punitive atmosphere of curiosity. Together, you and your clients are going to study a situation or "problem" so that you can understand it and influence it. Expect that the first interventions will be instructive but will not "solve" the "problem." Expect a few iterations of the cycle of assessment, brainstorming, intervention, and evaluation. It's all good.

2. As a coach, remember the power of the situation. Social psychology research makes it quite clear that the *situation* is more influential than personal qualities or individual character. Don't allow your clients to become self-blaming and punitive (but don't let them off the personal "hook," either). It is possible that you could plug almost anyone into certain situations and he or she will behave in roughly the same way. Examine the social environment as it pertains to the question at hand. Explore the possibility that some aspects of the environment should be adjusted in order to help your clients grow. Teach your clients' organization, if possible, about the organizational climate and culture. Make it open to examination and discussion.

   Help your clients examine social situations and how these influence them. Help your clients discern which aspects they are reacting to and why. Explore the ways that your clients are influenced by prevailing social trends, and help them think through which trends make sense and which do not. Provide a safe, sane place for your clients to think and talk about these things outside of the social situation that normally influences their behavior.

3. Remember that we all suffer from self-delusion. It is virtually impossible to live in the real and accurate world. It is too much mental work, and we are forced to use mental heuristics to economize and survive. These heuristics are vital and useful, but they often trick us, and cognitive dissonance causes us to make mental adjustments that are inaccurate, but comfortable. Help your clients

sort through the ways that they are tricking themselves and ways to get back to more accurate thinking. Help clients notice when they are stuck or when they are trapped by their own ideas.

4. Help your clients with self-presentation. Reinforce the importance of first impressions and physical appearance. Coaches are a crucial source of feedback. *You* can point things out to clients that others cannot (because of prohibitive social mores or role constraints; for example, how do you tell your boss that she has bad breath?). Your role as coach requires that you do just that. You must skillfully call attention to how your clients present themselves, and brainstorm for adjustments. This includes the way they dress, the way they speak—in person and on the telephone, the way they stand and sit, the way they make eye contact, the way they listen, even the amount that they smile. These are all examples of the kinds of self-presentation feedback that coaches are expected to provide to clients. According to social psychology research, it is invaluable.

5. Assess and teach Emotional Intelligence. Goleman's materials are quite useful in "selling" this concept. Goleman's books, an article from the *Harvard Business Review* (1998a), and cassettes are available to help you and your clients. Technical expertise and intellect are important, but they are threshold skills. They are expected, and they get your clients in the door. Social factors are more important to your clients' long-term success than are the technical ones. These include empathy, self-awareness, self-regulation, and social skills (such as the ability to accurately read the emotions of others). These skills are the bread and butter skills of the executive coach, and they are often the reason that coaching is requested in the first place, whether your clients acknowledge this or not.

References

Allport, G. W. (1954). *The nature of prejudice.* Reading, MA: Addison-Wesley.
Aronson, E., Wilson, T., & Akert, R. (1997). *Social psychology.* New York: Addison-Wesley.
Asch, S. E. (1951). Effects of group pressure on the modification and distortion of judgments. In H. Guetzkow (Ed.), *Groups, leadership, and men.* Pittsburgh, PA: Carnegie.
Axelrod, R. (1984). *The evolution of cooperation.* New York: Basic Books.
Cartwright, D. (1979). Contemporary social psychology in historical perspective. *Social Psychology Quarterly, 42,* 82–93.
Cialdini, R. (1985). *Influence: Science and practice.* Glenview, IL: Scott, Foresman.
Cormier, W., & Cormier, L. (1985). *Interviewing strategies for helpers.* Monterey, CA: Brooks/Cole.
Festinger, L. (1957). *A theory of cognitive dissonance.* Evanston, IL: Row, Peterson.
Goleman, D. (1995). *Emotional intelligence.* New York: Bantam.
Goleman, D. (1998a, November–December). What makes a leader? *Harvard Business Review.*

Goleman, D. (1998b). *Working with emotional intelligence.* New York: Bantam.

Haney, C., Banks, C., & Zimbardo, P. (1973). Interpersonal dynamics in a simulated prison. *International Journal of Criminology and Penology, 1,* 69–97.

Janis, I. (1971, November). Groupthink. *Psychology Today.*

Johnson, S. (1998). *Who moved my cheese?* New York: Putnam's.

Knox, R. E., & Inkster, J. A. (1968). Post decisional dissonance at post time. *Journal of Personality and Social Psychology, 8,* 319–323.

Krupp, S., DeHann, R. F., Ishtai-Zee, S., Bastas, E., Castlebaum, K., & Jackson, E. (1986). Action research as a guiding principle in an educational curriculum: The Lincoln University Master's Program in Human Services (pp. 115–121). In E. Stivers & S. Wheelan (Eds.), *The Lewin legacy: Field theory in current practice.* Berlin: Springer Verlag.

Lewin, K. (1951). *Field theory in social science.* New York: Harper & Row.

Lewin, K., Lippitt, R., & White, R. K. (1939). Patterns of aggressive behavior in experimentally created social climates. *Journal of Social Psychology, 10,* 271–279.

Milgram, S. (1963). Behavioral study of obedience. *Journal of Abnormal Psychology, 67,* 371–378.

Myrdal, G. (1944). *An American dilemma.* New York: Harper & Row.

Razran, G. H. S. (1938). Conditioned response changes in rating and appraising sociopolitical slogans. *Psychological Bulletin, 37,* 481.

Rosenhan, D. (1973). On being sane in insane places. *Science, 179,* 250–258.

Rule, B. G., Bisanz, G. L., & Kohn, M. (1985). Anatomy of a persuasion schema: Targets, goals, and strategies. *Journal of Personality and Social Psychology, 48,* 1127–1140.

Segal, M. (1997). *Points of influence.* San Francisco: Jossey-Bass.

Rosenthal, R., & Jacobson, L. (1968). *Pygmalion in the classroom: Teacher expectation and student intellectual development.* New York: Holt, Rhinehart, & Winston.

Silberman, M. (1986). Teaching force field analysis: A suggested training design (pp. 115–121). In E. Stivers & S. Wheelan (Eds.), *The Lewin legacy: Field theory in current practice.* Berlin: Springer Verlag.

Simonton, D. K. (1987). *Why presidents succeed: A political psychology of leadership.* New Haven, CT: Yale University Press.

Simonton, D. K. (1992). Presidential greatness and personality: A response to McCann. *Journal of Personality and Social Psychology, 63,* 676–679.

Witherspoon, R., & White, R. (1997). *Four essential ways that coaching can help executives.* Greensboro, NC: Center for Creative Leadership.

Recommended Readings

Deaux, K., Dane, F., & Wrightsman, L. (1997). *Social psychology in the '90s* (6th ed). Pacific Grove, CA: Brooks-Cole.

French, J. R. P. Jr., & Raven, B. H. (1959). The bases of social power. In D. Cartwright (Ed.), *Studies in social power.* Ann Arbor, MI: University of Michigan Press.

Gilbert, D., Fiske, S., & Lindzey, G. (1998). *The handbook of social psychology* (4th ed.). New York: McGraw-Hill.

Hayes, N. (1993). *Principles of social psychology.* Hove, UK: Erlbaum.

Janis, I. (1986). *Groupthink: Psychological studies of policy decisions and fiascoes* (2nd ed.). New York: Houghton Mifflin.

Stivers, E., & Wheelan, S. (1986). *The Lewin legacy: Field theory in current practice.* Berlin: Springer Verlag.

Taylor, S., Letita, A., & Sears, D. (2000). *Social psychology* (10th ed.). Upper Saddle River, NJ: Prentice Hall.

9

The Existential Stance

Existence precedes essence.

—Jean Paul Sartre, 1966

Existential philosophy offers a great deal to the coach who can effectively pick and choose amongst the many views subsumed under the title of "existentialism." This is no easy task, as the existential literature is varied and often complex, meaning different things to different people. The parable of the blind men comes to mind, as they describe an elephant differently based upon whether they had felt the trunk or the ear or the tail or the tusk. More often than not, existential ideas are written in a fictional form, and authors are unwilling to interpret them for the reader. Many of the most influential existential thinkers refused to even embrace the label "existential," as there is very little agreement among them. Most wrote in revolt or rejection of the ideas of those who preceded them. While classical philosophers advocate reason, existentialists call for passion. One can find numerous books and essays with titles such as "What is existentialism?" but one would be hard-pressed to come up with a single tome that adequately captures and digests it all. Existentialism is less an "ism" than a way of approaching things, a stance or a "posture." In spite of the fact that existentialism does not lend itself to easy application, existential philosophy has had a powerful impact on psychotherapy theory and practice, and it offers enormously useful potential for the executive coach.

The coach's first challenge is to figure out what existentialism is and just what it recommends. This can be a daunting task. The second step

155

is to choose a discrete number of views or principles and decide how to apply them to the workplace. These two tasks are the goals of this chapter. Such an endeavor necessarily requires (useful) oversimplification.

History and Background

It is fair to say that threads of existential thought run from Socrates through the Bible and on into modern culture. The cubicle philosophies of Dilbert were surely informed by Franz Kafka, and the motion picture "Groundhog Day," is an illustration of Friedrich Nietzsche's "eternal recurrence," a test used to determine whether any given day is being "lived" properly. (The test: How would you feel if you were to relive this day over and over again?) Prominent existentialists have been a varied lot, and most of them could have been called "characters." Some were Christians, some were atheists, some were Jews, and one or two were Nazis. Most philosophical historians trace the identifiable origins of existentialism back to the German philosopher Georg Wilhelm Friedrich Hegel, who lived from 1770 until 1831. Among other things, Hegel wrote about the human spirit and asserted that it is the history of our spirit (as expressed in custom, law, and art) that defines us (Barrett, 1964). Subsequent existential thinkers rebelled against this idea, focusing instead on the view that "existence precedes essence," meaning that each human has no fixed essence, except as it is shown through moment to moment behavior, which can always change. Our personality does not define us; that is simply a label. Our *choices* define us after we make them, and then we are free to make new ones in the next moment. We choose ourselves. Our essence is defined by our existence, not the other way around. Most existentialists steadfastly resist labeling people. Labels are for *things* (like a vase, which has permanent and consistent qualities).

People exist only in the present and can make new choices each day, and they exist in social contexts and roles. A teacher is only a teacher in the presence of students. In a casino, that same person becomes a gambler.

Existentialism raises issues most of us would prefer to ignore. Proponents were preoccupied with themes of death, anxiety, dread, failure, and the absurd.

A brief story (circa 1840) from Søren Kierkegaard (1813–1855) is illustrative. It is about how he became a philosopher while watching his cigar smoke disappear into the air of a Danish café. His friends had all chosen careers and were busy with their work, but he had not.

It occurred to him then that since everyone was engaged everywhere in making things easy, perhaps someone was needed to make things hard again, and that this too might be a career and a destiny—to go in search of difficulties, like a new Socrates. (Barrett, 1964, p. 21)

He realized that he did not have to look far for these difficulties, as they were right there in front of him in his own life, in his own concrete existence. He was aware of his own pain and choices and anxieties, and to focus on these aspects of his existence would require a rejection of Hegel and spirit. He resolved "to create difficulties everywhere." So, off he went. In the end, he was famous for his epitaph: *"That Individual"* (Kaufmann, 1956).

At about the same time (1844–1849) Fyodor Dostoevsky wrote ten novels and short stories before he was thrown into a Russian prison. He wrote of the tragic side of life (a life that he knew all too well), the less attractive qualities of humans (depravity), and the central importance of individual choice and freedom in human existence (Dostoevsky, 1992).

Kierkegaard's work was eventually translated into German, and Karl Theodor Jaspers (1883–1969) and Martin Heidegger (1889–1976) built upon it in the period following World War I. Friedrich Wilhelm Nietzsche was born in Germany in 1844, wrote until the late 1800s, and died in 1900. His work was profoundly influential in his time, is still controversial and, is largely misunderstood. Some of Nietzsche's ideas are actually offensive and objectionable. Of importance to this chapter, however, is his emphasis on independent morality, on making the most of who you are, and of excellence over mediocrity. It was his view that humans have a moral obligation to become "excellent" rather than give in to the inclination to inertia and the herd mentality. Nietzsche exhorts us to get up off the couch, get going, and to take life seriously (Solomon, 1995). He tells us to stop preparing for life and start living it, even to live dangerously (Kaufmann, 1956). He also described something he called "the will to power" (Nietzsche, 1968), advocating that each of us do what it takes to have a major say in our own lives, and that we develop, nurture, and use our willpower (King & Citrenbaum, 1993).

German work was translated into French in the 1930s and was met with great enthusiasm by French intellectuals who were turned off by bourgeois culture and were facing Nazi occupation and another absurd world war. Jean-Paul Sartre (1905–1980) fought against the German army and helped lead French underground resistance during World War II. His essays and fiction put existentialism on the American literary map, and he shocked and confused many readers in the 1950s with themes of authenticity (vs. self-deception), absolute personal responsibility, the inherent conflict in human relationships, and his notion that the existence or non-existence of God was irrelevant to the human condition.

At about the same time in France, the Algerian author Albert Camus (1913–1960) produced strange fiction about the absurdity and pointlessness of life. He concluded, somewhat paradoxically, that absurdity opens the door to happiness.

> One does not discover the absurd without being tempted to write a manual of happiness. . . . Happiness and the absurd are two sons of the same earth. (1955, p. 122)

Key Ideas

This operating summary of essential existential concepts is presented (at great risk of trivializing complex points-of-view) so that the coach can grasp the basics and choose and use valuable aspects. The interested reader is referred to Olson's *An Introduction to Existentialism* (1962) for a more complete (and still accessible) background and explanation.

Traditional philosophers typically assert that the values of the "ordinary man" (or ordinary person); that is, the pursuit of money, physical pleasure, and fame or social approval are bound to frustrate and disappoint. These values, which most of us seek to some extent in real life, are inadequate on several levels. First, success in attaining these goals is substantially outside of the personal control of most people. The essential determining factors are capricious, beginning with factors having to do with birth and ending with vagaries of luck. Second, even if you do achieve a certain amount of success in finance, physical pleasure, and fame, this can be swept away in an instant, sometimes by factors over which you have no control. Physical satisfaction is guaranteed to dissipate. Third, the satisfaction these values yields is transient, and they tend to generate a wish for "more." The small number of people who have achieved financial wealth, physical pleasure, and social approval (and are satisfied with these things) might view much of Eastern and Western philosophy as "sour grapes," but existential philosophy asserts that this simplistic orientation is unwise.

Philosophers have recommended several ways to emancipate one's self from the pitfalls of traditional values. Stoics and cognitive psychologists advocate that you should "wish for things to be as they are," rather than wishing life to be different (Olson, 1962). We cannot make life deliver what we want, but we can control what we think and desire. Rigorous, self-disciplined thought is key. Enlightenment philosophers advocate the opposite: that we should relentlessly strive to change our environment so that we get what we want. A hard look at the world and the history of human happiness quickly negates the likelihood that ordinary people can ever hope that society can be counted on to deliver consistent happiness. For others the secret is in "enlarging our perspective" (Olson, 1962, p. 11) and focusing all of our attention on some object of greater good, such as beauty, or nature, or love, or God. In this way, we are liberated from the problems of unreliable sources of happiness. This was where Hegel entered the picture with his advocacy of the "Absolute Spirit."

Existentialists typically mock and denounce the idea that there is any way for humans to live a completely happy or satisfying life. Life is characterized by frustration, disappointment, and loss. These things are an undeniable central aspect of everyone's life. They cannot be made to go away, neither by extreme real-world efforts nor by mental denial. They assert that "the only life worth living is one in which this fact is squarely faced" (Olson, 1962, p. 14). To be totally happy is not human. The values and perspectives that derive from this acceptance are the ones worth living for. It is through the acceptance of pain and the ever-present possibility of loss that we become fully alive. We cannot really love without exposing ourselves to the possibility of great loss. Love without such possibility is more like habit or routine. It is a going-through-the-motions way to love. It is likely to be numb. To have a satisfying career is to take risk. Without the risk, work becomes tedium. Existentialism urges us to take the risk (with eyes wide open) and avoid the tedium. Life is to be lived intensely, not tediously.

The values that derive from this point of view include free choice, individual self-assertion, authentic love, and creative endeavor. The practical implications of these and several other existential values will be outlined for the coach in the rest of this chapter.

Six Core Concepts for the Executive Coach

Individuality and Context

Existentialism points out that no one is a fixed person. *Things* are fixed. A pencil is a pencil in every context, but a person is different in different contexts. You think and behave differently when you are with your friends than you do when you are at an important meeting with bosses or potential clients. This is not simple phoniness; it is a function of "background," of role and relationship. Human behavior is best understood in context, and social psychology has highlighted the "fundamental attribution error," the tendency to overestimate internal (personal) factors and underestimate situational factors. Even though you may have excellent data from a 360-degree evaluation, as well as an earful from key people in the organization, be prepared to encounter your executive clients in an original way yourself. Clear out your preconceptions before you begin to work with them. Find out what makes them tick and find out what they are like when they are with you. Then compare the information you get with those impressions and figure out why they are different. Understand your clients in the context of their work relationship world.

Choice

To live is to choose, to make endless choices moment to moment, each and every day. Existential writers call attention to "the anguish of freedom," freedom made difficult because we have so much choice, with no guarantee that the choices we make will ever work out. Things could turn into disasters, and when we choose one thing, we forgo something else. What if the thing we don't choose would have been much better? This decision-making function of life is central to the existential view of things, and it is the cause of much of the anxiety we all feel. Existence is the process of choosing, and *existence* (the things that we do) precedes *essence* (the "way" we are). We create ourselves by our choices from moment to moment. We are not a certain "way" and must therefore *choose* a certain way. We are free to choose in each present moment, thereby defining our self. The way we were in the past does not constrain us (except in the form of restrictive thinking), and the future is just in front of us, waiting to be chosen in this way or that.

The ultimate choice is in our choice of meanings. We even choose what things mean. No one is locked in a previous identity or habit pattern. We are free to learn new ways, to make new kinds of choices. Even when we cannot choose what is happening, or the circumstances, we can still choose how to respond to those circumstances.

Coaches can observe their clients and notice the ways that they restrict themselves, the ways that they decline to choose, and then encourage clients to notice those things, too. Effective choosing requires constant self-examination, and coaches can teach their executive clients how to do that. They can serve as a constant reminder for self-awareness and deliberate self-consciousness. Help clients make wise, well-considered choices. Help them notice when they have stopped choosing or when they let others choose for them, or when they move along thoughtlessly from day to day, just to go with the flow.

Intensity

In existential thought, death is the great motivator. Death ends everything, and, since we cannot predict when we will die, it is ever-present in life. Each of us could die today, and some of us will. Death is a possibility at every moment. Therefore, we make every moment count.

Since death is frightening to most humans, we tend to create ways to avoid thinking about it, to avoid noticing its presence, in spite of the absolute fact that each of us will die. We distract ourselves, make ourselves numb, we become detached. But this doesn't work. It doesn't indemnify against death and it makes life less worth living. The existential view is to reject mediocrity and tedium and to become fully engaged in life, as if each day were our last (as it very well might be). This means that we take risks, we get involved, and we become actors rather than spectators. We can't wait, because we have no assurance that we have much time. We *just do it*, as Nike advertisements advocate.

Death's presence also serves as a values clarifier. If you are aware that your life is time-limited, does that influence what you do today? Do you choose A or B? The importance of one thing over another changes when you factor your own death into the picture. You might just make more "authentic" choices, choices that reflect the more "real" values that you possess. You might makes choices based upon the things that are more important to you, instead of the ones that are easier to choose, or the ones that others prefer, or the ones you made yesterday.

As Robert Olson (1962, p. 196) puts it, "death releases human energies only by revealing the insignificance of ordinary pursuits." When we realize that we are going to die, we commit to things, we create things, we connect to people, and we focus. We refuse to fritter time and relationships and consciousness. In this way, death is our ally. It sharpens living. It demands focus.

The Herd Instinct

One of the most misunderstood philosophers of the genre is Nietzsche, and some of what he wrote was clearly objectionable. But one of his key ideas is of great value to the coach. He observed that humans are inclined to be lazy, to be fearful, to seek comfort, and to hide behind habits that keep us safe and the same. He observed also that humans in society don't tend to think much for themselves. Instead, they tend to take the mentally easy way, and to let others think for them. They accept the prevailing wisdom rather than come up with their own point of view. They take the path of least resistance. He observed that most of us live with a "slave morality." Nietzsche advocated that we instead "live dangerously," that we avoid becoming the "organization man," that we resist being caught up in the corporate shuffle, or in the prevailing attitudes of the times. He would have shouted, "Think for yourself!"

Coaches can take the same point of view, can root out this viewpoint in a client's behavior, and confront clients about the ways they are simply acting out values that are not their own or taking viewpoints that they have not, themselves, chosen. Coaches are in a perfect position, as an outsider, to be outside of the organizational trance state and to help an executive cut through unexamined premises and conclusions. Coaches can be advocates for thoughtfulness and for individual decision-making.

Confrontation

Jean Paul Sartre's view was that confrontation is the basis for all authentic human relationships. Conflict isn't to be avoided—indeed, it is through conflict that we forge real relationships and relationships of trust. He makes this point most dramatically in his play, "No Exit," which takes place in Hell. Three characters are stuck with each other and are constantly in disagreement and disapproval, but, surprisingly, they find that they cannot exist without each other. There is no exit from human confrontation and conflict. The available exits such as accommodation, denial, and withdrawal are inauthentic and result in a numbing tediousness. We need the very people who drive us crazy. Conflict is not only essential to human relationships; it is the very foundation of authentic living. There is no benefit, to the existentialist, in "getting along." We must challenge, confront, and be real with others.

Authentic relationships encourage the other person to be free, to make whatever choices they find appealing in order to become their individual selves. Sidney Jourard observed that "manipulation begets counter-manipulation" (1971, p. 142), and this is wonderful advice for a manager or leader, especially as the American worker continues to evolve toward greater autonomy (in good economic times, at least).

Manipulation and control of others simply does not work in the long run, and in the short run, when it does seem to work, it creates unacceptable negative side effects. This makes leadership challenging. Other people are not to be used, and we are not to be used by them. We are not objects, none of us.

The Absurd

Several existential writers deal explicitly with the idea that fundamental aspects of life are simply absurd, and there is no escaping this fact, no matter how hard we try, no matter how much we pretend that things make sense. In Kafka's *Metamorphosis* (1996), the main character is surprised to wake up one morning to discover that he is a cockroach. In *The Trial* (Kafka, 1956), a man is arrested, tried, and convicted without ever finding out what he was accused of. In Camus' *The Myth of Sisyphus* (1955), a man is sentenced to roll a huge rock up a steep hill (for the rest of eternity), only to have it roll right back down again, once it reaches the top. In *The Stranger* (Camus, 1942) a man is convicted of murder, mostly because a jury felt that he had not properly grieved over his mother's death.

Existentialism highlights the utter unpredictability of things (including the fact that we could die at any moment) and celebrates it. The fact that the universe is inexplicable to us, especially when we so desire to make sense of it all, is the ultimate evidence of the absurd (Thody, 1957). We wish to understand, but we can't. Life is full of brutal contradictions.

Most of us are tempted to ignore this reality, to deny it or to pretend it is not true. We create order in things and we insist that our order be honored. But even though it is important to establish order as best we can, it is a mistake to insist that our order prevail. The very nature of life shatters our orderly illusion. The roof can cave in at any moment.

This fact is not depressing to the existential thinker, however. In fact, the absurd opens the door to happiness. It is in total acceptance of the uncertainty of life's contradictions that we become free enough to engage ourselves in the regular day-to-day events and pleasures and to really appreciate them. They are our life. They are where we live. Life is crazy, and it is a joy that way. There is a classic anecdote that makes this point:

> You know the story of the crazy man who was fishing in a bathtub. A doctor with ideas as to psychiatric treatments asked him "if they were biting," to which he received the harsh reply: "Of course not, you fool, since this is a bathtub." (Camus, 1955, p. 129)

Ten Existential Guidelines
for the Executive Coach

1. **Honor individuality.** First of all, approach each new coaching client with a freshness and willingness to see him or her as unique. Reinforce your clients' points of view. Help them figure out what they, themselves, really think and feel, and then support that point of view. Help them learn about themselves. Check to see if they value their own personal point of view or, rather, if they diminish its importance relative to the point of view of others in the organization. Strengthen their confidence in their own perceptions and conclusions. Their personal point of view is of intrinsic value, even if they should choose to reexamine and change it as a result of the coaching process. Help them to figure out what is really important to them. Then discern where that fits into their career and their organization's priorities. This process may frighten your clients (or it may not), but it must be done. Help clients avoid a "herd" mentality and a group morality. Help them choose their own point of view. In the existential perspective, autonomy in self and others is valued and promoted.

   Avoid typing people. Don't put too much stock in what others say about your clients. Experience them freshly for yourself. It is likely, of course, that you will have similar impressions and come to similar conclusions, but you must do this for yourself. Look for the truth about your clients inside of yourself.

2. **Encourage choice.** Remind your clients that they choose their identity each moment of each day. Existence precedes essence. Their reputation need not constrain them. They can remake their "self." They can make new choices and behave or prioritize in new ways, starting now. Once they establish a pattern of different choices and different behaviors, others will eventually begin to look at them differently, and they will establish a new reputation and a new identity.

3. **Get going.** Exhort your clients to take risks, to get involved, to act, even to "live dangerously" sometimes. Life is finite, short even, and we don't have any guarantee that we will be alive tomorrow. This means that we must squeeze each day for as much life as possible.

   When you enter the world of your clients, look for ways that they have avoided risk or danger, ways that they have made themselves numb, ways that they have withdrawn from the action or narrowed the field. Point these things out to clients and urge them to reconsider. Numb is no way to live, and the existentialist is wary of comfort. We are actors, not spectators in life's adventures.

4. **Anticipate anxiety and defensiveness.** Anyone who is a coaching client will feel anxiety. This is expected and "normal." Beware of a client who reports no anxiety, for it means that he or she is not able to notice or discuss feelings or his or her subjective inner state. It is appropriate for coaching clients to be anxious about coaching or about the situation they face, given that they must change or grow. Change is often frightening, and it adds to the "regular" anxiety associated with a life that is already understood to be out-of-control, in the existential sense. A coach need not make much of this anticipated anxiety, but can "normalize" or even welcome it.

   Resistance and defensiveness can also be anticipated in the coaching process, because, as Maslow (1968) pointed out, growth and safety often pull in opposite directions, and all humans are drawn to both of those goals. Assume that resistance in clients is always present to some extent and in some form, and don't be disappointed when it erupts. It is an essential part of the change process and coaches must actively contend with it.

5. **Commit to something.** Existentialism urges us to get involved with the regular activities of everyday life, and to do it with a passion. Don't accept it when your clients hang back. Urge them to get involved with those things that are important to them, even if others don't agree with their priorities. Help them to really "dig in" to something and to make it important. Such a commitment can lead to excellence and to exceptionality. Mediocrity, especially when it represents a dull, reactive, go-with-the-flow mentality is to be banished. Regular daily activities are understood to serve as a distraction from commitment to something that is really important. Activity and intensity are valued. We only find out what we are "made of" when we are tested.

6. **Value responsibility-taking.** Existentialism urges us to take responsibility for the choices we have made. We did it, we chose it, and we now live with the choices and implications. Assess your clients along this dimension. Ask them what their view is on responsibility, ask others about them in your 360-degree evaluation. Observe them in action. Ask them to describe the last time they publicly took responsibility for something that went wrong in the organization. Help clients take responsibility for the decisions they make and the actions they take. Help them become known as responsibility-takers in their organizations. Don't let them duck things. Coworkers and subordinates love people who take active responsibility and scorn those who don't. Certainly the act of data collection—and asking for feedback—along with the changes these might incite, represent an exercise in choice!

7. **Conflict and confrontation.** In the existential view, interpersonal conflict is unavoidable, yet many people characteristically avoid conflict. This is a mistake, and coaches must assess their client along this dimension. Ask your clients how they evaluate themselves. Do they enjoy conflict? Do they thrive on it? Does conflict make them feel like they are more fully alive? Or do they hate it. Does conflict scare them?

   Certainly no one would advocate unnecessary conflict, but most people are likely to avoid rather than confront. Existentialism sees conflict as an essential aspect of any authentic relationship, and confrontation is necessary from time to time in order to keep a relationship "real" and valid. Of course, there are better and worse ways to handle confrontation, and a good coach can help clients learn how to do it. It also helps to view conflict and confrontation as a potential positive aspect of organizational life, rather than merely a symptom of dysfunction. Pseudo-tranquility ought to be of more concern than active confrontation from time to time.

   There is another aspect of the conflict inherent in human relations. Sometimes the very people who drive you crazy are the ones you need the most, so it can be a terrible idea to reject them too readily. There may be important lessons to learn from uncomfortable or annoying others, and as Sartre concluded in *No Exit* (1989), we need each other, even the people we despise.

8. **Create and sustain authentic relationships.** This advice applies to coaches and clients, as well. Both will benefit from authenticity in work relationships. Coaches ought to strive for real relationships with clients, and clients ought to strive for realness in organizational work relationships. An authentic relationship occurs when both parties treat each other as autonomous entities to be respected. The truth is told, and neither manipulates for personal benefit. People are not instruments for the accomplishment of some work purpose. They are individuals to be met with respect rather than treated as interchangeable components in the "labor market" (Shinn, 1959). In the existential view, other people are neither to be manipulated nor obeyed. *Gemeinschaftsgefhül,* or the feeling that we all belong to the community of humans, is the existential view (Jourard & Landsman, 1980).

   Authentic behavior with a client means you put into words what you are experiencing with the client as you work. This is the most powerful thing you can do to have the leverage you are looking for and to build client commitment.

   —Peter Block (2000, p. 37)

9. **Welcome and appreciate the absurd.** Organizations are full of examples of absurdity, and anyone who has ever worked in a large (or small) organization knows how ridiculous things can get. This is simply normal. Assess your clients to see how well they understand this fact and what they do with it. Do they whine or complain when things don't go the way they were "supposed to?" Do they get angry when their planning goes awry? Help them appreciate how out-of-control life really is. Help them find humor in the contradictions. And help them become more flexible.

10. **Clients must figure things out their own way.** No one can tell you the answers to the most important questions. You have to figure them out for yourself, in your own way. Coaches have to figure out what that means to them, as well as how they can "teach" important things to clients, to help them learn essential lessons or skills. Such teaching is rarely direct, as most humans resist being told what to do. Kierkegaard advocated "indirect communication," and added that truth requires self-discovery. It cannot be handed from one person to another.

> *Suppose an artist, for example, explains to you that a certain picture is beautiful. You believe him. You go around repeating the conclusion, "That picture is beautiful." But you do not understand what you are saying unless you personally have discovered the beauty.*
> —Roger Shinn (1959, p. 92)

Strengths and Weakness of the Existential Viewpoint in Coaching

The existential way of being and living and coaching promotes a thoughtful and energetic approach to things. It can be exciting and productive and satisfying. It can promote creativity and action. It can result in relationships that are close, substantial, and enduring. It promotes organizations that are alive and exciting.

There are downsides, however, to the existential stance, and they must be recognized. First of all, the classic existential writers were ineffective at politics. They have a poor track record, as might be expected, in matters that require finesse, restraint, and compromise, and much of real-life corporate success requires a shrewd political savvy. In fact, it might even be said that the intense, committed person only fits into a small (but important) number of corporate "slots" (CEO being one of them). It is possible, sometimes, for the passionate one to mistake intensity for wisdom. It is true that existentialist writers often seemed to advocate any decision, as long as it was individually and authentically made, without much concern about the wisdom in the decision itself. Decision-making is valued over reason sometimes (Shinn, 1959).

Sometimes an existential view leads to a kind of individualism that is thoughtless or empty of direction. This kind of individualism for the sake of itself doesn't work very well in real life or in organizations. An authentic individualism requires extensive self-examination and the willingness to live with the decisions one makes as a result.

Lastly, many people have inaccurate negative stereotypes of existential ideas. They associate existentialism with nihilism (a negation of all values or a rejection of law or order) and with godlessness. They also see it as a gloomy point of view, which it most certainly is not. But the ideas of existential writers are complex, and it is easy to see how such misunderstandings arise, and the original writers often do little to clear them up. Nonetheless, it may be simplest and wisest to low-key the overt expression of existential ideas and simply bring the best of the existential approach to the coaching process without a label. Coaches might also consider going to the references and recommended readings to see for themselves.

References

Barrett, W. (1964). *What is existentialism?* New York: Grove Press, Inc.

Block, P. (2000). *Flawless consulting, A guide to getting your expertise used* (2nd ed.). San Francisco: Jossey-Bass/Pfeiffer.

Camus, A. (1942). *The stranger.* New York: Random House.

Camus, A. (1955). *The myth of Sisyphus and other essays.* New York: Random House.

Dostoevsky, F. (1992). *The best short stories of Dostoevsky.* New York: The Modern Library.

Jourard, S., & Landsman, T. (1980). *Healthy personality* (4th ed.). New York: Macmillan.

Kafka, F. (1966, ed., orig. 1901). *The metamorphosis.* New York: Norton.

Kaufmann, W. (1956). *Existentialism from Dostoevsky to Sartre.* New York: World.

King, M., & Citrenbaum, C. (1993). *Existential hypnotherapy.* New York: Guilford.

Maslow, A. H. (1968). *Toward a psychology of being.* New York: Van Nostrand Reinhold.

Nietzsche, F. (1968). *The will to power* (W. Kaufmann & J. R. Hollingdale, Trans.). New York: Vintage.

Olson, R. (1962). *An introduction to existentialism.* New York: Dover.

Sartre, J.-P. (1989). *No exit and three other plays.* New York: Vintage.

Shinn, R. (1970). *The existentialist posture.* New York: Association Press.

Solomon, R. (1995). *No excuses: Existentialism and the meaning of life, parts I and II* (Audiotaped lectures). Springfield, VA: The Teaching Company.

Thody, P. (1957). *Albert Camus: A study of his work.* New York: Grove Press.

Recommended Readings

Beckett, S. (1956). *Waiting for Godot: Tragicomedy in two acts.* New York: Grove Press.

Dohn, H. (1997). *Existential thought and therapeutic practice.* London: Sage.

Jourard, S. (1971). *The transparent self.* New York: Van Nostrand Reinhold.

Kafka, F. (1956). *The trial.* New York: Vintage.

Sartre, J.-P. (1966). *Being and nothingness: A phenomenological essay on ontology* (H. E. Barnes, Trans.). London: Oxford University Press.

10
CHAPTER

Lessons from Athletic Coaches

Everybody's a coach in some aspect of life, and that means you. So grab your whistle and clipboard, and let's get in the game.
— Ken Blanchard and Don Shula (1995, p. 15)

Executive coaching has its roots in athletic and performance coaching, and there is a gaggle of books written by famous coaches to be found in the business section of every bookstore. Therefore, it makes sense to check the sports "literature" to see what nuggets lie there. Your clients have bought some of these books, and may have even read a few.

The main reason that coaching is called "coaching" and not executive counseling or workplace psychotherapy is that hard-charging corporate types, especially men, are likely to be happy to have a coach, but unwilling to enter therapy. Most identify with sport and would love to see themselves as athletes, or at least, as high performers. Most grew up on sports, following their favorite team and imitating their favorite athlete. Counseling is associated with weakness and inadequacy, while coaching is identified with successful sports figures and winning teams. Great teams have great coaches, and Tiger Woods apparently visits his swing coach often.

These books have relevance. Books by athletic coaches are interesting sources for executive coaches because team sports at the highest levels, especially football, have become corporate in nature. The San Francisco 49ers have a person who serves as "Executive Vice President for Football Operations." Players are referred to as "personnel" and the teams are now "organizations." Forty-Niners' Head Coach Bill Walsh's book, *Finding the Winning Edge* is essentially a large, detailed corporate organizational-operations manual.

The premier coaches insist on total control.

It was agreed that if I was going to be coach, I would be in charge of all football operations.
—Bill Walsh (Walsh, Billick, & Peterson, 1998, p. 9)

Rather than cope with limited authority and meddling owners, athletic coaches now serve as "Presidents" of large, complex organizations. Much of what they do has significant relevance to the corporate executive. Most of these books make at least some reference to the business world, and football coach Bill Walsh published an extended series of management articles in *Forbes* magazine between 1993 and 1997 (Walsh, Billich, & Peterson, 1989). There is significant content overlap between the football coach and the executive coach.

Ninety percent of the game is half mental.
—Yogi Berra (1998, p. 96)

The reading of books by marquee coaches can be mind numbing. They all contain more than their share of clichés ("Failing to prepare is preparing to fail") and well-worn (worn-out) motivational mantras ("When the going gets tough, the tough get going."). To make matters worse, many of these books brim with quotes from famous military figures such as George Patton, Sun Tzu, and even Erwin Rommel (the Nazi Panzer commander).

In the real world, athletes tire of these clichés, having heard them year after year, and they simply turn them off. Even one of U.C.L.A. basketball coach John Wooden's stars reported that he never paid much attention to Coach Wooden's famous "Pyramid of Success" while he was at U.C.L.A. In tribute to Wooden, however, he admitted that the pyramid was meaningful to him later on, as a professional player (Walton, G. M., 1992, p. 52).

Frank Deford (Jones & Deford, 1997) notes that "some incredibly stupid coaches have beaten some demonstrably brilliant coaches," so we have to be careful about giving too much credit where it is not necessarily due. He remembers that long-time Boston Celtics coach Red Auerbach's theories were brilliant as long as Bill Russell played on his teams. But some of these coaches have produced highly successful records over long periods, and star athletes and luck simply cannot account for all of their success. Some of what they have done has been masterful.

These busy winners probably do not actually "write" much of what is in their books themselves, and that is a good thing, for they did not attain success on the basis of their writing skills. It is also likely that the vast majority of coach books rest forever unopened on coffee tables and nightstands. But there is a certain charm about these books, and each contains one or two real "nuggets" mixed in with all of the success-speak and the examples from games won or lost along the way. Most coach books stress the obvious, such as hard work, teamwork, attention to detail, and positive attitude. This chapter synthesizes the less obvious lessons common to sports coach books (as well as a few "nuggets") that are sure to be useful to the corporate coach.

Common Themes

There is a striking consistency to books by athletic coaches and, perhaps, to the philosophies of the successful ones. If that is the case, there may be some serious truths to be found there.

Theme One: Drive

There is one quality that nearly all successful athletes and coaches have in common. This quality actually *diminishes* their usefulness to the executive coach. Highly successful coaches and athletes are focused and driven to the extreme. Most normal humans do not possess their brand of single-mindedness. Regular people might not even possess the capacity.

> What I have learned about myself is that I am an animal when it comes to achievement and wanting success. There is never enough success for me.
>
> —Gary Player (Jones, 1997)

> I hate to say it because I don't think it's the best thing for developing a person, but the single-mindedness—just concentrating in that one area— that's what it takes to be a champion.
>
> —Chris Evert (Jones, 1997)

Virtually all of the popular sports or coaching books found in the bookstore say the same thing: Highly successful people are driven, focused, and single-minded in their dedication to their craft.

Most of these books stress the importance of *dreaming* and *setting goals*. It seems that drive and dreams are related, and it would do well for executive coaches to help clients decipher their dreams or lack of them. Certainly, we can't expect executive clients to be working away in the job of their dreams like basketball players or golfers often do. But it is a coach's job to help a client figure out where passions reside and whether they are too distant from the workplace. If dreams and drive can be harnessed and ridden like a fine steed, all the better. That makes the task simple. Align everything directly, and go for it. But when a client is working away at a career with great ambivalence, that is a different matter, indeed. It is also different when clients feel that their work is secondary to other aspects of life, such as family or triathlons or Girl Scouts. Coach books all stress the importance of balance in life, especially with regard to family. But, in some cases, coaches go on to say that they didn't do a very good job with their own family responsibilities, and others quietly got a divorce sometime after their book was published. One coach's book is dedicated to his father: "I never got to say goodbye or tell you that I loved you."

This can be a starting point in executive coaching: Where does work fit into your life and your dreams? How driven are you now and how driven do you want to be? Would you feel confused if your larger priorities limited your career success? Similarly, would you be ashamed if your career strivings produced family pathology or spousal resentment? Perhaps an intense career drive was feasible early in one's career, but incongruent later on?

None of this is meant to demean drive. It is central to excellence in anything, and positive mental health and self-esteem are greatly enhanced when a person is excellent at something. But that "something" doesn't necessarily have to be career, nor is it reasonable to expect obsessive drive in most clients.

If a client intends great success at work, single-mindedness should be considered, though. Coaches can help clients develop drive, once focus has been defined and established. But I say: consciously choose one or the other (single-mindedness or a balanced life) and remember that you made the choice. Take joy in the outcome, but don't make one choice and expect the fruits of the other. Each path has its benefits and its liabilities. As a coach, help clients clear this up, as it can be confusing and even demoralizing. Organizations often advocate work–life balance, but they rarely reward it. It is the coach's job to stimulate clarity.

Everyone has noted the astonishing sources of energy that seem available to those who enjoy what they are doing, who find meaning what they are doing. The self-renewing man knows that if he has no great conviction about what he is doing, he had better find something that he can have great conviction about . . .

—John Gardner (Robinson, 1996, p.31)

Theme Two: Teach the Fundamentals

If you keep too busy learning the tricks of the trade, you may never learn the trade.
—John Wooden (Walton, 1992, p. 46)

Coach Wooden is famous for starting each new season with a lesson on how to properly put on sweat socks. All of the coaching books stress fundamentals, the teaching and learning of the basics of the game that is being played. Famous coaches typically view themselves as teachers, first and foremost. Several felt that it was their teaching skills that separated them from less successful coaches. They stressed redundant coverage of the fundamental skills, even to highly talented players with huge egos. They repeated and repeated these lessons until the skills were second nature, so that they could be executed under the extreme pressures of white-hot competition at the national level. These coaches simply refused to accept an athlete's reluctance to go over and over the basics. They forced the issue, using their best teaching skills.

Executive coaches can do the same thing. With your client, establish a taxonomy of the basic skills and competencies. Your clients may lack basic listening skills (many people do), they might not send thank you notes, they might be poor time managers and show up late for meetings, or maybe they don't return phone calls promptly. Perhaps they don't know how to make an excellent oral presentation. Maybe they can't write an effective memo or proposal. Some people don't know how to behave at a meeting. Some don't know how to dress. Conduct an in-depth assessment of the relevant basics, and then go to work on them. Break jobs down into component skills and offer a few new ones. Teach these skills using your best teaching. Read pertinent corporate manuals and review them for your clients. Assign readings and go over them step by step. Practice the skills off-line where there's no risk or pressure. Model them for your clients. Problem solve when your clients get stuck. Sell the basics, especially when your clients think they seem simple or when it seems embarrassing to admit they are missing a skill. Some clients have been able to avoid confronting a skill deficit for years, but now it has finally caught up with them.

Teaching, first of all, requires an agreement between teacher and student. Each must agree to take on the appropriate role, along with its attitudes and behaviors. The teacher must first set the scene and create a learning atmosphere. He or she must then make a clear presentation, give examples, answer questions, and give guiding feedback. Sometimes the teacher exhorts, sometimes the teacher praises.

Teachers also respond to feedback about their own effectiveness, making adjustments as they go.

Theme Three: Use Individual Approaches, Flexibility, and Ingenuity

Psychologists sometimes get stuck in their primary theoretical point of view. This is professionally acceptable in the practice of psychotherapy, in part because it is a function of theoretical integrity. But this is counterproductive in executive coaching. Unlike many psychotherapy patients, coaching clients will quit the relationship when they aren't getting results.

> A teacher needs to find the trigger inside each student that will release his or her best work. Some students need to be pushed; others need space.
>
> —Tara VanDerveer
> Women's Basketball Coach,
> Stanford University (Walsh, 1998, p. 34)

Virtually all of the sports books emphasize flexibility in human relations. Don Shula refers to this as being "audible-ready" (Blanchard & Shula, 1995). (An audible is a change made in a football play at the absolute last moment—well after you've committed to a different plan.) Each coaching book stresses that absolute rules are counterproductive because athletes must be treated as individuals. Some people learn one way, some another. A coach with a limited or inflexible repertoire will not succeed. Even the athletic coaches with the most rigid reputations recognized this facet of their work, before the appearance of the free-spirited or "modern" self-centered athlete. Cookbook approaches are doomed, and executive clients will sniff them out and run for the door. Most executives have paid their dues in seminars and leadership classes. They've tried cookbook approaches, or they have bought the book but neglected to read it or have forgotten what it said. Coaches are hired and paid to bring a wide-ranging, creative, individually designed and compelling repertoire to the effort.

> . . . if something isn't working, we innovate. We try *anything* that will help. In coaching, we never give up. Never!
>
> —Jim Valvano (Krzyzewski & Phillips, 2000)

It is best to treat each new client as a unique adventure. Versatility is essential in executive coaching. There is no need to stick with one theory or one approach, as a psychotherapist might do. There are really no theoretical constraints in coaching. Be ready to try any innovative approach that has promise. Even if it doesn't work, both coach and client can learn from it. Communicate a sense that the coaching process is an adventure, and that it will be tailored for that specific client. Seek innovative ways to work with each client, and when something is not paying off, move quickly to a different method.

Theme Four: Play Against Yourself

One of the most intriguing aspects of sports is that at the end of a contest (not unlike the end of a business day) you can look up and see exactly how you did. There's always a large scoreboard, and it tells you (and the world) whether you won or lost. (Jones, 1997, p. 10)

Most coach books don't buy this harsh point of view. While some of these books obviously stress winning, often at enormous cost, the vast majority focus on playing against yourself; that is, striving to better your own best performance. They advocate setting goals relevant to your own progress and measuring performance against those, rather than against an opponent or scoreboard. They value a worthy opponent, as such an adversary offers the best test, but they don't vest much self-esteem in the outcome. One successful coach makes the point that if all the coaches in America choose the national championship as their goal, 99% of them will have to label their season a failure at the end of the year. John Wooden is the most steadfast advocate of this view (and is arguably the most successful basketball coach of all time). Wooden even emphasized the processes of preparing and playing as more important than the outcome—the journey over the destination. Wooden made it a point of saying (in public) that his team scored more points than the opponent, not that they beat them.

He never challenged us to win the game. He always challenged us to do the best we could do.
—Walt Hazzard (Walton, G. M., 1992, p. 65)

With so much at stake it seems implausible that big-time coaches would embrace this perspective, but apparently coaches believe it. For college teams, alumni are all over them to "produce" (read: *win*), and large amounts of money are involved. These books are quite convincing, though, and their coach-authors make a consistent case for the validity of unrelenting self-improvement. Most of these coaches stress goal setting, but the goals derive from an effort to improve relative to one's own gifts and past accomplishments, not to the performance of others.

> If you're always striving to achieve success that is defined by someone else, you'll always be frustrated. Define your own success.
> —Mike Krzyzewski (Krzyzewski & Phillips, 2000, p. 64)

This lesson is of obvious value to the executive coach and client. Rather than relying on the scoreboard of institutional personnel decisions, why not set your own personal learning and competence goals and then measure yourself against them? This is a much saner approach. You can't control the decisions that an organization makes about you, but you can control your expectations, goals, and effort. In this way, you can take some control of your own destiny. You choose the goals, you choose the standards, and you decide how well you are doing and how to respond. When you get passed over or "downsized" or offered an attractive opportunity, evaluate the situation based on how it fits into your own personal plan. Then decide how to feel and react. Coaches can teach this point of view to clients.

Theme Five: Visualize

Virtually all successful athletic coaches use covert imagery rehearsal, or visualization, as they call it. This technique has truly made it from cognitive psychology into the arena of big time sports performance. Athletes go through their entire performance ahead of time in their mind, step by step. John Robinson, the former USC football coach, calls this "rehearsal vision" and notes that diver Greg Louganis mentally rehearsed his dives forty times prior to the actual event (Robinson, 1996, p. 24). Athletes who have used visualization say that when they actually played they had the feeling that they had done it all before and that it was now second nature. One professional basketball coach described how he engaged in forty-five minutes of visualization at home prior to each game "to prepare my mind and come up with last minute adjustments" (Jackson & Delehanty, 1995, p. 121).

The guided imagery literature is available to executive coaches, and covert rehearsal is an essential tool in the coach's kit. Virtually anything can be rehearsed in the mind prior to execution. If coaches need a refresher in covert rehearsal, sources are included at the end of this chapter (see Bry, 1978; Lazarus, 1977). Assign these readings to willing clients. Coaches can teach and demonstrate covert rehearsal in client meetings and advocate its use at home and at work.

Theme Six: Video Feedback

Successful athletic coaches make extensive and creative use of video feedback to teach and support their lessons. Video provides us with information that is unavailable any other way, and it does so powerfully. No talk is necessary, and the feedback can be provided without much verbal criticism. Verbal feedback must be offered skillfully, lest the receiver experience it as "criticism." The tape is not critical, and it does not lie. Certain things simply cannot be communicated adequately with words, and sometimes a picture really *is* worth a thousand words. Athletic coaches would not think of coaching without tape. Big-time college and professional programs rely on video to understand what they are doing and what they need to change, even during contests, while the action is taking place on the field. Most use video to understand technical elements, but some creatively use it to change a player's attitude or to reward good performance or loyalty. For example, basketball coach Mike Krzyzewski once used it this way:

> So one day I had a five-minute videotape compiled of nothing but shots of Hurley's facial expressions during games. Then I sat him down in private and showed him how he looked to me and to everyone else on the court. He saw himself pouting, whining, pointing fingers, dropping his head, and losing his temper. When the tape finished, I leaned over to him and quietly said: "Bobby, is that the message you want to send to your teammates?" (Krzyzewski & Phillips, 2000, pp. 92–93)

On another occasion Krzyzewski spliced together a segment of the awful plays that a star had made during one bad performance and played it in front of the entire team. This seems risky, but perhaps this player needed a serious "wake-up call."

"Coach K" presents each senior with a video of the highlights of his best efforts each spring as a graduation gift to celebrate his career.

Bill Walsh once produced a video with a series of brief clips of stirring moments from several sports, focusing on the athletes' eyes and the way that they focused their concentration. He used it to motivate a complacent team (Walsh et al., 1998, p. 330).

Most psychologists and mental health practitioners underutilize videotape. It has enormous potential for executive coaches and should be used with virtually every client. Some measure of creativity is necessary, and many clients will be reluctant at first. But the benefit is worth it. Show clients how they look, how they act, and how they speak and sound. Tape meetings and evaluate them later. Practice new skills on tape and review them. Even audiotape is a powerful tool. With your clients' permission, tape messages that your clients send. Tape and practice them until they are perfect. It is much easier to learn how to leave an effective voice message when you can hear yourself and get a coach's feedback than it is to read about it in a book. Rehearse important conversations and interactions prior to execution. For example, audio-video rehearsal is useful when a client must deliver a difficult message to a partner or employee, when a client must sell something, and when a client must change a troublesome mannerism. Video is of particular value when an analyst or manager strives to become a partner. A move up the hierarchy often requires a shift in identity and style, and this is very hard to communicate without visual input. A recent *Harvard Business Review* essay makes the point that aspiring partners must "forge a new identity," but all the help they get is "snippets of vague advice" such as "If you want to be a partner, start acting like one." (Ibarra, 2000). This is easier said than done, but video feedback closes the loop between a comment like that and real learning. When you see how partners behave and then compare it to how you appear on a video screen, the changes are tangible. And the coach does not have to be the bearer of bad news. Just let the tape do the talking.

Theme Seven: Learning from Defeat

Virtually every coach's and athlete's book makes reference to the importance of adversity and one's response to it. They credit losses with great learning.

> To win, you have to lose and then get pissed off.
> —Joe Namath (Jones & Deford, 1997, p. 43)

Some of these books refer to personal tragedies such as the loss of a loved one or a hurricane as having been motivational. Duke's basketball coach calls failure a part of success (Krzyzewski & Phillips, 2000, p. 44). Pat Riley even has a name for sudden adversity or losses: He calls them "Thunderbolts." Such a thunderbolt can occur when a star athlete suddenly goes down with a major injury. These books make a great deal of how important it is to learn from negative events and to grow stronger from them.

This is of obvious relevance to the executive coach, especially when called in to help a client who has suffered a major career setback. There is a lot to be learned when you are passed over for a promotion or a prized assignment. A coach can help reframe the loss, while being careful not to trivialize it. First, empathize with how significant and disappointing the loss seems and feels. Next, discern how your client views it. Then find a way to introduce the possibility that the experience can be a turning point or learning point. What is there to learn from the event? What weaknesses does it expose? Does the loss imply that this client needs to move in a different direction or strengthen a skill or learn a new skill? The response of some people to a setback is to tell themselves that they simply must work harder. This is rarely effective, because they will then do more of the things that weren't working in the first place. It is more likely true that they need to sift through the wreckage and find ways to change, to do some things differently, to view other things differently, or to learn something completely new.

Pain and disappointment can generate energy, and the coach can help direct that energy toward a productive change rather than allow it to be squandered or used to further damage client self-esteem. Sports books are unanimous and clear about this. Everyone suffers setbacks, and the key is to take advantage of them, just as you take advantage of vitamins or the wind at your back.

Most of these books stress flexibility. One must be able to adjust to changes in order to succeed. When an opponent throws something your way that is new or unexpected you must be able to shift your thinking, make exceptions to the rules, and take a different approach. While many famous athletic coaches come across as steely taskmasters, their books typically contain examples of how they broke their own rules from time to time with good results. Often these exceptions were on behalf of a player who made a mistake, and were made on the basis of the coach's intuition rather than published rules.

Theme Eight: Communication, Trust, and Integrity

Sports coaching books stress the importance of communication, but then, so does everyone. The trick is to figure out what they mean when they emphasize it. In some cases it is possible that these big-time coaches have no idea what they mean and are, in actual fact, terrible communicators most of the time. Sometimes they simply mean that you should use clear language and a direct approach when you talk to an athlete.

> Coach K will always tell you the truth.
> —Steve Wojciechowski, Duke athlete
> (Krzyzewsk & Phillipsi, 2000, p. 221)

Several coach books emphasize the importance of direct, frank, and honest interaction. They point out that this may create difficult moments, but that the benefits clearly outweigh the negatives. Krzyzewski even goes so far as to recommend that you "Make the truth the basis of all you do." This would be hard to swallow from most big-time, big-program coaches, but Krzyzewski is a West Pointer, and you get the impression that he really means it.

Most of these coaches connect communication with trust, and trust with honesty. For several of these coaches, communication means looking the other person in the eye when you talk and listen, so that you fully understand his or her intention. They talk about clarity and checking assumptions, giving examples of what has happened when they failed to do so. They advocate confrontation of problems quickly and directly. Rick Pitino (Pitino & Reynolds, 1997, p.136) makes the recommendation that, in interpersonal confrontations "The goal is to connect, not defeat." This is an important insight because of the natural competitive dynamics that tend to lurk in male-to-male coaching or mentoring situations.

High-level communication skills are the primary set of tools for the executive coach. This means that you are able to model them as well as teach them. Directness, excellent active listening skills, and a commitment to the truth are as important to the executive coach as they are to the football coach. If you need a refresher in active listening, go get one. If you need to listen to yourself speak, tape some meetings and study how you sound. Upgrade the quality of your speaking and listening. Make it a point to read the latest on communication in business. Executive coaches are expected to know what the gurus are saying, and it is best if you can teach what they advocate (if you agree with it) or teach something better in response.

Executive coaches often find themselves in the role of consultant, and a lot of baggage accompanies that role. For many, the first reaction to a consultant is cynicism and distrust. Clients have had experiences with consultants that left a bad taste in their mouth, often because consultants over-promised and under-delivered. Then they disappeared or were "let go." Consider absolute honesty and frankness to be a core business skill. As the old expression goes, honesty shocks people. Serious, high integrity, communicated directly, enables you to stand out in the crowd, especially over the long haul. This is a tough standard, but it is absolutely worth it. Any embarrassment or loss of work or money over the short run will eventually pay off, even if the pay-off is only in the realm of your own sense of self. Your integrity is liable to be tested at least once with every client in some small or large way. Make sure that you pass the test.

Nuggets

Aside from the important themes common to this genre of books, many contain small and unique "nuggets" of advice for executive coaches. Here are a few that can be useful.

Nugget 1: Innocence

This is a very intriguing concept introduced by professional basketball coach Pat Riley. Although Riley's book (Riley, 1993) is never completely clear about his philosophy, it advocates an innocence regarding the basic tension between the human urge to take and to give. He recommends that his players take a chance on each other, giving—on the assumption that the gift will be reciprocated, resulting in a win-win outcome. Without this attitude of innocence, cooperation can't flourish.

Executive coaches would do well to experiment with such innocence. Begin with a commitment to integrity and assume that you can count on the same from others. Sometimes the results will disappoint. But without an innocent premise, long-term trust is unlikely.

Nugget 2: Clear Contract

Michael Jordan and Shaquille O'Neil's coach, Phil Jackson advocates a "clear set of agreed-upon principles" because they reduce conflict and "depersonalize criticism" (Jackson, 1995). Pat Riley advocates a "Core Covenant," and although his book is not exactly clear about what he means, he advocates the establishment of some central agreement between team members and coach—an agreement that all would hold sacred so that everyone could count on it (Riley, 1993).

This is excellent advice for the executive coach who is sometimes called into situations typified by their singular lack of clarity. Something is wrong or someone needs to be changed, but it is not exactly clear what that is. The effort required to make a clear pact and to agree on principles is well worth the time. It allows you to learn about your client at the same time you communicate and model the importance of clarity. Plus, as Jackson says, if you have agreement on principles, restrictions don't need to be personal. If your client has to miss a coaching meeting, you have already agreed on how it will be handled. There is no reason for either party to take it personally. The agreement is in place, so you just stick with it.

Nugget 3: Goal Setting Is Overrated

This one comes from Don Shula's book. Shula is old school, and a dean of American football coaching. His view is that goals can get in the way of present-moment living, of making the most of the opportunities and energy we have today. He feels that goal setting is important, but it is the follow-up and attention to details on a day-to-day basis that makes things work. He also advocates that goals, when set, should be small, clear, and well monitored, and that they shouldn't get in the way of immediate awareness.

He's right. Together with your client, choose discrete, do-able goals that are tracked. When you accomplish those, congratulate yourselves and move on to new ones with a sense of self-efficacy. Don't let them blind you to what is happening in the here-and-now. And don't pick goals that are global and difficult to accomplish or measure. They tend to hang over everyone's head and pollute the atmosphere when they aren't accomplished and won't quite go away.

Nugget 4: Curiosity and Confusion

Swimming coach James "Doc" Counsilman points out that curiosity is the first step in the learning process. He figures that curiosity must be present for learning to occur. Confusion follows when the learner is confronted with a situation that doesn't make sense, using the current knowledge available to the student. This is followed by a "quest for knowledge" (Walton, 1992, p. 78).

These factors are important to the executive coach who is often confronted with a client who is not necessarily curious about skills to be learned but is confused by what has happened. Instead of sorting out the confusion and helping clients to feel better immediately, it is probably a good idea to exploit these feelings of confusion to motivate the learner's curiosity. Reframe the situation so that it is perceived as an opportunity. Leverage the confusion to nourish curiosity.

Nugget 5: Perpetual Change

The older we get, the more we must change.

Rick Pitino, the basketball coach, makes this interesting point in his book *Success Is a Choice: Ten Steps to Overachieving in Business and Life* (Pitino & Reynolds, 1997). He writes that change becomes more important as we age, because it keeps us fresh and energized and young. This is often the opposite of how humans behave in real life, as we get older and more stuck in the same old dependable ruts. Pitino points out how quickly the business environment changes and how important it is to be ahead of the changes, or at least excited to move along with them. Mental health practitioners certainly must be willing to take heed and change with the times. This might mean a reexamination of important ideas and values, for the sake of surviving and thriving.

Nugget 6: Patience Is Not a Virtue

Although few of the marquee coaches seem to be patient human beings, Bill Walsh is explicit about it: "In reality, patience is not always a virtue" (Walsh et al., 1998, p. 355). He goes on to say that a proactive approach is better than giving the impression that things will work out in the end.

Executive coaches must pay attention to this factor and make difficult decisions about pushiness. How accepting should they be about the client's timeline and progress? Most business people expect to change and to grow faster than most psychotherapy patients. And they do. It is always possible, of course, that the pushy coach could alienate his client or foster resistance, but pushiness is more likely to be welcomed, especially when the fees are high. This can be difficult for former psychotherapists to learn and do, after years of patients and patience.

Nugget 7: Love, Fun, and Work

> *The master in the art of living makes little distinction between his work and his play, his labor and his leisure, his mind and his body, his information and his recreation, his love and his religion. He hardly knows which is which. He simply pursues his vision of excellence at whatever he does, leaving others to decide whether he is working or playing. To him, he's always doing both.*
> —James Michener (Blanchard & Shula, 1995, p. 67)

Most coaching books make this point in some fashion. Several point out the importance of fun—of having a good time while you work. John Robinson uses fun as a barometer: "Pay attention when you are not having fun," as this is an indicator that something is wrong (Robinson, 1996).

Executive coaching is the same way. Keep track of the level of humor and fun along the way, as well as the level of optimism and excitement. Use these qualities to measure the process. Add your style and the personality of your client to the mix. (Some people are very uncomfortable, at least at first, with mirth in the workplace.) Enjoyment does not necessarily mean laughter or jokes. It can simply be an attitude—that everything has an amusing or joyful element to it. Find an appropriate way to mix fun with the work. Make it a priority.

Nugget 8: Awareness Is Everything

Being aware is more important than being smart.
                    —Phil Jackson (Jackson & Delehanty, 1996, p. 113)

One coach book stands out from the crowd of others, in that it takes a distinctly "Eastern" perspective on big-time basketball. This is Los Angeles Lakers' coach Phil Jackson's book *Sacred Hoops* (Jackson & Delehanty, 1995). Jackson mixes the Pentecostal religion of his youth with Lakota Sioux culture and Zen koans and practice. The result is an intriguing take on how to align and motivate athletic mega-stars in order to win championships. One of the several valuable points he makes is that awareness is central to all that he teaches. You must be open to what is happening now—in the present moment, right here.

This is just as important to the executive coach as it is to the athletic coach. It is a fine idea to go into client meetings armed with extensive tools and tentative plans. But it is a mistake to allow those plans to interfere with observation and present-moment awareness. Take a posture of readiness—see what is going on and react.

Consider the following example. As an executive coach, you go to a session with a client, and you have clear ideas about what that client needs to do. But, as you pay attention to his physical movement and voice, you notice that he is fidgety and seems tense. Something about him tells you that he is not focused on what you are planning. So you stop what you are doing and ask questions. You inquire about his attention—what's on his mind? He tells you that he is facing a deadline. He has two days before his annual self-assessment is due, and he is immobilized. He doesn't know what to write or how to get started. So you shift gears (radically) and use the meeting to help him think about and write that document. You invite him to open up his laptop and you start to draft the assessment together. As part of the effort, you help him explore the issues you had originally intended to work on in the meeting. It is all related, and your client is highly interested and focused, because you are attending to the matter that is of highest priority to him at the present moment.

Prepare, and then be aware.

Summary and Key Points

1. Hundreds of sports books and famous coach's books flood the market these days. They are littered with clichés and well-meaning but simple motivational ideas. There is a sameness about them, but there are a few core ideas of great usefulness to the executive coach. Among these are:
   - Take the high road. Create honest relationships and protect your integrity.
   - Establish a clear working contract with your client and stick to it.
   - Learn, teach, and practice to perfection the fundamental building block skills required for success in the business world, even with "high-level" players.
   - Treat each client uniquely. Adjust quickly when things aren't working.
   - Consider the use of audio and video feedback with every client.
   - Pay attention to your own drive and single-mindedness. See if you can find a way to work that really "gets your juices flowing." Then watch your balance.
   - Pay attention to the level of excitement and fun. If it is not there, find out why.
   - Remain aware. Bring a tentative plan, but stay present. Don't let your plan get in the way. Notice what is happening in the here-and-now, and be ready to adjust.
2. Sample the genre of sports-motivation books. Find a few that you like and consider "assigning" them to clients for reading and discussion. Several are listed in the section that follows.

References

Berra, Y. (1998). *The Yogi book (I really didn't say everything I said)*. New York: Workman Publishing.

Bry, A. (1978). *Visualization: Directing the movies of your mind*. New York: Barnes & Noble Books.

Ibarra, H. (2000, March–April). Making partner: A mentor's guide to the psychological journey. *Harvard Business Review*, 147–155.

Jackson, P., & Delehanty, H. (1995). *Sacred hoops*. New York: Hyperion.

Jones, C. (1997). *What makes winners win. Thoughts and reflections from successful athletes*. New York: Broadway Books.

Lazarus, A. (1977). *In the mind's eye: The power of imagery for personal enrichment*. New York: The Guilford Press.

Pitino, R., & Reynolds, B. (1997). *Success is a choice: Ten steps to overachieving in business and life*. New York: Broadway Books.

Robinson, J. (1996). *Coach to coach: Business lessons from the locker room.* San Diego, CA: Pfeiffer & Company.

Walton, G. M. (1992). *Beyond winning: The timeless wisdom of great philosopher coaches.* Champaign, IL: Leisure Press.

Wooden, J., & Jamison, S. (1997). *Wooden: A lifetime of observations and reflections on and off the court.* Chicago: NTC/Contemporary Publishing.

Recommended Readings

Blanchard, K., & Shula, D. (1995). *Everyone's a coach—five business secrets for high-performance coaching.* New York: Harper Business Books.

Bradley, B. (1998). *Values of the game.* New York: Broadway Books.

Carril, P., & White, D. (1997). *The smart take from the strong: The basketball philosophy of Pete Carril.* New York: Simon & Schuster.

Cousy, B., and Power, F. (1970). *Basketball: Concepts and techniques.* Boston: Allyn & Bacon.

Chu, D. (1982). *Dimensions of sports studies.* New York: Wiley.

Davis, J. (1999). *Talkin' tuna: The wit and wisdom of coach Bill Parcells.* Evangelicals Concerned Western Regional Publishers.

Didinger, R. (Ed.), & Sheedy, B. (1996). *Game plans for success: Winning strategies for business and life from ten top NFL head coaches.* Chicago: NTC/Contemporary Publishing.

Gallwey, W. T. (1974). *The inner game of tennis.* New York: Random House.

Gopnik, A. (1999, September 20). America's Coach. *The New Yorker,* 124–133.

Hill, B. (1999). *Basketball: Coaching for success.* Champaign, IL: Sagamore Publishing.

Holts, L. (1998). *Winning every day.* New York: Harper Business Books.

Krzyzewski, M., & Phillips, D. T. (2000). *Leading with the heart; Coach K's successful strategies for basketball, business, and life.* New York: Warner Books.

Lombardi, V. (1963). *Run to daylight.* New York: Prentice-Hall.

Lombardi, V. (1995). *Coaching for teamwork: Winning concepts for business in the twenty-first century.* Bellevue, WA: Reinforcement Press.

Martens, R. (1987). *Coaches guide to sport psychology.* Champaign, IL: Human Kinetics Publishers.

Penick, H. & Schrake, B. (1992). *Harvey Penick's little red book: Lessons and teaching from a lifetime in golf.* New York: Simon & Schuster.

Penick, H., & Schrake, B. (1993). *And if you play golf, you're my friend: Further reflections of a grown caddy.* New York: Simon & Schuster.

Perry, J. M., & Jamison, S. (1997). *In the zone: Achieving optimal performance in business— As in sports.* Chicago: NTC/Contemporary Publishing.

Riley, P. (1993). *The winner within.* New York: Berkley Books.

Selleck, G. (1999). *Court sense: The invisible edge in basketball and life.* South Bend, IN: Diamond Communications.

Suinn, R. (1980). *Psychology in sports.* Minneapolis: Burgess Publishing Company.

Walsh, B. (1993). How to manage superstars. *Forbes,* June 7, 1993.

Walsh, B., & Dickey, G. (1990). *Building a champion.* New York: St. Martin's.

Walsh, B., Billick, B., & Peterson, J. A. (1998). *Finding the winning edge.* Champaign, IL: Sports Publishing.

CHAPTER

Bruce Peltier
Ana Maria Irueste-Montes

Coaching Women in Business

Women can transform the workplace by expressing, not by giving up, their personal values.

—Naisbitt & Aburdene (1986)

There are good reasons to consider the coaching of women as a special case. Although executives are (at this point in time) much more likely to be male, women are making serious inroads through the glass ceiling and into the boardroom. But men created the vast majority of companies, and the organizational architecture and culture of those companies reflect a distinctly male point of view. Male ways are often the norm, and women are faced with difficult and perplexing decisions.

- Should I try to act and talk and look more like a man?
- Can I have children as well as a serious or demanding career?
- Am I cheating my family and children for my own career interests?
- Should I hide my sexuality in order to succeed?
- Should I confront a system (or person) that seems unfair, or just try to work with it?

Men rarely consider these difficult questions. Most men aren't even aware that they are important questions.

Stereotypes and Misconceptions

Women face complex and powerful stereotypes in the business world, including these described by Reardon (1995, p. 77):

- Women aren't sufficiently committed to their work and career. They have conflicted motives (work vs. home).
- Women don't work well with other women.
- Women generally lack sports experience, so they can't be expected to understand teamwork.
- Women don't make compelling leaders.
- Women are too emotional (and insufficiently rational).
- Assertive women are difficult and demanding.
- Women aren't good at technical matters.
- Men resent female bosses.
- Women lack the killer instinct necessary for a successful business in a competitive climate.

There is another reason for a special chapter on coaching women: Women are more likely to welcome the help of a coach, while men are notorious help-rejecters. Men tend to see the acceptance of help as a sign of weakness, plus they often have access to important informal mentors, and they know it. Women are far more likely to grasp the value of a coach—someone outside of the organization who knows the ropes, someone who can give clear feedback, and someone who will listen to things that cannot always be spoken in public.

It must be stated at the onset of a chapter like this that generalizing and stereotyping are dangerous—and are as likely as not to be wrong in the individual case. There is no standard woman or typical man. There are even men who think more like women and women who seem more like men. Men and women who neatly fit the stereotypes are actually quite rare. If you pay attention, this can get very confusing. Nonetheless, some gender tendencies are worth noting, and the workplace undeniably perceives and treats men and women differently. Behavior is routinely interpreted differently based on gender, even if no one is quite aware of it at the time. These differences may be less visible in tightly controlled hierarchical organizations than in more flexible settings. There are also specific traps into which women and men inadvertently fall, and these are worthy of discussion. Coaches can be extremely helpful in the effort to sort through the gender swamp, especially if coaches are savvy, thoughtful, and not afraid to talk about unvarnished reality.

The problems of gender are not new. Thoughtful insights have been available in the literature for years. Take, for example, the work of Simone de Beauvoir (1952). She wrote fifty years ago about the role confusion that women experience when they enter the workforce. These confusions are changing, and as culture evolves, gender relations evolve, as well. But these confusions cannot be ignored, and it is unwise to pretend that the differences between men and women are insignificant.

Women in the Workforce

The playing field is more crowded now.

—Dayle Smith (2000)

Women have arrived in all arenas of the workplace, and they are not going back home, as they did after World War II. There are clear signs that women are major players in the current economy, and although the pipeline to the top of large corporations is twenty years long, women have made their way into powerful leadership positions. According to the U.S. Department of Labor, women will make up nearly half of the American workforce by the year 2005 (Smith, 2000), and most colleges report that enrollments are now more than half female. Recent reports indicate that women own nearly 40% of Silicon Valley tech companies and there are more than 60,000 female-owned firms in the San Jose area alone (She's the Boss, 2000). As companies require more good workers and managers, they are more likely to consider women than ever before, yet women still make up less than 5% of the senior players in large corporations. There are only three female CEOs on the Fortune 500 list; the evolution is far from over.

> Women in the corporation are about to move from a buyer's to a seller's market. (Schwartz, 1989, p. 68)

As women develop and expand their businesses, as they climb the corporate ladder, as they even the playing field and break the glass ceiling, coaching can be key. Coaches must understand how women function within an organization and how organizations view them. Coaches can be the essential go-betweens when a male organization meets a capable female executive. There is much to learn in this transition, and coaches can pave the way, translating the behavior of each gender to the other in the context of organizational effectiveness and career success. At the very least, coaches can provide a thoughtful sounding board for a perplexed and frustrated woman; at best, a coach can help an organization change.

This chapter focuses on important typical differences between men and women in the workplace and the problems those differences cause. The implications for coaches are discussed, and recommendations are made. Bearing in mind the fact that stereotypes, generalizations, and oversimplifications are dangerous, an examination of gender subcultures in the workplace is well worth the risk.

Problems and Challenges

Women face numerous special challenges in today's business organization. The first problem is at the macro level, where issues arise because men and women are raised differently. Obviously this is not true across the board (and it is possible that young, "modern" women are being socialized quite differently), but many women were raised to be "liked." They were taught to avoid making waves, to fit in and avoid sticking out, to smooth things out in relationships, and to "be nice." It is uncomfortable (if not impossible) for many women to call attention to themselves or to their accomplishments. To make matters worse, when they do take overt credit, some other women will feel that they have broken the unspoken rule of equality, and will find ways to informally sanction the offender. It is important for coaches to anticipate the complex reactions that women face when they deserve (and need) overt recognition, and to help them develop a strategy. In most work organizations, positive visibility is essential to one's career success.

More often than not, women are raised to become nurturers, and important aspects of their identity depend on this attribute. Women are stereotyped in this way. People expect nurturing behavior from women, and this expectation can lead to friction when a woman makes a tough business decision. The discrepant perception between female as nurturer and woman as decisive cost-cutter can be uncomfortable or disorienting to all involved, and unfair to women leaders. That same element of interpersonal relationship is minimized or even absent in the development of many young men, as they are socialized to compete and to win. When a man decides to downsize it is more likely to be viewed as smart, tough, and decisive.

The second overarching problem derives from the process of perception. Behavior is perceived and labeled differently based on gender. When Sally is decisive and direct, she is labeled a "bitch" or seen as "hard," severe, or cold. When Stan listens empathically, he runs the risk of being seen as "soft." When Sally works extremely long hours, people wonder what's wrong with her social life or why she neglects her children. (She might even feel those maternal concerns, herself.) When Stan makes a commitment to be home four nights a week by 6 p.m., his loyalty to the team is questioned. When women speak up, they run the risk of being seen as "mouthy." When they speak directly, they can be viewed as "pushy." When they express high standards, they can be called "picky," and when they are intense, they are called "moody."

Not surprisingly, research indicates that some women react to negative stereotyping by "disappearing" (Goffee & Jones, 2000). They wear clothes that disguise their femininity or hide their unique flair, or they try to blend in by behaving like men. This, of course reduces their chance of being seen as leader material, and it diminishes the likelihood that the unique qualities women bring to the workplace will be appreciated.

A third important gender challenge is that women usually do not get second chances. There is less tolerance for error or experimentation in the learning process. Others make a quick decision about their acumen in situations where men might get the benefit of the doubt. There are still officers in large organizations (and customers, too) who wonder whether women belong. After the first error or mediocre performance, the woman is effectively out the door.

The Testosterone Culture

Business organizations are typically male-led, and they are dominated by male culture and assumptions. Men invented the current rules. Even the office furniture is built for men (Evans, 2000, p. 128) as is the decor. American corporations reward a competitive approach to things, a direct, in-your-face mentality and communication style that puts measurable performance ahead of relationships. Here's a *Wall Street Journal* headline from August 8, 2000 that exemplifies this attitude. It is prevalent in the business milieu:

> "Competitive Drive: Palm Puts Up Its Fists As Microsoft Attacks Hand-Held PC Market"

Metaphors of war are common in the current competitive American business environment. Men play fighting games as children. They keep score, and there are clear winners and losers. The object of these games is to beat the other team or person, and then go on to the next game and do it again. Girls often play games for very different reasons: to develop, study, and cement relationships, or to nurture all involved. Observe your children if you don't think this is generally true.

Successful male leaders model self-promotion that is borderline boastful, and executives are expected to let people know about the important contributions that they have made. Aggressive verbal behavior at meetings is rewarded, and the stress is modulated with jokes about sports or sex or the ineptness of a colleague. The metaphors are often sports-based, and it is sometimes difficult to understand them if you don't know baseball or football ("Don't leave runners on base," or "I think we should punt," are two of a thousand such examples). Team building is done on the golf course or at sporting events, and a season ticket is a legitimate business expense in the eyes of the IRS. There is nothing that says women can't learn this culture, and many women love baseball. These days, women are increasingly involved with team sports at a young age. But it is less natural for women to think and behave in these typically "male ways," and there is an adaptation and accommodation required if they want to succeed. (When women interact in an all female setting, the topics and patterns are typically quite different.) It can all be overcome, but it is stressful and it takes extra energy for many women to succeed in a male culture. Some women resent this adaptation and would rather not have to bother with it in order to succeed. It represents an additional layer of barriers.

Glass Walls

In addition to the acknowledged "glass ceiling" that invisibly prevents women from rising too high, there are also "glass walls" in business organizations. Women tend to be clustered in a small number of areas including HR and marketing, the new "pink collar" jobs. Not as many women tend to make it into IT or Operations, which are typically male-dominated. The reasons are complex, and male managers and female workers both contribute to the problem. In many organizations, women do not have access to important streams of information, they do not have effective mentors, and they are not given challenging key assignments that are essential to promotion later. Many leaders have a blind spot when it comes to women. They are stuck in stereotyped views of female ability. At the same time, women sometimes cluster in comfortable places with other women in the organization. Some prefer jobs with a clearly nurturing purpose. Sometimes women are handcuffed by their own limited sense of their capabilities, which is reinforced by organizational culture. Coaches can be of obvious help in such circumstances. It is difficult to promote people to the highest levels of an organization if they have not succeeded in a broad range of positions. They will certainly lack the necessary perspectives, skills, and relationships to lead. If you have never been involved in Operations, how could you succeed as a CEO? It is possible, but a tougher sell. No company is going to install a CEO whose entire career has been in HR.

Men and women both make erroneous assumptions about women in the workplace. They assume that family is a woman's highest priority, and while that may actually be true, it may also be false. Leaders assume that some of their customers or clients might not appreciate the assignment of a woman to their work. Many assume that women will not be welcomed or effective in international assignments (there is literature that makes this assertion). None of these assumptions is necessarily true, and they must be "checked out" on an individual basis (Adler, 1994). Some women have to fight such assumptions in order to get important assignments.

Sometimes men misunderstand the attention of women, misinterpreting job eagerness or an ebullient personality for sexual interest. Little is written about this treacherous dynamic, but there are times when it gets in the way of effective work relationships, mentoring, and assignments.

Appropriate mentors are not always available to women, and it may be more difficult for women to get the informal help and advice that is essential to success in an organization or in the marketplace.

Women do not always have access to the experiences and the places where effective networking can happen. Are they members of the same clubs that prominent male leaders join? Do they dine or work out with them? Are they able to run in the same circles, go to the same lectures, take the same leadership training, and attend the same conferences?

Often, women are the primary caretakers in their families, and they assume the lion's share of the work and time required to raise healthy children. This places an enormous burden on them, and makes it difficult or impossible to be available for the same number of hours that high-performing male colleagues put into their jobs. The question of "balance" is one that is much more likely to be on the mind of a woman than of a man. Resolution of this question requires serious thinking and difficult negotiations with family members and work-team members.

> It is absurd to put a women down for having the very qualities that would send a man to the top. (Schwartz, 1989, p. 69)

Lastly, women are often blamed for these gender problems or challenges. Their plight is viewed as a personal weakness rather than a lost opportunity for the company. This makes it even more difficult to succeed without thoughtful discussion and assertive career planning. Women need to be reminded that they bring unique assets to the organization. Their presence tends to democratize a company, creating a clear competitive advantage over more hierarchical or autocratic firms.

Vive La Différence

> *. . . men and women are wired differently, and we are brought up differently.* (Evans, 2000, p. 21)

There are numerous ways that the general differences between men and women are important in the workplace. Coaches must be prepared to help female clients with these differences. These include differences in communication patterns, in focus, in orientation to task and relationship, image, taking credit, speaking up, and leadership patterns.

Communication Style

Women and men communicate differently in the workplace. Significant differences are described in Deborah Tannen's three volumes of work on male and female conversation. Her books are listed at the end of this chapter, and they are essential reading for the executive coach. She is a socio-linguist who has spent considerable time observing communication in business settings and she comes to the following general conclusions: Men and women tend to use different conversational styles, and when styles clash or are misunderstood, the problems they cause are mislabeled as bad intentions, lack of ability, poor character, or some other intrapersonal quality. The problem for women in the workplace is that, as Tannen puts it (1990, p. 15): "The male is seen as normative, the female as departing from the norm. . . . Furthermore, if women's and men's styles are shown to be different, it is usually women who are told to change." She notes that women are judged negatively because of their conversational style, a style learned early by many girls as a part of normal female development. Here are several of the prominent themes that Tannen describes. The reader is urged to consult the original sources.

1. Women are inclined to make requests or suggestions rather than make a direct injunction (e.g., "Would you mind taking a look at the Bull's-eye account if you get a chance?" instead of "Please audit the Bull's-eye account and let me know how it looks by Tuesday"). This can be confusing to men or women who don't understand what the request actually means (Tannen, 1994, pp. 78–94).

   Here's an example from everyday life (courtesy of Tracey Pomeroy):

   Jane: *Where would you like to go for lunch?*

   (Thinking, "Let's talk about it. I care about you and am trying to politely engage you in a friendly negotiation, so that we can agree on a place.")

John: *Let's go to Chevy's.*

>(Thinking, "You asked a simple, direct question and I gave you a clear answer. This is polite, because it lets you know what I want, plus it doesn't waste a lot of time haggling. I just want to eat, and Chevy's sounds good right now.")

Jane: *What about Tortolla's?*

>(Thinking, "He's being a little rude and pushy. Why didn't he ask me what I wanted to do? Doesn't he care at all about me and what I think?")

John: *Tortolla's might be crowed at this time of day*

>(Thinking, "If she wanted to go to Tortolla's, why didn't she just say so in the first place, instead of tricking me by asking what I wanted to do, and then ignoring my answer? What's going on here?")

This is an example of how different communication styles can get in the way of two well-meaning people and create confusion and bad feelings. Neither style is right or wrong, of course. They are just different, and they strive to get to the same place by a different route.

2. Some women apologize compulsively and unnecessarily (Tannen, 1994, pp. 43–51). This is a social convention, a kind of politeness, much like the greeting "How are you?" (No one really expects an direct, explicit answer to that question.) When women apologize (e.g., "Sorry I didn't get back to you yesterday"), men often see it as a sign of deference or even of weakness. Women simply use apologies to keep relationships balanced and to show respect. "When a guy hears *sorry*, he infers that you've made a mistake" (Evans, 2000, p. 147).

3. In this same way, women say "Thank you" as a way to sustain positive feelings in a relationship, not necessarily because something must be thanked (Tannen, 1994, pp. 54–57). This is sometimes confusing to men, when they figure that they must have done something to deserve gratitude. For men, thanking can put the thanker in a one-down position. In the competitive games of life, for men, thanking someone means that they've just lost a round.

4. Women sometimes ask for an opinion as a way to show consideration for another person, even when they don't intend to use the opinion when it is shared (Tannen, 1994, pp. 61–63). For women, a request for an opinion can simply be a tactic to show respect or to open a discussion. This can be confusing to men if they render

an opinion but it is not "used." Males may interpret such opinion-seeking as manipulative or as a sign of weakness or indecisiveness.

5. Men and women may use praise and criticism differently. Tannen describes the intrinsic trickiness in these behaviors, as people interpret and desire feedback in very different ways, depending on their personality and background (Tannen, 1994, pp. 66–70). Some people interpret lots of praise as manipulative or prying, while others are embarrassed by it. Others think they are performing poorly when no praise is given. Some bosses don't say anything to solid performers, because "everything is OK." Conversely, many men have had a coach or a father who told them not to worry when they are being yelled at or corrected. "Worry when I stop yelling at you, for that means I've lost interest in your development," they say. Tannen speculates that "many men feel women don't tell them directly enough if they are doing something wrong, and many women feel that men don't tell them directly enough if they are doing well" (1994, p. 68). This is confusing stuff, indeed!

6. Women use "trouble talk" as a form of rapport builder (Tannen, 1994, pp. 71–72; Evans, 2000, p. 23). They share difficulties as a way to connect with others. Men sometimes don't know what to make of such talk, and they often feel compelled to solve the problem presented in the talking. This is interpreted by the female participant as a lack of empathy, an inability to listen and care. Many men view such "trouble talk" as complaining or whining. In their view, real team players focus on the positives. They "roll up their sleeves" and get to work. For men, talk is more likely to be seen as the simple transmission of information, while women use talk to maintain relationship, support, and interaction. Evans (2000, p. 31) notes that you never heard *Dragnet* Sergeant Joe Friday say "Just the facts, *sir.*"

7. Women (although many men do this, as well) often communicate indirectly, and the indirectness is confusing to others (Tannen, 1994, pp. 78–95). Traditional male leaders, especially those who played on athletic teams or served in the military, are used to giving and receiving direct statements at work. Tannen gives several examples of women and men who "hint around" at important information instead of providing direct speech (including a transcript of a hypothetical airline crash that might have been avoided: "What do you think about that ice on the wings . . ."). Indirectness is not the same as weakness, but it can be interpreted that way in some cultures. Once again, women do this as a way to sustain relationships. It comes across as caring and respectful (e.g., "Would you mind getting the Anderson file when you get a chance, please?").

Dysfunctional Communication Patterns

In her book, *They Don't Get It, Do They?*, Kathleen Reardon describes five ways that male–female communication patterns damage women in the workplace. She refers to these dysfunctional communication patterns as "DCPs." They are:

- **Dismissive DCPs:** This is the most common pattern. It happens when men interrupt, talk over, or simply ignore what women say. Women are put in the difficult position of having to reassert their point, sometimes against resistance. Sometimes it is easier to relent and be silent, which perpetuates the problem. The trick is to find a way to create a culture that does not value this pattern or allow it to continue. Calling attention to the pattern off-line (later on, and behind closed doors) and commenting about it when it happens are two ways to start.

- **Retaliatory DCPs:** Sometimes men communicate with women in a manner that retaliates for all of the perceived slights that they have received at the hands of women in their lives. Sometimes they limit conversation as a way to avoid being bested by a women, which many men find extremely humiliating and unacceptable. When a woman has a bright idea, they abruptly find fault, and then criticize in a way that mystifies that woman. All of this happens without comment on the process.

- **Patronizing DCPs:** This problem derives from the traditional roles that women are perceived to play (mothers, wives, or daughters). Some men communicate with women as if they were communicating with their mother or wife or daughter, and sometimes women respond in kind. Men find it hard to view a woman as a colleague, so they diffuse the role discomfort by flirting or trivializing the conversation. Women then have to make the difficult decision about whether to go along with the role problem or confront and dispute it.

- **Exclusionary DCPs:** Reardon makes the point that men often have two different communications modes, one for use in an all-male situation, and one when women are present. This becomes clear when a man says something at a meeting and then apologizes to a woman who is present. This implies that certain things just can't be said in front of women, an exclusionary sign, when you think about it. This also happens when critical information is passed along at informal, all-male gatherings, of which women are well aware. Once again, the question arises: Should I confront this situation? If so, when and how? If not, what are the consequences for myself and other women (and men) in the company?

- **Undermining DCPs:** These are observations made about women that are disparaging or even devastating to a career. They are subtle and found in media reports that give organizations reason to sustain stereotyped responses to women in the work force. Examples include the evolution of the "Mommy track" for women who weren't assumed to be fully committed to their careers, and the highlighting of women who criticize other women in the workplace. It can be exhausting to have to deal with these subtly undermining influences in the media and the corporate culture.

Unless both parties are on the same song sheet, misunderstandings are likely. The best communication happens when both parties naturally understand what things mean (which is unlikely) or when they have discussed conversational style, made allowances, and gotten used to each other.

Task Versus Relationship

Women tend to pay more attention to relationships than to specific measurable outcomes. It's not that they don't care about measurable outcomes; it's just that relationships often seem more real and lasting. Plus, women are inclined to understand the impact that relationships have on the bottom line.

> The feminine mode of ethical decision-making is based upon the maintenance of relationships, upon the importance of cooperation, connection, and concern for others . . . . Responsibility to meet the needs of others lies at the core of the feminine perspective.
> —Anneka Davidson (Cooper, 1994, p. 415)

This runs counter to prevailing business trends that require close attention to the bottom line, to the stock price, and to quarterly performance measures. Men tend to pay attention to the bottom line, even if people or relationships are hurt by that priority. This is an interesting problem, because it is difficult to make a case for relationships over profit in the American corporation. Companies are not hobbies or social clubs, and they must deliver value to the stakeholders and stockholders. But the perception that profit and healthy relationships are mutually exclusive is a premise that women can help American industry challenge. Relationships are increasingly seen in the business literature as essential to long-term business success, more so than quarterly reports. It seems obvious that a strong team with solid long-term relationships makes sense. Here is the conclusion that Sally Helgesen came to in her classic study, *The Female Advantage* (1990, p. 5):

And so a picture of "feminine principles" emerges . . . .:
principles of caring, making intuitive decisions, not getting hung up on hierarchy or all those dreadfully boring business school management ideas, having a sense of work as being part of your life, not separate from it, putting your labor where your love is, being responsible to the world in how you use your profits, recognizing the bottom line would stay there—at the bottom.

Image

Various components of image play a role in success.

To a guy, everything counts. The size of his office, the size of his staff, the size of his salary, the size of anything that can be measured. And they are always keeping score. (Evans, 2000, p. 58)

Women need to pay attention to the ways that they create an image, as image often creates reality. Image may actually be more important to women in business, because they are so often in the gender minority. When you are one of only two women at a meeting, you are likely to be noticed, even if you are ignored.

If a client naively believes that all that really matters is performance, she is liable to pay a heavy career price (many men believe this, as well). Office space, office appearance, travel arrangements, and various other perks do not go unnoticed in corporate culture, and they imply a powerful message.

Clothing and personal appearance are also crucial, and some people are naturally better at this than others. Women are held to a higher standard than men in most business settings, and they have a more complex appearance code to which they must adhere. "Both women and men hold women to some very high standards in terms of dress" (Reardon, 1995, p. 112). The codes are different for men and women. Men presently have fewer options, the range of choice is narrow, and many males just don't care much about how they dress. They can wear any color, as long it is dark and gray, brown, or maybe blue or olive drab. If they wish, they can wear different colored ties each day. Not much thought typically goes into the process of choosing the male wardrobe each morning, and as long as they meet some fairly minimal standards, their appearance is deemed acceptable. This is not to say that men don't often need coaching about their appearance. They do. But the rules are simpler. (For more on this, see Chapter 8 on Social Psychology.)

Women have numerous choices to make, many of which have serious consequences. And there is no single mode or standard way for a woman to dress professionally in the workplace.

Taking Credit

They know what a good job I'm doing. Why don't they just reward me for it?
(Evans, 2000, p. 8)

Many observers note that women are much less likely to feel comfortable "blowing their own horn" (Smith, 2000; Tannen, 1994). In meetings, men in business often jump into a discussion, making their expertise and certainty explicit. They can sound quite positive, as they have been taught to do, while women can be more comfortable expressing doubts and uncertainty. Women are more likely to be polite to avoid seeming egotistical or presumptuous. Sometimes women allow themselves to be interrupted or ignored at meetings while men are elbowing each other for airtime. Women, according to Tannen and others, do not want to seem as if they are putting themselves "above" others. They seek, rather, for interpersonal balance, or at least, the impression of it. While men know that they must regularly assert their achievements to be taken seriously as a person with a future in the organization, women sometimes hang back, uncomfortable with this male posturing. Men and women even "boast" differently, with men playing a "mine-is-bigger-than-yours" kind of game, while women tend to promote themselves in a more understated way (Miller, Cooke, Tsang, & Morgan, 1992).

> When guys brag, it reminds them of being on a team. When women brag, men and women hear rudeness and pushiness. (Evans, 2000, p. 76)

Sometimes women aspire to success by working "behind the scenes." This stance may be comfortable for them, but it is unlikely to produce greatness or success beyond a circumscribed limit. Serious career effectiveness requires visibility. Once again, the key is in the interpretation. In certain male environments, when modesty is interpreted as inadequacy, the woman is the loser. Many women could benefit by learning to find a comfortable way to exhibit their strengths from time to time. Coaches can help them figure this out and find a style that works for them.

Speaking Up

This is a difficult gender area, and another in which differential perceptions hurt ambitious females. Males are taught to stand up and speak up. Plebes at West Point are made to stand on the bank of the

Hudson River and give commands that can be heard on the opposite shore. Many have trouble at first, but eventually all cadets learn how to do it. Women often learn the opposite: to hang back and let others take the floor, to speak quietly and modestly, and avoid sticking out in a crowd. When women do speak out, they run the risk of seeming boorish or obnoxious or pushy.

Occasionally, men can even yell at work and get away with it. Such an outburst might be seen as a "great leadership moment." But when a woman raises her voice, she runs the risk of being seen as out of control. She's *lost it*.

Even looking men directly in the eye can be risky for women. When men do it, it is seen as an act of good communication, even of honesty. Straightforward men reach out and offer a firm handshake and look you right in the eye. When women look men right in the eye, men don't always know how to interpret things. They get uncomfortable. It's confusing.

Many women have the experience of speaking, but not being heard. In order to succeed in the present business environment, women must find an assertive voice and find a way to navigate through these narrow waters. Too cautious and you are seen as inadequate; too loud and you are viewed as pushy. But modern business moves quickly, and you don't have time to wait for others to politely draw you out.

> It's very easy for them to ignore what you have to say. You have to be willing to speak up and occasionally make a fuss or they won't pay attention to you.
>
> —Shirley Peterson
> Northrup V.P. (Reardon, 1995, p. 5)

Leadership Style

There is substantial research evidence to indicate that women tend to lead differently than men, and this is no surprise, given the different ways that boys and girls are raised and socialized. Evidence implies that women are typically more inclusive and participatory in their leadership efforts. They are inclined to seek consensus and participation, and a case can be made that those qualities are truly modern and can be more effective in a creative, entrepreneurial economy. Women are also more likely to share knowledge and to solicit information from their team before they act. They are less likely to value domination or hierarchy in an organization, and tend to behave as someone in the center of a web of human resources. One female CEO calls her style "empathic enabling" (Betsey Cohen in Smith, 2000, p. 3). This is a far cry from the descriptions of leadership that male athletic coaches provide in Chapter 10 of this book. Several sources of research on leadership styles associated with women are listed in the reference section of this chapter (Carr-Rufino, 1993; Gilligan, 1982; Helgesen, 1990; Rosener, 1990; Smith, 2000).

Coaches are often called upon to help ineffective leaders or those who have been recently appointed to a leadership position. Good leadership is an acquired skill, and a detailed examination of a client's beliefs about leadership is extremely important. Most business leaders never actually examine the premises upon which their own leadership behavior is based. Coaches can help enormously when they conduct a 360-degree assessment for a leader. It is also important for coaches to actually observe the communication and style of leaders so that they can feed back accurate behavioral information. Most leaders never get accurate behavioral feedback because those being led are reluctant to provide it. It is difficult to adjust leadership behavior without accurate, direct feedback.

Successful and Unsuccessful Women

Research is available to help explain why women succeed or fail. The Center for Creative Leadership (Morrison, White, & Van Velsor, 1987/1992/1994) undertook a major study of female executives and found that the following factors were the most important to the success of women:

1. Help from above.
2. A track record of success.
3. Desire to succeed.
4. An ability to manage subordinates.
5. A willingness to take career risks.
6. An ability to be tough, decisive, and demanding.

It seems clear that a coach can be helpful in most of the areas listed above. A coach can help a female client to actively seek help from executives above her in the organization. If help is not available, perhaps this executive is in the wrong organization. Perhaps she needs to find help in other creative ways, including outside mentors and sponsorship. Risk-taking is something that a coach and client can examine together. The amount of risk must be optimal, never too great, and not too little. Sometimes it is difficult for a person to discover this without outside help. Toughness, decisiveness, and the ability to demand results are qualities that can be assessed and developed.

What a Coach Can Do

A coach can do many important things for a female executive client, whether she is in a large organization or on an entrepreneurial journey.

First, there is reason to believe that many women are somewhat unsure of themselves in the male business world, especially at first. Often, women are unnecessarily hard on themselves.

> When a man cuts himself, he throws away the razor. When a woman cuts herself, she blames herself.
> —Gail Koff (Smith, 2000, p. 263)

A coach can provide a calibrating influence. Help your female clients notice how they feel and how they want to feel, then work toward getting there. Sometimes just having a supportive confidant is enough to solve this problem; sometimes a change project must be mounted.

In many ways, the coach's job is to help clients assess and push their comfort levels. Often, a serious career upgrade requires a visit to the outside of one's comfort zone. Along those lines, a coach can often help a female client figure out how to become more visible in an organization without feeling too uncomfortable about it. Women cannot expect promotion to the highest levels of organizations if they have spent their entire career in places most comfortable for women. It is obviously important to have experience in marketing and, perhaps, HR. But it is at least as important to demonstrate success and expertise in Operations or Finance or IT or strategic planning, and it may not be easy getting there.

Coaches can help female clients communicate their career aspirations to those who "count" in their organization. Sometimes, because they have been "hanging back," key people in the organization misjudge a female's ambition or goals. This can often be fixed when an executive makes her desires clear. Sometimes this is as simple as sitting down with a leader and telling him. Occasionally this must be done repeatedly with several key people in the organization. Women cannot expect others to read their minds or guess accurately at their career goals, because, as often as not, others will get it wrong. Along those lines, a coach can help clients devise and suggest alternative ways for performance evaluation. Present methods may be based upon male norms and may be wholly inappropriate for a woman.

A wise and experienced coach can sometimes serve as a "gender translator." If that coach has been around organizations and has been observant, he or she may be able to translate rules, mores, codes, and the behavior of others for an executive client. This can save much heartache and heartburn.

A coach may even be required to help a female client evaluate her clothing, physical appearance, and image. This can be tricky. The key questions are these: Does the way you present yourself match your career goals? What is the message that you send when you walk into a room? Would you be comfortable if you presented yourself differently? Would a change be worth it? Does your office décor present you in an effective way? What messages does it send? At the present time these are very important questions for executive women. Videotape can be extremely useful in this area.

Coaches can help female executives become more comfortable with power and more creative in gaining and managing it. Many women would benefit from experimentation with how they present themselves and how they handle available power in an organization.

Coaches can observe, assess, and provide feedback to clients about their communication and behavioral style. This can be crucial. People cannot accurately judge their own style or impact, and a coach can be essential to this process. Watch your client on the job. Get real-time data and information. Synthesize it and communicate it to your clients in a way that energizes them and motivates them to make small but important changes. Create a change project with target behaviors. Monitor the changes and adjust the plan. Get more feedback and do it again.

Help your client with the "balance question," if it is relevant. This is an important challenge for most women, and it probably ought to be for most men. A neutral outsider—someone outside of job and home—can be very useful in this process. It can be gut wrenching, because success in some jobs precludes a healthy family life. Hard choices have to be made.

> You can't have it all. As a CEO, my work came first, my daughter second, and my husband third. Sometimes you don't feel very good about that.
> —Ann Spector Lief (Smith, 2000, p. 254)

Requirements for Coaching

Not every coach will be able to be useful to every client. Some men and some women may not be comfortable confronting the issue of gender as a coach. Some clients demonstrate no interest in gender issues, and others consider it to be irrelevant, or even a distraction. Some are exquisitely aware of the dangers related to gender politics in a male-dominated corporation or market, and they steer a wide course around these dangers. Many business people, including women, view attention to gender as a "liberal" or "feminist" agenda, and a distraction from the real matters at hand. Others seem to possess a macho attitude, dismissive of gender bias or problems. Some women detest any association with the victim role. In the business press, it is common to read newspaper articles containing quotes from successful women (and these are actual quotes), such as, "I never found myself disadvantaged based upon being a woman," "Do what you love. If you do, other things will take care of themselves"; and "When I encounter stereotypes, I put my head down and execute."

Assess your clients along this dimension. See how they view gender and the role that it plays. If there is a good match between your readiness and skill set as a coach with their interests and needs, proceed to study the gender question, head-on. If not, consider packaging gender issues in other, more acceptable ways. The same feedback and changes can be viewed as an individual matter, leaving the abstraction of gender out of the picture entirely. The same changes can often be made; the same development can take place, without calling it gender-based.

Effective coaching for women certainly requires a coach's awareness of these issues, as well as an interest in them. Gender is a central aspect of our identity, and it is extremely interesting. As Deborah Tannen notes (1994, pp. 13–14) "Few elements of our identities come as close to our sense of who we are as gender. When you spot a person walking down the street toward you, you immediately and automatically identify that person as male or female." You could misjudge someone's racial or ethnic identity or not care about it (which is not to diminish the relevance of ethnicity). But it is virtually impossible to miss gender. It simply cannot be ignored.

The effective coach surely must study the gender-in-business literature to prepare for the role of coaching women. It is a complex landscape, and nearly everyone has a powerfully felt opinion. Several books in the References and Recommended Readings that follow this chapter are important enough to be considered "required reading." Of special note are Harragan (1976), Helgesen (1990), Tannen (1994), Reardon (1995), Smith (2000), and Evans (2000).

Summary and Key Points

1. Remember that men and women often see things differently. They have different impulses, different views of how to get things done,

and different ideas on what is most important. At the same time, remember that stereotyping and generalizing are quite dangerous. There is no single "typical female" or "typical male." In fact, some women think and act more like the stereotypical male than females, and you can't tell who they are at first glance. Most of us possess some aspects of both genders. Study this question and help clients evaluate themselves. The key is to ask, listen, and watch. Encourage active discussion of the ways that gender influences things. Put gender on the table. Organizations that are male-run tend to favor male mores. Even in such organizations, however, a "female" style can flourish. In some cases, it can have a transformative impact on the organization.

2. Help female clients decide what to do about the gender problem on a case-by-case basis. Help them think through the rules and decide how they want to handle things. There are usually several options. Don't try to force people to behave in ways with which they don't agree, or find objectionable. It is best to take advantage of one's own style rather than to try to make a radical change. Small adaptations are usually possible, but wholesale gender style changes are ill advised. There are many ways to succeed.

   An option that often makes sense is to help a female client enter into discussions with key others to clear things up. "What do you think I mean when I say . . ." is an example of the kind of discussion that can clarify and strengthen work relationships between the genders. "Why do we do things this way or that?" is another. The key is to establish a culture that welcomes open gender talk, even when disagreement is involved. Most people find it intriguing, when presented properly.

   A gender-based 360-degree evaluation is a creative way to discover some of the gender-based trends and "ways" of the organization.

3. Avoid the impulse to blame and scapegoat. Don't blame the person and don't blame the organization. It is a waste of time and energy, and it tends to create costly negative emotions. If changes can be made in the organization, work on making those changes. But, be willing to help your clients accept the organization just as it is, without self-pity. Help them become savvy about gender politics and relations. It is unwise to take these things too personally.

4. Help female clients figure out the unwritten rules and gender codes. Do a research project. Ask others in the organization about these rules. Most people have their own slant on them and are happy to reveal them to a coach or a coworker.

5. Encourage your client to find an informal mentor within or outside

of the organization. This is nearly essential to career progress and development.

6. Create a career plan or succession plan with your client. If this is not possible, at least open a discussion about where she is headed. Be careful about glass walls—invisible barriers that keep women in career ghettos. A successful rise to the top of a hierarchical organization usually requires time in key organizational positions (revenue-generators, decision-making, make-or-break jobs).

7. Coaches would be wise to support female executives at times when they become discouraged or demoralized by the prospect of swimming upstream in a male-dominated organization. The day-to-day toll can be exhausting, and it helps to have someone in your corner.

Finally, there may be small advantages available to women in the workplace these days, and coaches can help women find them.

> The fact that I am a female may give me an unfair advantage due to my "scarcity" value. The redhead may be far more memorable than a zillion investment bankers who all look alike. Genetic dice work that way. It's up to me not to screw it up.
> —Christina Morgan (Smith, 2000, p. 259)

References

Adler, N. (1994, Autumn). Women do not want international careers: And other myths about international management. *Organizational Dynamics,* 66–79.

Carr-Rufino, N. (1993). *The promotable woman: Advancing through leadership skills.* Belmont, CA: Wadsworth.

de Beauvoir, S. (1952) *The second sex.* New York: Vintage Books.

Evans, G. (2000). *Play like a man, win like a woman.* New York: Broadway Books.

Goffee, R., & Jones, G. (2000, September-October). Why should anyone be led by you? *Harvard Business Review,* 63–70.

Harragan, B. (1976). *Games mother never taught you.* New York: Warner Books.

Helgesen, S. (1990). *The female advantage: Women's ways of leading.* Garden City, NY: Doubleday.

Miller, L., Cooke, L., Tsang, J., & Morgan, F. (1992, March). Should I brag? Nature and impact of positive and boastful disclosures for women and men. *Human Communication Research,* 364–399.

Morrison, A., White, R., & Van Velsor, E. (1994). *Breaking the glass ceiling: can women reach the top of America's largest corporations?* Reading, MA: Addison-Wesley. (Original work published 1987; Fev. Ed., 1992)

Naisbitt, J., & Aburdene, P. (1986). *Reinventing the corporation.* New York: Warner Books.

Reardon, K. (1995). *They just don't get it, do they?* Boston: Little, Brown.

Schwartz, F. (1989, January–February). Management women and the new facts of life. *Harvard Business Review,* 65–76.

Smith, D. (2000). *Women at work: Leadership for the next century.* Upper Saddle River, NJ: Prentice Hall.

Tannen, D. (1990). *You just don't understand. Women and men in conversation.* New York: Ballantine.

Tannen, D. (1994). *Talking from 9 to 5. How women's and men's conversational styles affect who gets heard, who gets credit, and what gets done at work.* New York: William Morrow and Company.

Recommended Readings

Blum, D. (1997). *Sex on the brain: The biological differences between men and women.* New York: Penguin Books.

Davidson, A. (1994). Gender differences in administrative ethics. In T. Cooper (Ed.), *Handbook of administrative ethics.* New York: Marcel Dekker Inc.

Engendering a debate. (2000, June 4). *San Francisco Examiner,* J–1, 2.

Gilligan, C. (1982). *In a different voice.* Cambridge, MA: Harvard University Press.

Gray, J. (1992). *Men are from Mars, women are from Venus: A practical guide for improving communication and getting what you want from your relationships.* New York: Harper Collins.

Henning, M., & Jar dim, A. (1977). *The managerial woman.* New York: Pocket Books.

Rosener, J. (1990, November/December). Ways women lead. *Harvard Business Review,* 119–125.

Ryan, W. (1971). *Blaming the victim.* New York: Random House.

She's the boss. (2000, August 4). *San Jose and Silicon Valley Journal,* 29.

Tannen, D. (1986). *That's not what I meant! How conversational style makes or breaks relationships.* New York: Ballantine.

Tavris, C. (1992). *The mismeasure of woman.* New York: Simon & Schuster.

Willen, S. (1993). *The new woman manager. 50 fast and savvy solutions for executive excellence.* Lower Lake, CA: Asian Publishing.

12

Workers, Managers, and Leaders

Leadership is different from management, but not for the reasons most people think.
—John Kotter, 1990

People generally don't understand the essential differences between leaders and others. Much of what they do know is wrong and problematic. Since coaches are often called upon to help line workers make the transition from follower to manager and to help managers move into leadership, it is essential that coaches clearly understand the different sets of skills and behaviors required at each level. Many executives have not thought much about the distinctions between leadership and management. The old "industrial paradigm" sees leadership as simply excellent management or management that is particularly popular or effective.

The skills and the differences between leadership and management are not generally taught in school, and people are supposed to pick them up, somehow, as they move through their career. This is impossible to accomplish without independent study, partly because of myths related to the leadership function, myths like the following:

Myth: Leaders are born, not raised.
Myth: Leadership skills develop naturally as one moves up through an organization.
Myth: You must thoroughly understand (and preferably master) the content skills of those you lead.
Myth: Before you become a leader, you must learn how to be an excellent follower.

Myth: Managers must be leaders.

Myth: What we really need is more leadership and less management.

Myth: Real leadership cannot be taught.

Myth: There is no unique set of leadership skills. It's common sense, and for the most part, consists of good personal and work habits.

Myth: Managers and leaders do about the same thing in an organization, just at different levels (and for different compensation).

These myths create problems for organizations, as they inhibit good leadership as well as good management. It is clear that leadership skills can be learned by motivated learners. It is also clear that, as John Kotter (1990, p. 109) puts it, "the on-the-job experiences of most people actually seem to *undermine* the development of attributes needed for leadership." There is little evidence that good followers make good leaders. The required skill sets seem to be nearly independent of each other. Some great leaders have been notably poor followers (George Patton being the paradigm example). In today's busi-ness culture, there is virtually no way that leaders can possess the technical skills of those they lead. The requisite skills change too quickly. Do you suppose that Bill Gates can still write useful computer programming code? Leaders and managers perform uniquely different functions using different sets of skills, and both are crucial to organizational success.

The last myth in the list, that managing and leading are essentially the same, is the one that coaches must thoroughly understand. Coaches are often called upon to help a bright, promising executive move from worker to manager and from manager to leader. They must be able to teach clients the important differences and help them develop leadership skills that will enable them to excel. In fact, the skills that make for a great line worker might actually get in the way of someone in the manager's role, and the skills and personality of a terrific manager can be counterproductive when that same person is thrust into the leadership role. The following section outlines some important distinctions between workers, managers, and leaders in a typical hierarchical organization. Table 12.1 summarizes these differences.

Differences Between Workers, Managers, and Leader

The Line Worker or Professional

A review of the important skills required by workers at the entry level is necessary. There are extensive sets of personal habits and behaviors

TABLE 12.1. Differences between workers, managers, and leaders

Worker/professional	Manager	Leader
Performs basic tasks	Controls things	Creates things
Performs repetitive tasks	Keeps track of things	Changes things
Needs and uses resources	Budgets, makes ends meet	Finds resources
Develops specific task expertise	Plans	Gets the mission defined
Finds new business	Organizes	Creates an environment
Creates product/provides service	Solves problems	Shakes things up
In contact with customers	Copes with complexity	Sets the direction and tone
Enlists new clients, customers	Staffs jobs and tasks External locus of control Conservative and cautious	Aligns people Internal locus of control Creative risk taker
Follows rules	Rule oriented, system based	Imagination based
Needs managers (and leaders)	Needs leaders (and workers)	Needs managers (and workers)
Interacts with outsiders	Interacts internally Keeps people in line with systems	Interacts with outsiders Inspires people
Responsible for own effort, production and sales	Responsible for performance of organization	Responsible for overall outcome
Works independently	Deductive process	Inductive process
Lacks overarching viewpoint	Creates structures Risk averse	Creates mandates Risk taker
Takes direction from others	Uses authority and rules Gives direction Keeps everybody lined up	Uses influence Convinces Shows the direction
Provides feedback to organization	Monitors organizational culture	Monitors outside culture

that ought to be in place before a professional worker shows up. This is, of course, not always the case, and coaches can certainly help workers identify and develop the necessary skill set. Certain skills are essential, because they are the fundamental basis for the organization's success. New customers and clients must come in, and work must go out. Employees must possess energy to get things done, and they need basic communications skills, basic content skills, and basic computer skills. They must be well organized and reliable. Some require extraordinarily complex skills and a drive to succeed. Some jobs require workers to develop a serious expertise. They must be adequately loyal to the organization and its goals, even when they don't agree with current tactics. They need to be willing to be told what to do, to "follow orders" often when the orders don't make sense or when they disagree. They need a positive attitude, to be able to see things in a good light and to behave pleasantly. Increasingly, workers must be able to make a good impression with customers through a service orientation and the ability to go the extra mile to provide exceptional customer service. They also need to be able to provide feedback to the organization when something is amiss or is being done poorly. They need to be reasonably well organized and able to cope with paperwork efficiently. They have to be able to learn new tasks as demand arises. They must avoid the destructive behavioral traps like substance abuse, sexual harassment, and entangling office romance. They must be able to effectively manage the written word. And they need to be able to get things done, to see projects through to their completion.

The Manager

> Managers seek order and control, and are almost compulsively addicted to disposing of problems even before they understand their potential significance.
>
> —Abraham Zaleznik (1992, p. 131)

Managers, as Abraham Zaleznik wrote in the *Harvard Business Review* (1998, p. 61), "ensure that an organization's day to day business gets done." Managers are about *control*. They create order out of potential chaos and translate leadership's vision into productive reality. They tame complexity. They direct people, reinforce desired behavior, and punish that which does not conform. They are the gatekeepers, and often say "no," when an idea is out of conformity with the system. They limit things and they dislike disorder. They make sure that the organization has "the right products in the right places at the right time and in the right quantity" (Sloan, 1964, p. 440). They regulate and safeguard the company's resources, and pay close attention to what is happening in the present moment. They know where everything is, and they work hard to meet established goals. They set goals that are aligned with organizational strategy, as they understand it. Much of what they do and think is data-based these days, and they rely on spreadsheets. They are highly interested in what leadership is thinking and are likely to be involved in bureaucratic politics and intrigue. They know where the bodies are buried. When something works, they keep doing it, and they can be hostile to change, for change causes them problems. They've got systems in place that have worked well, and changes force them to adjust their systems.

The managerial personality is best when it is calm, rational, and analytical. Managers are tolerant, but demanding. They are on the lookout for problems, for shortages, and for deviation from the system. The successful ones are diplomatic. They are sensible and reliable. They tend to be realists, and they don't much like risk. They are very much focused on *how* and *whether* things get done rather than *why* or even *what*. Tell them what needs to be done and they will find a way to get their system and people to do it.

None of this is meant to disparage managers or managing. Excellent management is essential for organizational success, and it is not easy to do. Recent business literature and training has given the impression that leadership is a good thing and management a bad thing (Bennis & Nanus, 1985). In this view managers are associated with bureaucracy, and that is seen as bad. Leaders save the day by cutting through red tape and creating action. Good management, however, creates systems that work, and people rarely complain about those. Nor do managers get much credit. Management is not as glamorous as leadership, that's for sure, but is exceptionally important. If you have a great idea and hard-working employees, but you can't get a product to market, you die. If you have a great product but you can't get it delivered on time, what's the point? If your resources are squandered through laxness, how could your organization possibly succeed? Leadership can motivate people to try harder, but a good system is required. What good is a mayor who charismatically urges good public transportation if there is no one in place who knows how to manage such a complex system?

Although good management is not as rare as good leadership, it is not common. Managers organize and coordinate complex systems that are essential to our well-being. Disorganization and poor coordination drives people crazy, damaging morale and running customers off. Organizations need effective management in order to survive and succeed.

People hate to work for dictators, of course, and the set of personal and functional skills required by effective managers is extremely valuable. Humane efficiency is worth its weight in gold, yet it is often taken for granted.

> Effective managers are a joy to behold and a pleasure to work with in any organization. People love to work for well-organized managers who facilitate getting the job done by coordinating the work of various people, and they hate to work for managers who are ineffective, uncoordinated, or incompetent. (Rost, 1991, p. 106)

Managers exhibit leadership behaviors, but those behaviors are not necessarily found in their job description, nor are they essential to their function. Those behaviors are often helpful but sometimes counterproductive. While a manager might be charismatic, and his or her charisma might be helpful, it is not an essential component of effective management performance. Sometimes the charisma of a manager can get in the way, causing jealousy and resentment from above. Managers might be visionaries, but that is not an essential management quality. While it is often best to influence subordinates, a manager influences people to conform to a system that is in place, not to change the basic arrangements. When a manager influences people to work harder or to do things in a new way, he or she is using leadership skills, but this is not a leadership function. When everyone in an organization exercises leadership, the resulting changes must still be managed.

> Of course, leadership from many sources does not necessarily converge. To the contrary, it can easily conflict. For multiple leadership roles to work together, people's actions must be carefully coordinated . . . by strong networks of informal relationships. . . . (Kotter, 1990, p. 109)

Leaders, hopefully, have established overarching mores and relationships for followers to use. Too much leadership behavior (in the wrong places) can create the very chaos that managers are paid to control.

The Leader

> *Leadership is not equivalent to office-holding or high prestige or authority or decision-making. It is not helpful to identify leadership with whatever is done by people in high places.* (Rost, 1991, p. 98)

Leaders are responsible for the overall outcome, and they determine the overall direction for the company. They create the organization's vision, and they align people and things to make it come true. They create a process by which the social order of the organization is formed or shifted (Rost, 1991). Their focus is usually on change. They sometimes create chaos for managers to clear up. Leaders influence the reality and direction of an organization. While management can coerce you, you must volunteer to be led.

Classic leader behaviors include breaking paradigms, motivating people to see things in a new way, causing others to shift priorities, and disrupting the status quo. Leaders are not always comfortable to be around or to hear. They can disturb and frighten. They upset things, they point out faults in the way things are. They *intend real changes* (Rost, 1991).

While there may be times when minimal leadership is required, in the modern environment, where change seems rapid and normal, leadership takes on an essential role. It is a rare organization that can survive by simply doing something well for long periods in the same ways. Other companies catch up or find a better way.

Leaders tend to be restless as a personality style. They love change and hate mundane, repetitive work. They like to use their imagination and they trust their own intuition. They enjoy being alone and like to reflect on things. They are comfortable with risk and understand its role and importance. They tend to be competitive by nature, and this translates into a desire to be "the best," to be on top of the heap. Competition gets their juices flowing. Sometimes they act without thinking things through. They don't always realize that they must follow all of the same rules as everyone else. Their work life and workplace might even be disorganized, so they hire someone to organize them.

Although it is a plus when leaders are also good managers, it is not essential. If real leaders are rare, then real leaders with good management skills are even more rare. An organization simply can't wait around for such a person to evolve, so it hires a leader (or follows an emergent one) who lacks management skills. It is then essential to hire excellent managers to compliment and administer the leader's vision. In many cases, great leaders could never put their ideas into practice (or if they could, it wouldn't be for long), and great managers could never think up the ideas that they are now managing. Leaders and managers need each other.

Leaders communicate with organizational outsiders. They present the vision and image of the organization to stockholders, funding sources, government agents, and the public. They pay attention to the interests of those parties and bring feedback to the organization so that adjustments can be made. They manage boards. They establish life-or-death interpersonal relationships with important outsiders. Effective leaders are able to create trusting relationships that become resources in times of trouble.

Leaders do one more thing that is not typically associated with the management function: They think. They reflect, they synthesize, they develop and use their imagination. They take in information from wide-ranging sources (including newspapers and best-selling books), and they integrate it into the organization they lead. Managers have no time to think. They are paid to be on top of things. They don't have much time, and they are not paid to take time. Leaders are paid to reflect.

The "Modern" View

Certainly this model represents a traditional view of the hierarchical organization. Newer versions of business organizations stress a flatter structure, with shared responsibility for leadership throughout the organization. Each member of the company team is responsible for providing vision, motivation, and direction. Such a structure can be enormously effective in some markets and environments. But it is probably not suitable for all business situations, and it often does not survive as a company matures.

Similarly, many managers find it important to serve as leaders of those who report to them. Certainly they must motivate and find creative ways to accomplish their tasks. But most of the critical leader functions are still most appropriate for those in leadership positions.

The Coach's Opportunity

Leadership coaches are hired for two reasons. They are either paid to help "fix" problem people (or remediate deficits) or they are brought in to help a person make the transition from one career step to another.

Coaches thrive most when they are seen as an essential component in the developmental process of the organization's leadership. If you (as an individual) have a coach, the organization sees you as having promise, and is willing to invest in your transition from worker to manager and from manager to partner or leader. The distinctions between these roles offer an important opportunity for the coach.

Most organizations are poor teachers of leadership, and few are organized to grow real leaders. Many actually punish those with real leadership inclinations. The leadership literature points out that people desiring leadership development cannot learn their skills in school or at institutes or by reading (although these activities must certainly help). They need to have guided leadership experiences, and they need help to learn from their own inevitable mistakes. They require challenging assignments early in their career, and they can use extensive mentoring and time for reflection. A coach can be of enormous help in this ongoing process, especially when mentors are not available.

The Roles Coaches Play

In 1997, Witherspoon and White wrote a defining booklet on executive coaching at the Center for Creative Leadership (*Four Essential Ways that Coaches Can Help Executives*). They describe the following four essential roles that coaches can play. These roles should be contemplated and discussed with clients early in the coaching relationship.

Coaching For Skills

Witherspoon and White recommend skills coaching when workers (and occasionally managers or leaders) need quick help learn a skill. This process can start from the basis of a self-perceived deficit or as the result of an assessment. Examples of such skills include public speaking, listening, personal organization and time management, presentation of self (appearance or behavior), teaching how to cold-call, even providing an in-depth understanding of the product or service that the organization offers. Sometimes a professional becomes aware that he or she is not "coming across" effectively. Coaches can perform an assessment, present the results, collaborate in the creation of a learning plan, and help the client put his or her learning into effect. This aspect of coaching tends to be brief and circumscribed. When the executive learns the skill, the coaching is finished.

Coaching for Effect

This form of coaching focuses on the executive's current job and his or her performance in it. Such coaching is appropriate for managers who face difficult obstacles. Clients often do not know what is wrong or lacking, but they have reason to believe that they need to improve what they do. This form of coaching is more comprehensive, and it, too, begins with an assessment, but this assessment is likely to seek input from a wide range of sources. A 360-degree evaluation is often useful. It tends to be intermediate in time-span, lasting over several months or as long as a year. It has specific goals, and the goals are organizational in nature. For example, the coach and client will know that they are successful when specified organizational outputs improve. Coaching might focus on analytical skills or tasks, problem solving measures, team-building, organizational architecture, or operations manage-ment problems. Such a coach must possess expertise in the arena of focus, or at least must be able to locate someone with task specific skills for consultation.

Coaching for Development

This role is appropriate for workers, managers, and leaders, alike. It strives to prepare a person to move to the next level. It involves an analysis of the essential skills required for the future, an evaluation of skills in place, and a comparison of the two. Coach and client work together to develop those necessary skills and the experiences required to gain them. As Witherspoon and White point out, it may even involve the unlearning of a behavior that was once useful but will be a liability in the future (p. 9). The goals may be less clear and more personal in nature, and they might even involve an examination of where the client wants to go with a nascent career. It might call for a clear-eyed look at how realistic the client's goals are.

Coaching for the Executive's Agenda

This is the coaching role most closely related to the leader function. A coach can be used by a leader on an on-going basis to help that leader develop and to help him or her evolve the organization. This role is likely to be on-going, with ambiguous and ambitious goals. The coach may be available regularly or on an as-needed basis. He or she may help that leader to think things through, to reflect, to make decisions, and to provide support when problems get difficult or the process gets lonely. The coach can act as a sounding board and reality test.

Summary and Key Points

1. Management and leadership are different, and the relationship between the two is widely misunderstood. Coaches can bring useful clarity to an organization, even in modern "flat" organizations.

2. Coaches can help clients move from one level to another. It is nearly impossible to learn adequate management and leadership skills without mentoring and growth experiences. You can't learn to ride a bicycle without getting on and falling off a few times. Mistakes will be made. Coaches can serve as important mentors and teachers in this process.
3. Coaches must help clients accurately determine the appropriate purpose for coaching and then apply the right interventions. Significantly different interventions are useful in different circumstances.
4. The role of coach as developmental mentor is important to the coach, for it removes him or her from the negative role of remediator of "losers" or people the organization will eventually shed. Coaching can be a resource for "fast-track" people.
5. Most organizations do not breed leaders. Coaches can help them create a leadership development culture.

References

Bennis, W. G., & Nanus, B. (1985). *Leaders: The strategy for taking charge.* New York: Harper & Row.

Goffee, R., & Jones, G. (2000, September–October). Why should anyone be led by you? *Harvard Business Review,* 63–70.

Kotter, J. P. (1990, May–June). What leaders really do. *Harvard Business Review, 90,* 163–176.

Rost, J. (1991). Leadership and management (pp. 97–114). In G. R. Hickman (Ed.), *Leading organizations.* Thousand Oaks, CA: Sage.

Sloan, A. P. (1964). *My years with General Motors.* New York: Doubleday.

Witherspoon, R., & White, R. (1997). *Four essential ways that coaching can help executives.* Greensboro, NC: Center for Creative Leadership.

Zaleznik, A. (1992, March–April). Managers and leaders: Are they different? *Harvard Business Review,* 126–135.

Zaleznik, A. (1998). Managers and leaders: Are they different? *Harvard Business Review on Leadership.* Boston: Harvard Business School Publishing.

Recommended Readings

Bennis, W. G. (1977, March–April). Where have all the leaders gone? *Technological Review,* 3–12.

Bennis, W. G. (1989). *On becoming a leader.* Reading, MA: Addison-Wesley.

Bennis, W. G. (1989). *Why leaders can't lead.* San Francisco, CA: Jossey-Bass.

Goleman, D. (1998, November–December). What makes a leader? *Harvard Business Review,* 93–102.

Harvard Business Review on Leadership. (1998). Boston: Harvard Business School Publishing.

Mintzberg, H. (1990, March–April). The manager's job: Folklore and fact. *Harvard Business Review.*

Phillips, D. T. (1998). *Martin Luther King, Jr. on leadership.* New York: Warner Books.

Syrett, M., & Hogg, C. (Eds.). (1992). *Frontiers of leadership, an essential reader.* Oxford, UK: Blackwell Publishers.

Weinstein, B. (2000, August 27). What a techie gives up to be a manager. *San Francisco Examiner and Chronicle,* CL 23.

Ethics in Coaching

The search for excellence, whatever it may be, begins with ethics.
—Robert Solomon, 1997

Clinicians are used to formal ethics codes and standards. Each subspecialty within psychology has a written code, and members of professional organizations are generally well aware of them. Therapists take required ethics courses in graduate school and clinicians take mandatory continuing education in various ethical and legal topics as they evolve. Psychotherapists of various types are members of longstanding professions, and these professions have rules, traditions, mores, and a culture. The American Psychological Association has been publishing ethical codes and standards since 1953. In psychotherapy, there is even a complex "standard of care," the unwritten normative behaviors expected of members of the professional community. Practitioners are held to those standards.

This is not so true in management consulting or executive coaching. Coaching is too new for well-defined group norms or formal professional structures, so coaches must monitor themselves. Ethical standards are in the process of development. In the mean time, individual coaches are on their own to make difficult moral decisions. Clinical codes and standards are available as a reference point, but they do not suffice. This chapter outlines areas where clinical and coaching ethics are similar or the same, along with several difficult areas where they differ. References and published guidelines are provided at the end of the chapter. As the practice of executive coaching evolves, so will the need to clarify and codify ethical standards. For now, coaches must use thoughtful individual judgment and healthy doses of collegial consultation. In general, honesty and avoidance of exploitation are probably the single best general guidelines for coaching practice.

Two Different Cultures

There is a cultural problem one encounters when making the transition from clinical counseling to management consulting or executive coaching. It has to do with primary value orientations in the two fields.

In business, there is a proprietary culture, one based upon a *competitive* market premise. Buyer and seller compete for the best deal they can get. Each expects the other to compete. They don't expect the other to look out for them or for their interests.

This is very different from the culture of psychotherapy. Clinicians use an "ethic of care" to guide their work. In this model, doctors or therapists take care of patients or clients. They look after their clients' best interests. These interests are central to the arrangement, and the arrangement is *cooperative*. The clinical relationship includes essential fiduciary dynamics. Clients must trust therapists to look after their interests, and clients are not always in the best position to know whether this is actually being done. Therapy clients are often in a weakened or vulnerable position. Think about how competent you might be (as a client) just after your spouse has announced an intention to divorce, or when you seek counseling because your child has died, or because you find yourself seriously depressed, and you can't discern why.

Executive coaches must navigate between these two cultures. On the one hand, they are working in a business culture, where the profit motive rules. It would be considered unethical for a business, particularly a corporation (which is a public entity), to place any value above that of delivering a return to the shareholders. That is the primary purpose of the corporation. Other purposes come second. This point of view is well understood by corporate officers and leaders. Coaches must understand it, as well. On the other hand, however, executive coaches must apply some aspects of the ethic of care to their individual clients. This balancing act can become confusing.

Consider the circumstance where executives must severely cut costs in order to protect profit or to protect the survival of the company, itself. Even though downsizing—the release of good people—is heartbreaking to the executive as well as to the person who will lose his job, it must be done. A coach must be able to understand the point of view of the corporation and find a way to synthesize the competitive with the cooperative point of view.

Areas of Similarity

There are numerous areas where clinical and coaching ethics overlap. The usual virtues of integrity, honesty, and responsibility are urged by consulting codes (Institute of Management Consultants, 1999) as well as clinical codes of ethics (American Association of Marriage and Family Therapists, 1998; American Counseling Association, 1995; American Psychological Association, 1992; National Association of Social Workers, 1999). All professions advocate such values. There are three particular areas of similarity that deserve attention.

Similarity 1: Clear Agreements

Clear agreements between practitioners and clients are recommended and they are required by ethics codes in both cultures. These make good sense and good practice. They do, however, require sophisticated communication skills and a solid professional self-esteem. Clients will appreciate such clarity, though, and it is worth the effort. Clients in the business world are often used to clear agreements and written contracts, perhaps more so than most psychotherapists. In any case, the need for clarity at the beginning of the coaching relationship is quite real. When this seems difficult, colleagues or mentors can help. A guidebook for formal consulting contracts is posted at the end of this chapter (Holtz, 1997).

Similarity 2: Whistle-Blowing

Both cultures, business consulting and clinical counseling, advocate whistle-blowing, particularly when colleagues behave poorly or are found to be incompetent. Both cultures recommend that one step in and say something to a colleague or report unethical behavior to a professional organization or board, even though most practitioners are loathe to actually do so when faced with this situation.

Similarity 3: Know Your Limits

Psychotherapists are taught to practice within their own personal limits. They are taught to use techniques only after adequate training and supervision. They learn which clients or patients to accept for treatment and which to refer, based upon their training, experience, and (their own) personality. No ethical psychotherapist would attempt to treat every patient who calls for an appointment. The standard of care requires an intake interview in order to assess and evaluate the fit between professional and client. When the fit is suboptimal, a referral is made on behalf of the best interests of the client (and, from a pragmatic point of view, in the best interest of the clinician, as well. Most seasoned psychotherapists recall the occasions when they took on a patient, against their better judgment, and suffered for it later).

Business and consulting standards require that coaches decline work for which they are not qualified and, further, that they represent their skills honestly. Deceptive advertising is expressly prohibited, but business people are used to hyperbole when consultants hawk their services, and nearly everyone has been burned by a consultant who could not deliver that which had been promised. However, it may be difficult for coaches to accurately assess the limits of their expertise. If you have never worked with a certain kind of client or have never worked in a particular industry, how are you to know if you have the expertise in advance? Do you err on the side of a conservative presentation of your skills, or do you take a risk, present a confident front, and hope that you can figure things out when you get on site? Since coaching is so new, both to coaches and clients, an aggressive approach seems more defensible, especially since the mental health of a person in a fragile state is not typically at stake, as is often the case in clinical psychology. An experimenting tack is certainly more acceptable when the coach has a mentor or support group in the wings.

Areas that Are Unclear

There are many more areas of executive coaching where the ethics of clinical practice can be instructive, but inadequate. Clinicians are likely to be naïve about them, and without deliberate preparation, could wade into an ethical minefield. As a result, they could end up harming clients or client companies.

Who Is the Client?

This is a practical, as well as a philosophical issue. It is similar, in some ways, to the problem that occurs in clinical practice when third party payers become involved in treatment. Loyalties become stretched and twisted. When a company hires a coach to work with an individual executive, who is the client? Is it the company, who hires and pays the coach to help with a business need? Or is it the individual executive, who is seeking to grow and move forward in his or her career? This question is easily answered when the executive personally pays the coach's fee. But, what about when the company pays the bill, as is usually the case? In a 1999 doctoral dissertation, Macmillan posed this question to business consultants and found widespread uncertainty and disagreement. To whom does the coach owe loyalty? What happens when a client's interests or intended behavior are at odds with those of the company? For example, what if a client wants to focus on skills that the company clearly does not need—or skills that the client would like to use in her next job or as an entrepreneur? What happens when a client is angry and contemplating legal action against the company, or is plotting his next move to a new company? How does a coach work with that client? These are difficult questions, indeed.

Clear contractual arrangements, spelled out in advance, are one antidote, especially when such problems can be anticipated at the onset. However, specific difficulties are often unforeseeable in this area. A second guideline is to favor openness. Direct discussions between coaches and clients about such problems, at the beginning and as they arise, can help enormously.

For example, a coach can raise the issue: "Jane, I'm concerned that what you and I are talking about may not be aligned with the company's goals. What you want to work on with me doesn't seem to be in the firm's best interest, yet it is the company that is funding our work together. What's your thinking about this? Does it seem fair to you? What should we do?"

Such a discussion might cause the focus of coaching to change. It might necessitate a discussion with the person in the company who authorized the coaching, in order to seek "permission" to wander a bit. Some organizations would have no problem with coaching that serves to enhance the skills of a valued executive even when there is only a small chance that the effects will be immediately applicable to current business needs. Some companies will figure that by providing coaching to a smart, effective executive they will create good will and cement a long-term positive relationship—or smooth over a bad relationship prior to a parting of the ways.

There is also a chance it might precipitate termination of the coaching. It is certainly difficult to justify a coaching process that is contrary to the best interests of the funding company. Coaches in that position should make a reasonable adjustment when that happens. Change the focus, rethink the content and purpose, and move in the direction of integrity. Ask the question: "How would I feel if I had to honestly describe what we are doing to the boss or to a group of senior managers?" If the answer to that question is uncomfortable, reconsider and realign. Occasional forays into tangential territory seem inevitable and acceptable, but when the focus is wrong, the work is wrong.

Confidentiality

An associated problem is this: to what extent is the relationship between coach and client confidential? In clinical practice, both the *fact* of the counseling relationship and the *content* of the relationship are confidential, and the rules are pretty clear. Psychotherapists do not even reveal the names of their clients. There are a few exceptions, and these can be communicated verbally and in writing. But what about the coaching relationship? Many people in the company are aware that coaching is happening and for whom, but the rules for content confidentiality are, to some extent, up for grabs. Coaches often tell clients that they will treat communication confidentially, but is such a promise always realistic? Coaches and clients must somehow establish the working arrangement as they go along, and clients vary with regard to their interest in privacy. Some (naively) don't seem to care. Others are positively paranoid about it. Even when clear arrangements are struck at the onset, difficulties can arise. What do you do about information that you (the coach) wish the "boss" (of your client) could have?

There is a second difficult aspect of confidentiality in executive coaching. To what extent does the coach owe the organization a confidential relationship? Coaches come across important information about the company, not just the client. For example, how should coaches handle proprietary secrets and insider stock information? What about a merger in the wings? What about illegal activities proposed by your client or illegal activities by the company? Information of sexual harassment or problematic office romances? This is a swamp, and the coach should be thoughtful and careful. Adequate guidelines, specific to executive coaching, aren't yet available.

There are two preliminary (and admittedly inadequate) answers to these questions. The first is the "cure-all": direct, frank, explicit discussions at the onset of coaching. It is the coach's responsibility to bring confidentiality up, and to do so in a way that does not unnecessarily alarm. Clients might not initiate such a discussion, because they don't want to give the impression that they have something to hide or that they are too private or not open enough. Others haven't given the matter any thought, but would have concerns if they did. Many cannot anticipate the difficulties around the corner, while a good coach certainly should.

So, a frank discussion about the demand for confidentiality (if demand exists or should exist), complete with examples, must be initiated by the coach. This discussion can start with the prospective client and include essential others, such as seniors, colleagues, and human resources personnel who might later inquire about progress. One way to head off problems is to offer regular progress reports, done collaboratively by coach and client. The format can be devised at the beginning and based upon established goals. That way, if someone asks about coaching, the answer can be, "We'll have a written progress report for you in a couple of weeks."

It is often a good idea to encourage clients to be open about the fact that they are getting coached. This can be framed as a positive—something that healthy, realistic, ambitious people do from time to time—and it is a compliment that the company is willing to fund it.

In reality, most people are happy to cooperate with the confidentiality arrangements that coaches and clients establish. They are generally aware that much is at stake, and few desire to do anything that might "gum up the works." Most others in the organization realize that they, too, have a vested interest in the positive development of the client.

The second "cure" for this problem requires that groups of coaches work together to establish consensus norms. These can be hammered out in professional meetings or through discussions in journals, but, in any case, written guidelines are sorely needed. Coaches with experience should begin to make their thinking about this matter public.

Consent

In clinical practice, nothing is done without clear client consent. In business coaching, clients may participate in coaching without such a clear consenting agreement, especially when told that they need coaching in order to advance their career, to make partner, or to simply survive with the company. What executive would decline such an "opportunity?" It is likely that clients sometimes participate in coaching with mixed motives and ambivalence, yet they are generally unwilling to reveal these motives to coaches. This is akin to mandated therapy when clients are referred to a clinician by a court or government body. The consent is not really voluntary, in the strictest sense of the word.

Coaches must remain alert for this mixed-motive scenario and confront it appropriately from the point of view of the client (rather than the company). Help clients figure out what to do. Such a discussion obviously depends upon the level of trust established in the coaching relationship. But even without trust, a coach can offer a well crafted statement to alert a client and open the "bidding." For example: "You know, sometimes it seems like you are not completely engaged in the coaching. I think about it a lot and wonder if you don't have some mixed feelings." One could add, "If I were in your position, I might have mixed feelings, too, given _____ (*the relevant specifics of the situation*)."

It may also be useful to develop a written consent form, appropriate to the corporate culture. This form could be used as a format for discussion of the important issues at the onset of the coaching relationship.

Boundaries

In the past decade, the standard of practice in psychotherapy has moved toward increasingly rigid professional boundaries. This change evolved because some therapists damaged clients by blurring or ignoring appropriate boundaries. Clinicians generally avoid mixing therapeutic relationships with social or other kinds of additional relationships. When you treat clients in therapy, you avoid all other relationships with them. You don't have dinner with them, you don't play golf with them, you don't sell things to them or buy things from them, and you don't go to cocktail parties or receptions with them. There are legitimate theoretical and practical reasons for this policy. The therapeutic process, as well as clients themselves, are often hurt when boundaries are violated.

Things are different in business consulting and executive coaching. Consultants and coaches are expected to attend business or social events with clients and their companies. To miss these events would seem odd to business people, and would isolate a coach from the company's culture and from other opportunities to observe. When a group of executives invite a coach to an event sponsored by the company, that coach needs to think twice about declining. A no-show might be seen as unsupportive of the organization or unenthusiastic about the work. Plus, you might miss out on an excellent opportunity to assess your client in an important working situation. In other words, executive coaches must, after careful consideration, attend social events with clients and other important "players" in the organization. There are valid coaching and business reasons to do so.

This different set of expectations does not, however, indemnify the coach or client from some of the difficulties that can arise in such "dual relationship" situations. They simply must be managed with sound judgment and a commitment to avoid any role exploitation.

Once again, a preemptory discussion about these matters is a good idea. Psychotherapists bring a special expertise to this situation, as they have generally given more thought to the pitfalls of mixing one's settings. They have seen, firsthand, how problems of dual relationships can evolve, and many therapists have engaged in frank and open discussions with clients about them. They have learned about the potential for misunderstanding, resentment, and embarrassment. Most business people do not have this experience and have no idea that problems can occur. Although consultants are generally welcome at corporate "outings," it is certainly possible that a client may wish that his or her coach stay away. Check with your client. Ask his or her preference, discuss what it means, and honor it.

It must be said, however, that executive clients are not as vulnerable as psychotherapy clients. They are not in the same position with respect to the coach as a patient is to a therapist. They are usually not hurting or scared or depressed. Their self-esteem is usually (but not always) intact and high. When tricky social events occur, they are in a better position to interpret things in a healthy way or to let something roll off their back or to even ignore a small embarrassment. Therapy patients are often uncomfortable when confronted with their therapist in settings outside of the consulting room, while executives are quite unlikely to feel this way.

Beware, however, of letting your guard completely down. Remember, as business people learn to do, that a social outing with the company is still work. It is not purely a social event, even if people act like it is, and mistakes can be made that can ruin a perfectly good business relationship.

Consider the following example:

> You join your client at a golf outing. You are not a good golfer, although you enjoy the game from time to time. You and your client play a friendly match, and he sets up a wager with the other team. On the last hole, you play terribly, and your team loses a substantial amount of money.
>
> Conversely, imagine the same scenario in reverse. You are an excellent golfer, and your client plays poorly, causing your team to lose the wager. These events complicate your relationship, but do they damage it, or is there potential for a deeper and stronger bond, or even a learning experience?

Other Areas in Question

There are numerous other areas where clinical guidelines might help out, but don't neatly apply. The following areas must be sorted out in the future.

Record-Keeping

What kind of records should executive coaches keep, and how should they be managed and protected? Certainly, notes can be important and useful to the coach, especially when a coach works with multiple clients simultaneously, or when an executive calls for additional coaching after a few years away. It is probably a good idea to apply the basic rules that therapists use for record keeping, although there is certainly no mandate for process notes, as there is in the practice of psychotherapy. Accurate financial records are obviously essential, and assessment data, goals, and notes about observations should be maintained and safeguarded. Hopefully, the need for notes and records will be driven by a coach's interest in his or her client, rather than a perceived need to protect one's self from criticism or future harm, as is sometimes the case in the healthcare arena.

Termination of the Coaching Relationship

What is the best way to wrap things up when goals have not been met or when corporate money runs out? Often companies are not willing to finance coaching that goes on and on, without timely and demonstrable results. What do you do when progress is stalled or nonexistent? What happens when a coach or a client is reassigned or relocated? Sometimes nearly random events cause premature termination. Does a coach have any obligation to continue the coaching relationship after a client leaves the company? Is there ever an obligation to continue coaching at a reduced fee (if the client is to personally take over payment)?

Certainly, a clear discussion of how and when coaching will end is appropriate material for initial discussions in the relationship.

Assessment

What level of psychological testing skills must a coach possess before using instruments with coaching clients? Are the rules the same as for psychologists or master's level counselors? Coaches generally use instruments that do not require that the user hold a clinician's license, so there really are no legal constraints. But the general rule for clinicians is helpful: Use an instrument only under the following circumstances:

1. The instrument has been shown to be valid, reliable, and appropriate for the purpose intended. Coaches must be wary, as there are many unvalidated instruments available to business consultants.

2. The user possesses adequate skills and experience (including supervision, when appropriate) to use the specific instrument.
3. The testee is properly informed about the instrument, ahead of time, and the results are provided in language that he or she comprehends.

Duty to Warn

Do coaches face the same obligations as clinicians when clients become a danger to self or others? Is there a duty to safeguard an executive from harm to himself or a duty to warn others in order to prevent danger? Some executive clients can become quite depressed when major downturns occur in their industry or personal career. Are there other duties in industry that clinicians can't anticipate? Is it fair to hold coaches to the same legal standards that clinicians are held to, given that coaches often aren't privy to the same depth of interpersonal information that therapists possess about their patients?

The guidelines used by clinicians in this area can be extremely useful in the very rare circumstance when a client is psychologically troubled. Such clients are lucky to be in the hands of a coach who has clinical training and experience. Generally accepted principles for clients who are a danger to self or others ought to be applied. Examples of workers who have exploded or assaulted after being terminated or slighted cannot be ignored. Sometimes business organizations ask business coaches to help out with difficult employees or disgruntled managers, and coaches must evaluate such clients for impulse control, emotional range, perception, and attribution.

Pro Bono Services

Shouldn't coaches, who command higher fees than clinicians, have an obligation to give back to the community? What community? Should coaches provide some services to non-profit organizations at a reduced fee?

It seems clear that many ethical aspects of executive coaching are not clear, and that the ethical principles and methods used by clinicians may be extremely useful, if not universally applicable. Significant areas for thoughtful discussion exist, and as coaching becomes more widely accepted, professional standards must be developed and disseminated. As groups of coaches evolve, it will become increasingly important that they create explicit standards and guidelines to express aspirations and to limit problem behavior or damage. These standards will enhance the prospect of long-term survival for coaches and coaching. It is time for professional organizations to draft prototypes of formal ethical guidelines.

In the mean time, coaches must use good judgment, consult with a trusted colleague or mentor, and take care.

Summary and Key Points

1. Coaches and clinicians live in different ethical cultures, and this requires small, but significant adaptations by clinicians.
2. Well-developed codes, standards, and guidelines do not exist for executive coaches. Coaches must adapt existing standards as they go, applying some, as is, and adjusting others.
3. Clear initial agreements between coaches, clients, and the client's company are essential, and they help to avoid many ethical problems.
4. Coach–client confidentiality, while not absolute, must be respected, discussed, and managed.
5. Boundary expectations are quite different in the corporate world, as executives often expect consultants to join them on company outings and social events.
6. Psychotherapists possess useful skills when it comes to record-keeping and record management. Although clinical standards are more extensive and restrictive than might be necessary, it would be a good idea to keep them in mind when managing coaching notes and records.
7. Most of the instruments used by coaches are less complex than those used by psychologists, but the same practical requirements apply. Coaches should only use instruments that they understand to be appropriate, valid, and reliable.
8. Psychotherapists possess sophisticated and useful skills for the rare occasion when an executive becomes a danger to self or to others. These skills should be applied in much the same way as they are in the clinical situation. Be careful about the potential embarrassment and weigh it against the potential danger.

References

American Association of Marriage and Family Therapists. (1998). AAMFT Code of Ethics. Washington, DC: Author. (Available on line at http://www.aamft.org/about/ethics.htm).

American Counseling Association. (1995). Code of ethics and standards of practice. Alexandria, VA: Author. (Available online at www.counseling.org/resources/codeofethics.htm).

American Psychological Association. (1992, December). *Principles of ethics and code of professional conduct.* Washington, DC: Author. (Available online at www.apa.org/ ethics/code.html). The APA also publishes specialty guidelines for Industrial/Organizational Psychologists.

Holtz, H. (1997). *The complete guide to consulting contracts* (2nd ed.). Chicago: Dearborn Financial Books (Upstart Publishing Company).

Institute of Management Consultants. (1999, January). *Code of ethics.* New York: Author. (Available online at www.imc.org.au/)

Recommended Readings

Bennett, B., Bryant, B., VandenBos, G., & Greenwood, A. (1990). *Professional liability and risk management.* Washington, DC: American Psychological Association.

Bersoff, D. (Ed.). (1999). *Ethical conflicts in psychology.* Washington, DC: American Psychological Association.

Brotman, L., Liberi, W., & Wasylyshyn, K. (1998). Executive coaching: The need for standards of competence. *Consulting Psychology Journal: Practice and Research, 50*(1), 40–46.

Clinical Social Work Federation. (1997). *Code of ethics.* Arlington, VA: Author. (Available online at www.cswf.org/ethframe.htm).

Corey, G., Corey, M., & Callahan, P. *Issues and ethics in the helping professions.* Pacific Grove, CA: Brooks/Cole.

Devine, G. (1996). *Responses to 101 questions on business ethics.* Mahwah, NJ: Paulist Press.

Gorlin, R. (1999). *Codes of professional responsibility: Ethics standards in business, health, and law* (4th ed). Washington, DC: BNA Books (Bureau of National Affairs).

Keith-Spiegel, P., & Koocher, G. (1998). *Ethics in psychology: Professional standards and cases* (Vol. 3). New York: Oxford University Press.

Macmillan, C. (1999). *The role of the organizational consultant: A model for clinicians.* Unpublished doctoral dissertation, Massachusetts School of Professional Psychology.

Messick, D., & Tenbrunsel, A. (1997) *Codes of conduct: Behavioral research into business ethics.* New York: Russel Sage Foundation.

Nagy, T. (2000). *Ethics in plain English: An illustrative case book for psychologists.* Washington, DC: American Psychological Association.

Nash, D. (1994). A tension between two cultures . . . dentistry as a profession and dentistry as proprietary. *Journal of Dental Education, 58*(4), 301–306.

National Association of Social Workers. (1999). Code of Ethics. Washington, DC: Author. (Available online at www.naswdc.org/code.htm).

Peltier, B. (2001). The ethical responsibility of professional autonomy. *Journal of the California Dental Association, 29*(7).

Peltier, B., & Dugoni, A. (1994). A four-part model to energize ethical conversation. *Journal of the California Dental Association, 22*(10).

Rest, J., & Narvaez, D. (Eds.). (1994). *Moral development in the professions: Psychology and applied ethics.* Hillsdale, NJ: Earlbaum.

Snoeyenbos, M., Humber, J., & Almeder, R. (Eds.). (1992). *Business ethics: Corporate values and society.* New York: Prometheus Books.

Solomon, R. (1993). *Ethics and excellence: Cooperation and integrity in business.* New York: Oxford University Press.

Solomon, R. (1997). *It's good business: Ethics and free enterprise for the new millennium.* Lanham, MD: Rowman & Littlefield.

CHAPTER

Making the Transition

When you come to a fork in the road, take it.

—Yogi Berra (1998, p. 48)

Coaching is here to stay. Several powerful trends support that statement. The workplace has become a faster-moving, more independent, more creative, and more demanding place. Job security, at every level, has disappeared. Thirty-four year old chief executives are not uncommon. Staff levels are lower than ever, and smaller numbers of people are expected to get the work done. The job market is tight and valued employees switch companies in a heartbeat for a better offer. Diversity is finally coming of age. Customers are more demanding. International markets are opening, and the Internet is connecting us all.

Now that you know what mental health types have to offer the business community, it is time to look at how to make the transition from therapist to executive coach. You may want to stick a toe in the water first. Just because a new market has "buzz" doesn't mean there's a fit. Coaching might not suit you, because the business world is different from the psychotherapy world. There are some lovely aspects about working as a psychotherapist, and you just might miss them. As a therapist, you help people who are struggling and in pain. You heal wounds. You fill in gaps left by inadequate parents. You occasionally dissuade someone who is seriously suicidal. There are the smaller perks, too. You can call most of your own shots, choose your own hours, and wear comfortable clothes that express who you really are. You can "give away" your work gratis or at a low fee, from time to time, to someone who really needs it and is appreciative.

You could certainly do some executive coaching "on the side" or on a part-time basis without making a total commitment to life in the consulting world. This might involve some measure of dissociation on your part, but it is a viable option. The consulting world includes two kinds of coaches: one who is an employee or independent contractor for a large consulting firm; the firm finds and sells work and controls the action of the coach, while paying that coach some percentage of the total fees. The other kind of coach is the individual consultant, referred to by the large firms as the "boutique" operator. This person must find and sell his or her own work, and then keep all of the profits. Fees tend to be substantial relative to those paid to psychotherapists, and there is no managed care broker or associated paperwork with which to contend (although the consulting world has its own forms of onerous paperwork, to be sure).

The fact that many therapy skills are transferable to executive coaching should not encourage you to jump in, willy-nilly, or to take the dilettante's approach. You can spot articles in the newspaper, from time to time, highlighting a therapist who has gleefully transformed her psychotherapy practice into a "coaching practice." Instead of struggling along with depressed, low-fee patients, she now does executive coaching from the comfort of her home, over the telephone! No more difficult people, no more managed care, no office hours. One such recent success story showed a photo of an ex-therapist doing phone coaching in Bermuda shorts and expensive sunglasses from the hull of her sailboat. She's gazing off over the water for inspiration and speaking to a client whom she's never actually met in person! One brochure depicts a coach sitting on a sandy beach, breeze blowing through his hair, telecoaching in the sun. One flyer calls coaching "The hottest market niche for the new millennium." Much of this kind of coaching is actually personal counseling, outside of the business world, with clients who are mentally healthy but looking to get an edge or make a change. Such personal success coaching is a fine activity, but it is not executive coaching, and it is potentially damaging to the corporate coach's reputation (and focus) to mix them up.

Transition A: The Business Culture and the Profit Motive

Executive coaching requires considerable involvement in the business and corporate world.

Money

The most important difference between the therapy world and corporate culture is fundamental. Simply stated, *the purpose of a corporation is to return value to stakeholders and stockholders*; that is, to make a profit. In business school, students are taught that this is an *ethical* issue. To confuse the profit motive with other tasks or motives is to do a disservice to shareholders, who are counting on you. To place other functions ahead of profit is unethical. That's how important the bottom line is to a publicly held corporation. Small businesses are not held to this profit-oriented standard, but the point still stands. You must make a profit or stop doing business, properly labeling what you do as a "hobby." The IRS insists on this. If you don't make a profit after a certain period of time you cannot deduct expenses against revenues, because the government would then be underwriting your hobby. Small business owners, in many ways, are even more serious about the importance of the bottom line. If they don't make money, they go out of business and they "lose their shirt." Such risk tends to focus one's attention. The bottom-line profit orientation in the business world runs deep, it is powerful, and no one makes apologies for it.

In the therapy world, money is seen as a by-product of having provided a useful service and for caring. The service is central and the money is a happy bit of a "necessary evil." Few revel in it, and no one brags about how much money he or she makes as a psychotherapist. Therapists are timid about greed. Most would love to make more money, but they don't talk directly about this. Most psychotherapists probably chose their profession because of a desire to help people, to make a positive difference, or because they were fascinated with the theories and ideas. Money was secondary to all of that.

Business people (always, but especially after about 1990) have no such pretensions about the role of money. It is the way to keep score. The money you take home tells you (and others) how you are doing. It is a clear and simple standard, and few apologize. That's just the way it is, and most think it's a pretty good way. Of course many business people are doing work that is intended to improve the world, but the money is still how they keep score. Read Ayn Rand for the overarching perspective. Read the *Wall Street Journal* (called "The Journal" by business folks) to get the day-to-day point of view.

Speed

The business world tends to move more quickly than the world of psychotherapy. "Getting from point A to point B" prevails over a "peeling the onion" metaphor. While therapists tend to value contemplation and reflection, the business world insists on results . . . soon. Business people tend to be action oriented; they trust activity. Psychotherapists work with abstractions; they reflect. Therapy constructs are difficult to quantify and measure. Business people are taught to be goal oriented and to measure progress. They like benchmarks and "metrics." They move as fast as they can. Thoughtfulness sometimes gets lost in the shuffle.

Executive coaches must be able to swim in these waters. You don't have to agree with this point of view, but don't disparage it if you want to work in the business culture. Find a way to live with it. Find a way to let it energize you, too, without compromising the values you cherish.

Transition B: Presentation of Self

Marketing consists of all activities by which a company adapts itself to its environment—creatively and profitably.
                                                        —Ray Corey (Kotler, 1997, p. 1)

You cannot go into business organizations and act, look, or speak like a psychotherapist. Therapists have patients, and business people are reluctant to take on the qualities associated with the role of "patient." The two main areas on which to focus are appearance and speech.

Appearance

First, you must dress and behave like a businessperson, to some reasonable extent. Initial impressions are powerful (remember social psychology), and you will make a poor impression if you dress like a stereotypical "bohemian" therapist. If you are serious about coaching and feel you need help in this area, get a clothing coach. It is entirely possible that you don't have good judgment about this. If you view clothing as a mode of self-expression, take care to express business savvy. If you view clothing as a tool, sharpen and focus it. You don't need to try to look like a banker, and there is ample room for self-expression, but your appearance must convey a sense of seriousness and substance, and to some extent, conformity. Outliers frighten business people. Happily, dress codes are changing, and many firms are dumping ties and high heels. Find out how they dress at the places you want to consult and match them, especially when you intend to physically enter the workplace to coach or to "shadow" your client on-site. Business people tend to respect those who know how to "dress sharp."

Speech

Second, you must change your vocabulary. Psychotherapy, like all professions, has its own jargon. This vocabulary is not clear to non-psychotherapists, and its use can become a distinct "turn-off" in the business environment. Businesses and specific industries also have their own way of speaking, and you must learn the language. You don't need to speak it yourself (and attempts to do so can come across as phony), but you must be comfortable with the vocabulary of the industry. For example, if you consult or coach in a dental office, you need to learn what they mean by terms like "perio" or "fixed," and you need to call patient files "charts," and know the difference between hygienists and assistants. No one will expect you to know these things immediately, but you must learn quickly.

Table 14.1 contains examples of generic business language changes to consider. Some examples of how this works:

Instead of saying "You have issues around performance under stress" you might instead say, "One of the challenges you face is how to take advantage of unanticipated opportunities."

Instead of saying, "I get a sense that you are feeling anxious," you might consider, "You seem nervous about this." Or "You look nervous. What was your reaction? What's your thinking?"

Transition C: Marketing and Sales

Marketing's job is to convert societal needs into profitable opportunities.
—Kotler (1997, p. 1)

You must learn to market and sell your services. Most people don't understand the difference between these two essential tasks. Marketing is not the same as "sales," and many psychotherapists hate the idea that they must sell something. They don't see themselves as able to do it, either. Marketing is an umbrella function, and it includes sales. But it involves much more, and it can be very interesting.

> Marketing is so basic that is cannot be considered a separate function. It is the whole business seen from . . . the customer's point of view.
> —Peter Drucker (Kotler, 1997, p. 1)

TABLE 14.1. Language differences between therapy and coaching

Therapy language to avoid	Business language to learn
• Issue ("What are your issues?")	• Challenge, solution ("What challenges are you facing?" "What solutions are required?")
• Why ("Why is this happening?")	• How ("How does it happen?")
• Sessions (with clients)	• Meetings
• Way I work, way of working	• Method
• Sense ("I get a sense that . . .")	• Idea ("Here's my idea." "Here's what I think.")
• Feeling ("What are you feeling?")	• Reaction ("What is your reaction?")
• Around ("I have feelings around this issue.")	• About ("I am concerned about this.")
• Tasks ("What do we need to do?")	• Results and deliverables ("What are the deliverables?")

Marketing means that you must figure out what consumers need and what they are willing to buy and then match those things with a service that you are willing and able to provide.

This requires constant adjustment as consumer demands evolve. Executive coaching is an example of how mental health providers can fit evolving business needs, and most of the heavy lifting has already been done for you. The coaching market has already been developed. Corporations are now well aware of executive coaching and of their need for coaching, especially in a shrinking employee market. They know how much it costs to hire and train a good executive, and they don't like it when employees leave, taking their knowledge with them. They are also generally aware of the havoc and damage a poor or inappropriate leader can cause. They also know that they cannot simply "promote" an excellent analyst and expect him or her to make a quick and easy transition to partner.

There is work left to be done in marketing, however. First you must figure out just what it is that you have to offer. Then add to it or adjust it to meet the needs of prospective customers. That might involve research about what customers want. It might involve serious introspection and self-assessment. It might even allow for creative development of new services that you could offer to clients (still close enough to your core competencies), once you have made them aware of a need that you can fill. You may want to offer new "products" or new ways to provide coaching. Or you may decide to offer coaching to a subset of potential clients that others have not considered (e.g., dentists or attorneys or accountants or hardware store owners or hotel managers or family businesses). It really helps to enter a niche that you know or with which you have some experience.

The Core Competency

At the same time you must decide on one or two *core competencies*. This is a central concept, as it defines what you do and keeps you pointed in the proper direction. A core competency (sometimes called a distinctive competency) is the single thing that you do the best. It is what you are all about, and it includes your unique strengths and qualities. It is your specialty, that which you have organized your efforts around for a long period of time. It is what you know best and do best. It includes your skills and your resources, and it is difficult for others to imitate. Every successful business has one, whether acknowledged or not. (If they don't have one, they probably won't survive.) Leverage that distinctive competency; don't spread the energy all over the place and become mediocre. Focus on your core competency; become exceptional at it. This creates an interesting tension between evolving needs of the marketplace and the solid constancy of your core skills. Pay attention to this. The idea is to create a *sustainable competitive advantage*.

Marketing includes "The Four Ps." Together they form the basis for comprehensive marketing planning. They are *product, place, price,* and *promotion.*

Product

Decide what it is that you want to offer. This can include a "product mix" of several services and tangible products such as books, videos, or cassettes.

It is especially important to be able to describe what you do. You must be able to define coaching, and you should choose a definition that is results oriented. This is not an easy task, for the service coaches provide is intangible by nature. Here are some thoughts to help you construct your definition.

First of all, consider the *tasks* a coach can accomplish. A coach can enhance a client's

- listening skills
- interpersonal skills
- delegating
- behavior in meetings, and ability to run meetings
- public speaking
- ability to give feedback
- understanding of company politics
- self-understanding
- presentation of self
- strategic thinking

Coaches must be able to also talk about what they offer in terms of client company *outcomes*. For example, coaching can

- enhance an executive's performance.
- help increase market share.
- enhance the company's image or reputation.
- increase customer satisfaction.
- decrease complaints.
- improve productivity.
- increase efficiency.
- retain high-performing executives.

In other words, coaching must be explained to potential clients in terms of *what's-in-it-for-them*. What will be different (better) after you have done your coaching?

Place

Figure out where you will operate and how customers and clients will find you. For example, decide whether you will operate as a consultant to a larger consulting firm, as an independent operator, or as an in-house consultant to the company whose employees you will coach. Consider an Internet "place" for your efforts. Decide how much you are willing to travel.

Price

Decide how you will price your services. Consult with others in your geographic area and in your target industry. Consider a wide range of pricing alternatives including a daily rate, an annual rate, acceptance of stock options instead of cash, and strongly consider value-based fees. A value-based approach sets a fee amount based upon the total worth in specific and general outcomes to the client. Read Weiss (1998) for a detailed explanation of this approach to pricing. Be careful about locking yourself into an hourly fee. It can become too restrictive after you have established your reputation and value in the marketplace. Project pricing is the model most often used these days in management consulting, and businesses are used to paying consultants on this basis.

Promotion

Decide about how you are going to inform and educate potential clients about your services and their value. You cannot expect clients to find you, and although self-promotion is anathema to many psychotherapists, it is an essential aspect of successful consulting. Think this one through. Find a way to understand the key idea: You have a valuable and important service—something that can make a very positive impact for the right client. (If you don't believe this, rethink what you are doing and why you are doing it. This must be true—as a baseline requirement.)

You have to connect with a potential new client. Promotion does not mean bragging or hustling people. It means that you match services and clients in a win–win paradigm. There really are many clients out there in the world who would benefit from excellent coaching. Remember that you have much to offer the business and corporate world. And don't limit your target to mainstream businesses. There are many small or individual business people who can dearly use your services, including dentists, physicians, entrepreneurs, attorneys, nonprofit organizations, family businesses, print shops, and politicians. There are books available to help with this process, and some are listed in the reference section of this chapter.

In any event, here's what you have to accomplish:

1. **Figure out what the market wants and needs.** You could do this by reading, taking coaching training, or interviewing business people. The goal is to figure out where opportunities exist and how to assess the existing barriers. What forces or factors exist in the market environment that will make penetration difficult? Where is the opportunity greatest?
2. **Figure out what you have to offer.** Decide if you are willing to adapt or learn new skills to fit the need. Take a clear look at your strengths and weaknesses relative to the opportunities in the market. Some companies or businesses are likely to be more accessible than others, given your contacts and skill set. Match your skills and resources to the existing opportunities and barriers.
3. **Differentiate your services from psychotherapy and from the**

services of your competitors. Decide about your distinctive competencies, the things that you are really good at. Be able to succinctly explain how you are different and what kind of situations you are best suited to handle. When you are not the optimal coach for a particular client or industry, be ready to recommend someone else. Take a service orientation, and help customers solve their problems, even when you are not going to get the current piece of work. Direct your efforts toward their success. They will remember your help and be more likely to come back when they need your skill, or to recommend you to someone else.

4. **Make your presence known.** Let companies know about the services you offer. Companies need consultants. Consultants help them solve problems they do not know how to solve. Consultants save them money.

5. **Constantly assess the value of your service.** Adjust as you go along. Work hard to match what you offer to what clients need. Help them discern their needs, as well.

6. **Spend time with business people.** Don't spend most of your professional time with other psychotherapists. As Weiss (1998) notes, that's like trying to sell stamps to the post office. Skip meetings of therapist organizations, and start to attend meetings of management consultant organizations. Better yet, attend meetings of business people. Seek out chambers of commerce or rotary club or human resource trainings. Let people know what you do, and let them help you structure your service.

7. **Find a mentor.** Establish a relationship with someone who knows what you don't. Nourish the relationship and pay attention. (Be prepared to pay for this help.)

What You Have to Offer

Although "connections" and reputation are the two main ways that you will get work as a business consultant, if you don't have those, you must start somewhere. Consider the sources of your *authority*. What is your authority as an executive coach? Why should someone take a risk on you? There is much more than money at stake for most coaching clients. They (or their organization) need serious help, and they need it to work quickly and effectively. They need it to be able to succeed in a new job, they need it to keep their present job, or they need it to keep an organization afloat. People depend on them to succeed. Ask yourself why they should listen to you. Why should they put themselves and their organizations in your hands?

Here are some possible sources of your attractiveness:

Possibility 1: You have a track record. Maybe you have demonstrated effectiveness under the same or similar circumstances. You may even be able to produce letters of support or recommendation from former coaching clients. This is the most effective kind of authority in the marketplace. Some prospective clients will demand it.

Possibility 2: You (yourself) have experienced the same circumstances as your client. You have worked in the corporate world and served as a VP of marketing or HR or finance. You have been there and you understand what it takes to succeed. Or, perhaps you ran a small clinic or a university counseling center or a drinking driver program. Maybe you served as an officer in a professional organization. Perhaps you managed a budget and a staff.

Possibility 3: You have taken (or given) a lot of training in business coaching. It is increasingly easy to find training in coaching. Take some of your mandatory continuing education credits in this area.

Possibility 4: You have written about the subject. Maybe you have conducted a study in the field of coaching. Perhaps the newspaper printed an article you wrote, or better, you write a regular column for the business section. Perhaps you have your own newsletter about business coaching and related topics.

Possibility 5: You have a website that highlights your accomplishments and presents information and news about coaching. There are already many of these on the Internet from which to learn.

Possibility 6: You have years of experience as an effective psychotherapist. This one is quite valuable, especially if you are the kind of therapist who can readily translate previous work into business coaching, but it is a hard one to sell to many corporations. They typically aren't interested in sending their execs to therapy.

Possibility 7: You are smart, shrewd, and know how to develop rapport quickly to influence people. This is a very important set of skills, but it is hard to convince people that it is true ahead of time. When you do, you are liable to come across as bragging or as needy. Smart people don't advertise their smarts, they demonstrate them, and other smart people notice. But those who keep their talents hidden don't fare well, either.

Transition D: Mixing Relationships

Psychotherapists develop a special relationship with their clients, and they rarely, if ever, mix professional relationships with social ones. They do not party with clients, do not go out on clients' boats, they don't play golf with patients, and rarely attend weddings or graduations with clients. There are good reasons for these restrictions, and in some situations, social contact with clients is actually against the law.

But things are different in the business-coaching world. Consultants are *expected* to socialize with clients. It is an essential and important part of the culture, and serious feelings will be hurt if you routinely decline invitations. You really must do some socializing with clients in the business environment.

This has two important implications. First, when socializing you have to behave in a way that engenders confidence in your judgment and ability. You are always "on" in these social situations. They are work, not necessarily play or fun. Business people know this; they are used to it. Second, this means that you must be especially conscious of the level and kind of confidentiality that you can offer clients. In therapy, the very *fact* that you have a professional relationship with a client is, itself, confidential. Not so, in the business world. People will know that you are a coach and they will know that Bill or Sally is working with you. Discuss this with clients at the beginning of the relationship. Be clear about how you will handle confidences. Don't present this in a way that pathologizes the information they will discuss, and don't make promises you can't keep. Just let them know that you intend to respect their confidence and their reputation. You are in their corner and your main goal is to enhance their career. It is usually possible to frame the coaching as a positive. Only those with high potential get this service, therefore it is prestigious to be coached.

Transition E: Contracts and Business Arrangements

Negotiate explicit contracts that are fair to all parties. The service you provide is a valuable one, especially when it goes well. Do not under price or undervalue your work. Skills that may seem relatively simple or second nature to you are quite valuable to many business people who have never spent a day in a psychology class or a human relations seminar.

Create contracts that are clear. Make expectations explicit for you and for your client. Agree on a policy for no-shows, as they are inevitable (and don't take them personally, unless they are chronic). When an opportunity pops up for a client to close a lucrative "deal," they will certainly miss their appointment with you. Be prepared to charge them fairly. They will understand, especially if you have a contract and an agreement.

Your agreements ought to include "deliverables," explicit ways to know if and when you have accomplished your goals. What will you deliver, and how will you know when you have done so? This will require clear thinking and conversations about those goals. Choose them carefully so that they are measurable and achievable. Make them modest at first, and build on success. This is not often easy, but it is always possible. Think in terms of what will be different as a result of successful coaching.

Finally, check with your malpractice or liability carrier. Let them know that you are doing executive coaching as part of your practice. They, too, know about coaching, and may have a policy in place, although it is unlikely that it will place any demands on you. You will not be the first new coach to call them. Do not give up this insurance policy (assuming that it covers your coaching).

Endnote: Be Exceptional

Develop a vision. Make this vision real by writing it down in a sentence or two. Massage it until it speaks for you, motivates you, and keeps you focused. Refer back to it regularly. Keep it real. Turn this vision into a concise mission statement, if you wish.

Remember that all consulting is relationship based. Nurture personal relationships in business. Put long-term relationships ahead of narrow or momentary business matters.

Go the extra mile to become excellent at what you do. Get feedback from trusted clients and friends and listen to it. Then make changes or get more training or skills. Read extensively in the management consulting area. Certainly this book alone is insufficient preparation for successful coaching. Find a mentor. Use him or her, and pay for his or her time, if necessary.

Study the leadership and management literature. Become familiar with the core readings as well as the popular books that executives read on airplanes. Keep up with the latest *Harvard Business Review*. Learn the business of business, along with its vocabulary.

Tell the truth when you coach. A large study of senior managers in Fortune 250 companies found that the most important factor in effective coaching was *"honest, straightforward communication"* (Peterson, Uranowitz, & Hicks, 1997, p. 1). This may not be altogether easy, but it is extremely valuable, and people will notice it. Don't be too afraid to say the unpopular thing. Your observation skills, listening skills, and your honesty could turn out to be your *inimitable sustainable competitive advantage*. In the long run, clients will hire those they trust, and they will trust those who tell the truth.

Aim high and enjoy the ride.

References

Berra, Y. (1998). *The Yogi book: I really didn't say everything I said.* New York: Workman Publishing.

Kotler, P. (1997). *Marketing management: Analysis, planning, implementation, and control.* Upper Saddle River, NJ: Prentice Hall.

Peterson, D., Uranowitz, S., & Hicks, M. D. (1997). *Management coaching at work: Current practice in multinational and fortune 250 companies.* Minneapolis, MN: Personnel Decisions International Corporation.

Weiss, A. (1998). *Million dollar consulting. The professional's guide to growing a practice.* New York: McGraw-Hill.

Recommended Readings

Barney, J. (1997). *Gaining and sustaining competitive advantage.* Menlo Park, CA: Addison-Wesley.

Benton, D. (1999). *Secrets of a CEO coach.* New York: McGraw-Hill.

Block, P. (2000). *Flawless consulting, a guide to getting your expertise used* (2nd ed.). San Francisco: Jossey-Bass/Pfeiffer.

Douglas, C., & Morley, W. (2000). *Executive coaching, an annotated bibliography.* Greensboro, NC: Center for Creative Leadership.

Doyle, J. (1999). *The business coach.* New York: Wiley.

Farson, R. (1996). *Management of the absurd: Paradoxes in leadership.* New York: Simon & Schuster.

Gilley, J., & Boughton, M. (1996). *Stop managing, start coaching! How performance coaching can enhance commitment and improve productivity.* Chicago: Irwin Professional Publishing.

Hargrove, R. (1995). *Masterful coaching.* San Francisco: Jossey-Bass/Pfeiffer.

Holtz, H. (1997). *The complete guide to consulting contracts* (2nd ed.). Chicago: Upstart Publishing Company.

Kerin, R., & Peterson, R. (1998). *Strategic marketing problems: Cases and comments.* Upper Saddle River, NJ: Prentice Hall.

MacMillan, C. (1999). *The role of the organizational consultant: A model for clinicians.* Unpublished doctoral dissertation, Massachusetts School of Professional Psychology.

Martin, I. (1996). *From couch to corporation. Becoming a successful corporate therapist.* New York: Wiley.

Miller, J., & Brown, P. (1993). *The corporate coach.* New York: St. Martin's Press.

Peters, T. (1999). *The brand you 50.* New York: Alfred Knopf.

Sperry, L. (1996). *Corporate therapy and consulting.* New York: Brunner/Mazel.

Tobias, L. (1990). *Psychological consulting to management: A clinician's perspective.* New York: Brunner/Mazel.

Waldroop, J., & Butler, T. (2000, September–October). Managing away bad habits. *Harvard Business Review,* 89–98.

Wallace, W., & Hall, D. (1996). *Psychological consultation: Perspectives and applications.* Pacific Grove, CA: Brooks/Cole.

INDEX